D0885934

PRAISE FOR THE FIRST EDITION OF *THE CHACO MERIDIAN*

"Once every generation or so a new work appears that radically changes how we perceive some aspect of the world. [*The Chaco Meridian*] is one of those 'paradigm-shifting' events in archaeology. . . . It is a fun yet thought-provoking book, a must-read for anyone interested in modern archaeology." —**David Anderson, National Park Service**

"Lekson is one of a few active archaeologists who have the experience, perspective, and creativity to think this big. A truly significant book." —**Keith W. Kintigh, Arizona State University**

"Lekson is one of the few archaeologists who writes with a distinctive voice, one of the few who prefers to work without a net. . . . His account of political history of the ancient Southwest . . . is a reconstruction that cannot be ignored by those interested in ancient Pueblo history and in the development of political complexity and social inequality."—**Mark D. Varien**

"Not only does Dr. Lekson's scheme imply a degree of regional unity unsuspected heretofore but it casts a new light on several archaeological features . . . and also, perhaps, on the lore of the region at the time of contact with the Spanish." —*Antiquity*

"Provocative and challenging. . . . I recommend this book to anyone interested in the American Southwest; it is an exciting exercise in the possible."—**K. Kris Holt**

"Lekson presents a unique perspective on the Southwest. . . . [His own] work is well-published, and it is the lesser-known information about Aztec and Casas Grandes that makes the book worth reading and the meridian question worth pondering. . . . [T]his book is worth reading for its effort to look at old data in new ways and to incorporate new data in looking at old questions. . . . *The Chaco Meridian* is a highly personal exploration of Southwestern archaeological data that will motivate a new level of discussion. . . ."—**Winifred Creamer, Northern Illinois University;** *Journal of Anthropological Research*

"His proposed political history of a significantly expanded Pueblo world . . . is intended to make us think globally and escape the confines of 'feeble provincialism.'"—**R. Grinn Vivian, Arizona State Museum, University of Arizona;** *Cambridge Archaeological Journal*

"*The Chaco Meridian* effectively addresses some questions and spawns others, as seminal works are inclined to do. Lekson provides a compelling argument, meticulously laid out with some fun terminology and observations."—**Kevin S. Blake, University of Wyoming;** *The Geographical Journal*

"Lekson's narrative style is clearly a refreshing departure from the typical archaeological discourse of careerist gravitas and pretentious sanctimony. Lekson, in his own way and language, is surely seeking converts to his Chaco Meridian, but he is also challenging others to test his model and come up with a better one. To do either or more, one must first read this book."—**J. Jefferson Reid, University of Arizona;** *Journal of Arizona History*

"*The Chaco Meridian* gives me hope for the survival of archaeology in this postmodern, new millennial world. It vindicates the approach of the lone scholar and harks back to the great strides made by the independent foundations and scholars of bygone years. Let there be more books like it. . . . If others will be inspired to follow Lekson's lead and tackle the unknown and unpopular, the profession, the public, and all of us will be the better for it."—**Stephanie M. Whittlesey, Statistical Research, Inc.;** *Journal of Field Archaeology*

The Chaco
Meridian

Cardinal Mazarin smiled, holding out his hands, as if to convey the expectation that such things would happen only on the correct meridian.

—*Umberto Eco*, The Island of the Day Before

The Chaco Meridian

One Thousand Years of Political and Religious Power in the Ancient Southwest

Second Edition

STEPHEN H. LEKSON

Foreword by Ruth M. Van Dyke,
Phillip Tuwaletstiwa, and Severin Fowles

ROWMAN & LITTLEFIELD
Lanham • Boulder • New York • London

Published by Rowman & Littlefield
A wholly owned subsidiary of The Rowman & Littlefield Publishing Group, Inc.
4501 Forbes Boulevard, Suite 200, Lanham, Maryland 20706
www.rowman.com

Unit A, Whitacre Mews, 26-34 Stannary Street, London SE11 4AB, United Kingdom

Copyright © 2015 by Rowman & Littlefield
First edition 1999.

All rights reserved. No part of this book may be reproduced in any form or by any electronic or mechanical means, including information storage and retrieval systems, without written permission from the publisher, except by a reviewer who may quote passages in a review.

British Library Cataloguing in Publication Information Available

Library of Congress Cataloging-in-Publication Data

Lekson, Stephen H.
 The Chaco meridian : one thousand years of political and religious power in the ancient Southwest / Stephen H. Lekson. — Second edition.
    pages cm
 Includes bibliographical references and index.
 ISBN 978-1-4422-4644-7 (cloth : alk. paper) — ISBN 978-1-4422-4645-4 (pbk. : alk. paper) — ISBN 978-1-4422-4646-1 (electronic) 1. Pueblo Indians—Antiquities. 2. Pueblo Indians—Politics and government. 3. Pueblo roads. 4. Mimbres culture. 5. Chaco culture. 6. Chaco Culture National Historical Park (N.M.) 7. Aztec Ruins National Monument (N.M.) 8. Casas Grandes Site (Mexico) I. Title.
 E99.P9L44 2015
 978.9004'974—dc23
                                                                          2014047175

∞™ The paper used in this publication meets the minimum requirements of American National Standard for Information Sciences—Permanence of Paper for Printed Library Materials, ANSI/NISO Z39.48-1992.

Printed in the United States of America

For Alden C. Hayes, who noticed the Meridian years ago:
he had the good sense to let it lie.

For J. Charles Kelley, who warned me about Culiacán.

For John R. Stein, who had all the right ideas long before anyone else.

And for Peter Pino, who traveled the Meridian and wrote a song about it.

Contents

Figures

Foreword in
Three Movements

I

It has been fifteen years since Steve Lekson first jolted the world of Southwest archaeology with the initial publication of *The Chaco Meridian*. As predicted by pundits at that time, the work has since played a significant role in setting research agendas, not to mention raising blood pressure, across the Southwest. Lekson is the best and brightest among us—a scholar with the creativity, the vision, and the audacity to challenge traditional notions about the scale and scope of movements and interactions in the ancient Southwest.

Like it or loathe it, you can't just leave it; *The Chaco Meridian* is a witty, irreverent, inspired piece of scholarship that cannot be, and has not been, ignored. Lekson's intellectually invigorating ideas have impacted Southwest archaeology in several major ways.

First, *The Chaco Meridian* forces readers to think beyond the provincial boundaries that govern the work and thought of many Southwest colleagues, mired in the myopia of their own particular river valleys or desert plateaus. Just as Chaco did not stop at the edge of the San Juan Basin, the ancient Southwest did not stop at the contemporary US-Mexico border. Lekson is one of the few who have long been cognizant of that fact. There is nothing unreasonable or unlikely about ancient Southwest interactions that spanned 500 km or more.

Second, *The Chaco Meridian* has inspired Southwest archaeologists (including myself) to work at the scale of landscape, not site. Past peoples were concerned with more than making a living in the desert: they imbued places with memories and meanings. Today's investigations into sacred geographies, viewsheds, soundscapes, social memory, roads, and movement owe a debt of inspiration to Lekson, who was perhaps the first widely recognized scholar to build a model around a meaningful cosmographic alignment with deep history and far-reaching implications. Lekson takes landscape and cosmography seriously—as do the contemporary indigenous inhabitants of the Southwest.

Third and more locally, *The Chaco Meridian* motivated a bevy of scholars to head to the Middle San Juan, where we are still in the midst of a research boom carried out by archaeologists seeking to both support and refute Lekson's ideas about Aztec as Chaco's successor. The basic fact of Chaco-to-Aztec is now widely accepted, but there are still many questions around when, how, and why.

This new and improved version of *The Chaco Meridian* expands Lekson's original vision to the north and south, to time periods both earlier and later. Southwest archaeological scholarship has proceeded apace over the past decade and a half, and the second edition is replete with up-to-the-minute information and discoveries. Orchestrated by powerful ancient elites, Lekson's original meridian stretched across time and space to link Chaco to Aztec to Paquimé. In this new and expanded vision, elites now initiate the meridian in Chaco Canyon in the Basketmaker III period, head north to Sacred Ridge–Blue Mesa for the Pueblo I period, return to Chaco for Pueblo II, rebound to Aztec for Pueblo III, travel 630 km south to Paquimé for Pueblo IV, and keep going for another 630 km to meet the Spanish at Culiacán.

The Chaco Meridian bears the hallmarks of postmodern theory's incursions into the conservative empiricism espoused by a previous generation of Southwest archaeologists. Lekson's thought is evolving with, not against, the times. As he points out, this is a narrative argument, not a testable hypothesis—nor does it need to be. Lekson is right about at least four things: ancient Southwest people did care about cosmography; ancient Southwest people did communicate and move across long distances; ancient Southwest people did have the technological means to carry out this program; and finally, the alignment of these five very large, very weird sites in sequential time and space is certainly odd. Cardinal alignments over long distances were *de rigueur* in the ancient Andean world, and there is no reason why they could not have been important in Southwest North America. To refute Lekson's argument requires us to engage with motives, not means or opportunity, and this brings us back to the crux of the issue: the nature of socio-politico-eco-ritual organization at Chaco. Although I (like many others) balk at the connotations of calling Chacoan leaders "kings," I heartily concur with Lekson (and many others) that Chaco was not just a big pueblo full of pseudo-egalitarian farmers. In the new *Chaco Meridian*, Lekson introduces the Mesoamerican *altepetl* as a unit of governance involving a rotating cadre of noble families who collected tribute from a small territory in hierarchical fashion. This sounds an awful lot like how some of us have always envisioned Chaco working but with the added benefit of an actual historical (and historically appropriate?) ethnographic analog. The new ideas in this second edition are likely to continue to invigorate Southwest archaeological scholarship for the next fifteen years.

Lekson's prose is peppered with self-deprecating witticisms, irreverent asides, and bad puns. Copious notes are loaded with gems of insight and historical anecdotes. Lekson clearly enjoys thinking, working, and writing as an archaeologist. His wordplay is a breath of fresh air on an archaeological landscape where most scholars of his stature labor to build arguments one passive, colorless sentence at a time. Lekson's prose, by contrast, is nothing if not engaging. Readers may shout with outrage, groan with dismay, chuckle with recognition, or leap up to respond, but they will certainly have an opinion. Yes, "uniquity is unsettling," and *The Chaco Meridian*, second edition, is nothing if not unique. If you've read it before, read it again, in this new and improved version. And if you haven't read it yet, get ready for a rollicking ride.

—Ruth M. Van Dyke, Binghamton University, State University of New York

II

This complex book is a major contribution to Southwestern historical and archeological literature; it transcends traditional archaeology through an original approach that synthesizes history and science. Steve Lekson presents a plethora of sweeping concepts while creating a line-by-line evidentiary examination of everything that is important in Chaco archeology. Block by block, he builds a Unified Theory.

When Lekson begat the original *Chaco Meridian*, I had mixed reactions. I puzzled about a basic question: Why would the ancestors create a long alignment between Chaco and Paquimé? Finally, I asked a question I felt I could answer: Could they actually create this alignment?

Before the global positioning system rendered America's small pool of geodetic scientists obsolete, we measured distance and directions on a continental scale. Initially, we did it with invar tapes and theodolites. Putting my archaic knowledge to use, I wrote a paper in 2000 (unpublished) analyzing whether the Chacoans could create a long north-south alignment. I concluded they could.

With that off my chest, let us now concentrate on the more substantive questions the second edition of *The Chaco Meridian* raises and responds to.

I approach this task from three perspectives. First, I am trained in the physical sciences. Second, I am a Hopi. Third, I relish Steve's perspective: He is liberal, humorous, creative, courageous, smart, and direct.

In this seminal work, Steve approaches the Chaco Conundrums of who, how, where, when, and why like an attorney arguing a case before us, the jury: He says, "Well, yes: I'm making an argument, building a narrative. Not science, more like a legal case. Not scientific certainty but a preponderance of evidence."

Does he succeed? Not if he were arguing a case where the criteria for guilt is "no reasonable doubt." However, as a civil case, he presents powerful arguments. His circumstantial evidence for the Chaco Meridian, and much more, is convincing. In saying this, I anticipate a muted swell of murmuring voices, evolving into a chanting chorus, and ending in a high-decibel crescendo shouting, "But where is your proof?" To all the Naysayers, I say, where is your contradictory proof?

In 1999, just before the original *Chaco Meridian* made its appearance, I wrote, "Of the many who have tried to fathom Chaco's enigma, a few people have provided insights that, to me, are original, evocative and creative: I highlight Steve Lekson, Mike Marshall, Anna Sofaer, and John Stein."

The strength of their views resides in their intuitive and unorthodox thinking. Guided by their "feel" for a place, an understanding of human nature, an intuitive sense of where to go, and a willingness to embrace the unconventional, they see what many of us miss.

However, in going this route, they have paid a price, because their reasoning is subjective and supporting data is sparse. Therefore, colleagues do not rush forward with warm embraces. The irony is that some of their harshest critics eventually copy, modify, amplify, or borrow their ideas.

I have thought about Chaco since I first traveled there in 1961. I have worked over the years to develop my "theory" to explain Chaco's origins, organization, constructs, and closure.

I reasoned that a "Unified Theory" should have these characteristics:

- Make no unreasonable leaps in logic.
- Seem plausible.
- Conform to the "facts" as we understand them.
- Offer a broad and coherent explanation for the phenomenon.

In other words, the theory should stand tall until confronted with contrary evidence or usurped by better idea.

Drawing on my earlier writing, I want to reinforce some of Steve's ideas.

"The Mesoamericans invented writing, a calendar and zero. During the Classic Period, AD 150–900, they built civilizations comparable to any other great civilizations in the world. This was also a time of social strife, warfare, and conquest. During this time of upheaval, there were migrations away from the heart of Mesoamerica toward the frontier regions."

Ben Nelson helped me understand this. In a long telephone conversation, I described my beliefs about the origins of Chaco. He referred me to his essay in which he states, "Frontier developments may be related to rearrangements of core Mesoamerican power structures associated with the disintegration and collapse of the megalopolis of Teotihuacan around AD 600. . . . The local polities that formed in the Hohokam, Pueblo, and Mogollon areas around AD 775–1150 can be seen as the final and most distant reverberations of phenomena occurring in . . . Mexico . . . around AD 500–900 " (Nelson 2000).

Steve's book is sweeping in concept and addresses all of the reasonable arguments for and against his own ideas about origins, alignments, movement, interaction, hegemony, history, integration—the list goes on and on. I was left with one overarching conclusion: reasonably, it could have happened that way.

Having offered these thoughts I have a few quibbles. Steve mentions the astronomy at Chaco but does not address fully the role it may have played. I contend that it was a major factor in the elite's ability to establish and maintain power. By demonstrating their esoteric astronomic knowledge and using it to razzle, dazzle, and befuddle the locals, they had a powerful tool. I am certain they exploited it; otherwise, there would be no Chimney Rock and other lunar or solar alignments. If Steve developed the role of astronomy, he could also clarify and deepen the Mesoamerican connection.

Steve brings the Chaco roads into his evidentiary lexicon. He wrote, "Populations were concentrated in Mesoamerica, [but] spread out in Chaco's region. Chaco developed technologies to make it work: roads and line-of-sight communications networks ensured the coherence of the polity form over the huge Chacoan region."

I am uncertain what Steve meant by his statement about roads: I would be surprised if he intended to place the roads in a utilitarian context.

John Roney, in his excellent paper, "Prehistoric Roads and Integration in the Chaco System," described seventy roads (Roney 1992). Only fourteen roads were longer than 3.0 kilometers, and 67 percent are less than 1.0 kilometer. Roney references are to the visible formalized sections of the roads, usually entering or exiting the Great Houses and other features. The roads, however, as spiritual pathways, could extend for miles to physical or abstract places.

I believe roads were symbolic and metaphorical. The purpose of the roads formally entering a Great House was to anchor that place in spiritual space and to serve as a portal between worlds. Roads acted as reminders of a common belief system that held Chaco culture together.

Steve promotes the *altepetl* idea. I am not a Naysayer, but I am not fully on board. Yes, it seems to fit. No, I do not have a better idea. Yes, it has historic precedence. Maybe I resist because it is conceptually foreign to my Hopi thinking. I shall buy into it until something better comes along.

I close with this gem from Steve: "Pueblo societies developed, historically, in reaction to and rejection of Chaco, after 1300." When I read this, it leapt off the page and seared my synapses. This short sentence synthesized a conglomeration of ideas I could not assemble into a unified thought. To me it explains much.

—Phillip Tuwaletstiwa

III

The first edition of Stephen Lekson's *The Chaco Meridian* created little explosions throughout Southwest archaeology when it appeared in 1999. Perhaps you thought debates over the organizational complexity of pre-Columbian societies in the region were somehow settled; Lekson was there to tell us that we haven't even begun to inquire into the sorts of ambitious political geographies and complicated historical contingencies that guided Ancestral Pueblo development. Perhaps you thought Southwest archaeology had entered a synthetic stage when large regional databases were finally revealing the true nature of past social interaction; Lekson stepped in to tell us not only that we must think continentally rather than regionally but also that regional patterns must be threaded together with a unifying historical analysis if they are to make any sense at all. And perhaps you had simply resigned to letting the general public revel in the "enigmas" of the Pueblo past; well, here was an empirically rich narrative that drew a wide readership into the thick of archaeological debate over models rather than mysteries.

The Chaco Meridian is as much about a line of thought in the development of one of archaeology's most original scholars as it is about a line through space that organized the political history of the pre-Columbian Southwest. In this much-anticipated second edition, both of these lines are greatly extended. Mobilizing a swirl of new research from the past fifteen years, Lekson not only responds to his critics but redoubles his argument for reading Southwest history spatially as a movement along a north-south axis that cosmologically anchored and legitimized an emerging noble class in this northern periphery of the post-Classic Mesoamerican world. To his prior account of a progression from Chaco Canyon to Aztec Ruins to Paquimé, Lekson adds key new discussions of earlier Basketmaker III and Pueblo I developments within the same geo-historical corridor, as well as a provocative expansion of his argument for a subsequent leap south along the meridian from Paquimé to the late pre-Columbian site of Culiacán on the Pacific coast. In the course of these travels, he introduces us to an important new model for understanding ancient Southwestern political formations—the *altepetl*—which was there all the time within the wider Mesoamerican tradition. As with the first edition, Lekson presents us with an intellectual call-to-arms; this is a book that demands response.

Read Lekson's study of the Chaco meridian—again, for the first time—to be taken in by the stunning vision of a Pueblo past that finally overcomes the belittling provincialism of so much twentieth-century archaeology in the Southwest. Or read it beet red in the face as a provocation to hone one's own position on Chaco (and the rest of the Southwest) through creative disagreement. Or read it for the sheer joy of listening to one of the most distinctive literary voices in contemporary archaeology. But do read it again to absorb its central teaching: that compelling narrative histories of "prehistory" are, in fact, possible.

"There's a story to be told here—a history—if we can read the ruins."

—Severin Fowles, Columbia University

Acknowledgments, Apologies

When the thought first came to him, Farmer Hoggett dismissed it as mere
whimsy . . . but, like most of his harebrained ideas, it wouldn't go away.

—*Babe*

This book's a rip-off: it's other people's work. Charles Di Peso advanced the idea
of Paquimé-Chaco connections forty years ago; John Stein, Jim Judge, and others
nominated Aztec as Chaco's successor; Stein, Mike Marshall, Anna Sofaer, and
others recorded the North Road; Peter McKenna and Tom Windes got hundreds of new dates (and new data) from Aztec; Jeff Dean and John Ravesloot put
Paquimé in its chronological place; Pueblo people passed their histories down
through the generations; God made north. I just put it all together.

Illumination came while I was defacing a page of the *National Atlas*, adding Paquimé's location to the margin of the "Arizona and New Mexico" sheet.
The margin was, of course, blank white; I needed Paquimé's coordinates to plot
my dot. When I scaled out the latitude and longitude, I noticed some alarming
geography: the plotted dot was hot, potentially important, and (mildly) danger-
ous, professionally. After several months of cold feet, I decided to plunge in: just
another dent, after all, in my junkyard reputation.

Something this dicey—for let me be frank: this argument skates the thin ice
of a globally warm and fuzzy New Age—needed special treatment. There is the
Science strategy: keep it close to the vest until the truth is revealed (presto!) like
a new car at an auto show. But this argument, unlike a shiny new Dodge, is not
immediately compelling. It's complicated, it grows on you—or, at least, it grew
on me. So I decided on plan B: market saturation. I presented innumerable papers

and posters, preached to meetings and chapters, invited myself to universities and museums, published in newspapers and magazines, corrupted graduate students. I sent out early drafts to a select list of Southwestern archaeologists. Most, understandably, did not respond; but two-pound manuscripts are impossible to ignore. I spent a small fortune in photocopies and postage, not so much fishing for converts as beating the bushes.

Like Holmes's giant rat of Sumatra, this was a story for which the world was not yet prepared. I tried to prime my audience, to dull the sharp edge of reaction and yet whet the appetite. There's more than one way to make a case. *Science* works for quantitative hard-science blockbusters; complicated semihistorical, semianthropological diatribes require a different approach.

My arguments received polite interest at professional meetings (actually, a poster version won the "best of show" award at an SAA meeting, a fact of which I am inordinately proud). I sensed a reaction among my colleagues much like that which greeted Edward Ferdon's argument, at an early Pecos Conference, linking the Southwest and Mexico: "He called across the table and congratulated me for having put some life into the session, and then added, 'of course I knew you didn't believe a word you were saying'" (Ferdon 1955:10). Well, Ferdon did, and so do I. I'm not just stirring up the waters to see what floats and what sinks: I think the Chaco-Aztec-Paquimé business is/was real. This might have been easier had I simply demonstrated the remarkable material similarities and sequential chronology of Chaco, Aztec, and Paquimé and then footnoted the alignment as a possible subject for future research. Where's the fun in that? I admit that one of the appeals of this work is seeing how far I can push the boundaries of polite research before I'm on the outside looking in. Life's too short to play safe.

Time to name a few names. For services real and imagined, I would like to thank: David Armstrong (monkey ID, figure 2.14), Doug Bamforth, Bruce Bradley, Dave Brugge, Jim Byrkit, Linda Cordell, Darrell Creel, Bill Davis, Jeff Dean, Joey Donahue, Chris Downum, David Doyel, Andrew Duff, Patucche Gilbert, George Gumerman, Lou Hacker, Al Hayes, Alice Kehoe, Klara Kelley, David Kelley, Jane Kelley, Ed Ladd, Fred Lange, Bob Leonard, Brad Lepper, Bill Lipe, Kim Malville, Joan Mathien, Randy McGuire, Peter McKenna, Barbara Mills, Paul Minnis, Ben Nelson, Ben Patrusky, Lori Pendleton, David Phillips, Stella Pino, Rene Reitsma, Carroll Riley, John Rinaldo, Dean Saitta, Curt Schaafsma, Jason Shapiro, Payson Sheets, Rolf Sinclair, Anna Sofaer, John Speth, John Stein, Steven Swanson, John Taylor, Wolky Toll, Sharon Urban, Mark Varien, Gwinn Vivian, Barbara Voorhies, Michael Whalen, David Wilcox, Chip Wills, Tom Windes, Norman Yoffee, and the participants at the 1996, 1997, and 1998 CU Field Schools, the 1996 Oxford V meetings, the 1995 Southwest Symposium, the 1996 34th Annual New Horizons in Science Briefing, various Pecos and Mogollon and Anasazi conferences, colloquia audiences at ASU, UNM, UA, NAU, and CU, the Colorado Archaeological Society, Edge of the Cedars Museum, the CU

Center at Cortez, Colorado, and CU classes who got guest-lectured. My particular thanks to Roger Kennedy and Peter Pino—scholars and gentlemen—who offered encouraging counsel when most needed. None of these people, institutions, or convocations are responsible or liable, but they all had a role in shaping the argument. Thanks!

I thought about these matters while flying back and forth to Chicago, Washington, New York, and other pots of gold in the service of Crow Canyon Archaeological Center. Thanks for the bonus miles and airline meals! I had my "aha" moment in 1996 shortly after I left the employ of that fine organization; but the joke was on me. After a couple of years of circulating drafts, hitting the lecture circuit, and hitting walls, I finally found time to write it all down in the summer of 1998. When not fleeing militiamen or digging Great Houses, I spent that summer in Bluff, Utah (supported by a JFDA grant from the University of Colorado) trying to tame this beast.

Several people slogged through this manuscript near the end, when it was getting really ripe: reviewers Mitch Allen, Brian Fagan, Keith Kintigh, Bill Lipe, and Dean Saitta; and several volunteers: Chris Pierce, Dan Falt, and Chris Ward. The reviewers improved things for both author and reader by insisting on compressions, truncations, and digestions (this is a lot shorter than it used to be) and asking for more pictures. Mitch Allen was a great publisher, Patricia Rechtman an excellent editor, and Marjorie Leggitt an outstanding illustrator.

My wife and colleague, Cathy Cameron, has been wonderfully patient with my fads and enthusiasms. She is blameless, not culpable for this book; I couldn't have written it without her support and kindness—but these sins are my own.

Who haven't I thanked? Probably lots of people; if you actually want to see your name here, associated with these heretical ideas, but I missed you, let me know. I may be forgetful, but I'm not an ingrate. Happy trails to you until we meet again.

—S.H.L.

Preface to the Second Edition

And so we meet again, Dr. Jones. (Was that Belloq or Duke Nukem?) The franchise continues, and here comes the crystal curveball. There is much new material to ponder, and much to talk about. The new data seem (to me at least) to support the arguments of the first edition. As you will see, fifteen years later I think the facts remain as stated, with of course some very important updates, and I've honed my interpretations in ways that make it easier for me—if not you—to deal with them. Some of this material was published as a series of disconnected footnotes to *A History of the Ancient Southwest* (2009), and the new edition of *Chaco Meridian* reflects the Southwest presented in that book. But most of the new material in this edition is just that: new material. I estimate by word count that the second edition is over two-thirds new and improved—bigger, better, and brasher than the first edition. (I was struck, revising the book, how temperate and restrained was my 1999 prose.)

I've updated the references with new titles cited in the second edition, and with published versions of what was unpublished in 1999 (in press, theses, etc.); but I've not tried to bring the literatures for various themes up to date. So there are a lot of missing references from 1999 to about 2009 (for these, see Lekson 2009).

Since the first edition in 1999, I've been busy with projects in several parts of the Southwest: the Chaco Synthesis Project; the Bluff Great House in southeast Utah; Pinnacle Ruin in south-central New Mexico; analysis of the Yellow Jacket site in southwestern Colorado; Chimney Rock near Pagosa Springs, Colorado; and Black Mountain and Woodrow Ruin in southwestern New Mexico. And ten years of NAGPRA. While I was the PI on all the field projects, I deferred as much as possible to my co-PIs and PDs: Cathy Cameron, Karl Laumbach, Katy Putsavage, Jakob Sedig, Brenda Todd, and Richard Wilshusen. And for

NAGPRA, deferred always to the Tribes and Nations. My thanks to all those excellent professionals, young and not so young, and to all the crew chiefs and students who worked on those enjoyable projects. And to all the endlessly patient Tribal representatives. Each project, in its own way, is represented or at least reflected in the new material here.

I travelled the Meridian in October 1997 with Peter Pino and Roger Kennedy and a group of interesting Crow Canyoneers; that trip helped a lot on the first edition. I did the route again in 2004 with David Roberts and Bill Hatcher; and that journey got me thinking about retelling the story. Then in 2012, we sparked Meridian ideas at an NEH Summer Institute, "Mesoamerica and the Southwest," organized by George Scheper and Laraine Fletcher—a large and lively gang of historians, art historians, ethnohistorians, and scholars of every stripe—and *nary an archaeologist*, save Katy Putsavage and me! That did it: revise and resubmit, a second edition. Thanks!

I am happy to name, with thanks, those who shared ideas and shared data, and who honed my arguments for this second edition: Larry Baker, Erin Baxter, Larry Benson, Gary Brown, John Carpenter, Jason Chuipka, Jim Copeland, Darrell Creel, Patty Crown, Chris Downum, Dabney Ford, Rich Friedman, Pat Gilman, Kathy Durand Gore, Gerardo Gutiérrez, Winston Hurst, Jane Kelley, Roger Kennedy, Timothy Kohler, Mike Marshall, Mike Mathiowetz, Randy McGuire, Peter McKenna, Paul Minnis, Ben Nelson, Matt Peeples, John Pohl, Paul Reed, David Roberts, Michael Smith, Anna Sofaer, Karl Taube, Wolky Toll, Ruth Van Dyke, Mark Varien, Chuck Wheeler, Richard Wilshusen, and Tom Windes. All can honestly deny any association whatsoever with the odd notions presented here, but they helped me—a lot! I thank Michael Whalen and Paul Minnis, and Suzy Fish and Paul Fish for sharing with me drafts of "in press" books—very important books indeed! And particular thanks to Sean Rice, for his support and encouragement. Thanks!

Since 1999 and the first *Chaco Meridian*, I've been at the University of Colorado Museum of Natural History. I've greatly enjoyed and benefited from my archaeological colleagues at Boulder: Doug Bamforth, Cathy Cameron, the late Linda Cordell, Beth Dusinberre, John Hoffecker, Sarah James, Art Joyce, Scott Ortman, Payson Sheets, Paola Villa, and Tim Webmoor. Various bits and pieces of the second edition were bounced off these fine people, who mostly bounced 'em right back. My day job (which I love) in the Anthropology Section of the Museum: Jen Shannon, Christie Cain, Debbie Confer, Stephanie Gilmore, a long line of excellent graduate assistants, and our NAGPRA guru, Jan Bernstein. None of them were involved in the Meridian brouhaha, but I knew I could wool-gather about archaeological foolishness and the Anthropology Section would operate efficiently and professionally. (It's like . . . they don't really need me.) Thanks to all!

And the fine crew at Rowman & Littlefield: Leanne Silverman, Andrea Kendrick, Jehanne Schweitzer, and Ina Gravitz (indexer extraordinaire), pulling it all together. And, of course, my thanks to Ruth Van Dyke, Severin Fowles, and Phil Tuwaletstiwa for their very kind foreword(s). Thanks!

My apologies to anyone I've forgotten: my mind isn't what it used to be, and it wasn't that all that great to begin with . . . a bear of very little brain.

I've added (with his kind permission) Dennis Holloway's magnificent computer graphics of Casas Grandes. He's done wonderful things for many Native American sites: http://www.dennisrhollowayarchitect.com/VirtualRealityArchaeology.html.

I owe chapter 4's title to Paul Minnis, a debt I failed to acknowledge in the first edition of the book. Dr. Minnis was riffing on a quote by Thomas Huxley. Thomas Huxley was grandfather to Aldous Huxley, whose book *Brave New World* I've riffed on, more than once. I've been a thorn in Paul's side from time to time, which I regret: he's a fine fellow. In the foreword to *Brave New World*, Huxley advised: "If you have behaved badly, repent, make what amends you can and address yourself to the task of behaving better next time." I repent and make amends, but I'm not sure I'll behave better next time. My thinking on Chaco-Aztec-Paquimé has involved learning from my mistakes—very selectively.

James Q. Jacobs, of Central Arizona College, informed me that he discovered and named the Chaco Meridian in 1990. He didn't publish his discovery, and I don't see how I could have known; but I try to be fair, so: let it be known that Jacobs noticed that the Big Horn Medicine Wheel, Chaco, Aztec, and the Mimbres Valley were on the 108° longitude in 1990, and in 1991 he noticed that Casas Grandes and Mount Wilson were also on this longitude. He further notes that the distance from Mount Wilson to Pueblo Bonito was 1/200th of the circumference of the earth. Jacobs and I are talking about (some of) the same alignments, but I hope it is clear to the reader that our interpretations of meaning differ markedly. There is little glory and much grief in the Chaco Meridian; for my part, Jacobs is welcome to both. His website: http://www.jqjacobs.net/southwest/chaco_meridian.html.

1

Pourparlers

Trust me, Wilbur. People are very gullible. They'll believe anything they see in print.

—*Charlotte the large gray spider (as reimagined by a Hollywood hack)*

This book is not for the faint of heart, or for neophytes. If you are a practicing Southwestern archaeologist with hypertension problems, stop. Read something safe. If you are healthy, but new to the region, I highly recommend starting with Stephen Plog's (2008) *Ancient Peoples of the American Southwest*, or John Kantner's (2004) *Ancient Puebloan Southwest*. Fill up, because we're diving into the deep end and not coming up for air.

THE ARGUMENT IN BRIEF

In Pueblo prehistory, there were three "capitals"—small ceremonial cities where low-grade political complexity encompassed and organized surrounding regions: Chaco Canyon, Aztec Ruins, and Paquimé (also called Casas Grandes) (figure 1.1). These capitals were sequential, and historically related. Each was by far the most important settlement of its time and place. Chaco, Aztec, and Paquimé together spanned five centuries, from about AD 900 to AD 1450. (All dates are AD or CE, and hereafter I dispense with those abbreviations.) A variety of symbols and architectural forms were used to signify historical continuity from each successor capital back to its predecessor. The three capitals were all built on the same meridian.

So too were two earlier centers (but not capitals) and one later Mesoamerican city, altogether spanning more than a millennium. Pueblo, Navajo, and colonial

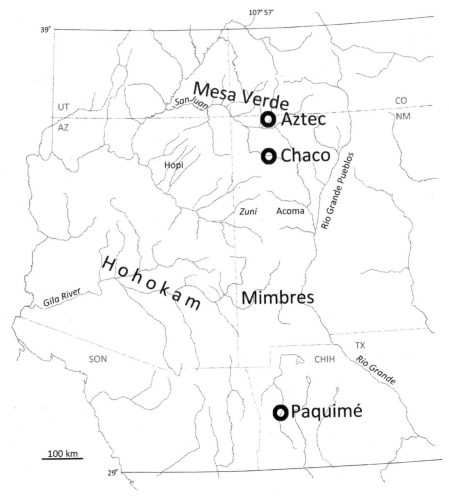

FIGURE 1.1
The Southwest, with the usual suspects.

Spanish traditions and histories allude to the three capitals, the Mesoamerican city, and their histories. That's all simple enough, I think.

PLAN OF THE BOOK

The story behind that story is not so simple, or so neat. It emerged piecemeal over the last twenty years, and continued to change and evolve during the writing of the first and second editions of this book. My own work, four decades in

Chaco's region, the Mesa Verde area, and southwestern New Mexico, prepared the ground, hoed the long row. Other people's research—Charles Di Peso (1974), Earl Morris (1919–1928), Neil Judd (1954, 1964), Frank Roberts (1929), and dozens of other "old" reports—fell into line, like seeds in a furrow. The research of John Stein and his associates (Fowler and Stein 1992; Stein, Friedman, Blackhorse, and Loose 2007; Stein and Lekson 1992; Stein and McKenna 1988; Stein, Suiter, and Ford 1997) was critical to the growth of my ideas. At this point in my strained agricultural metaphor, it could be said that my friend John Stein's work was the manure—but that might be misunderstood, so let's say Miracle-Gro. This second edition is informed by (irrigated by?) recent work at Aztec Ruins (e.g., Brown, Windes, and McKenna 2008), a series of new reports on Casas Grandes archaeology (e.g., Whalen and Minnis 2001, 2009), remarkable excavations by the Animas-La Plata Project (e.g., Potter and Chuipka 2007a, 2007b), new-data-from-old-data at Chaco (e.g., Plog and Heitman 2010), and many others acknowledged in the pages that follow. Most of the data and many of the interpretations are not mine: they are others', but I do not expect the original researchers (dead or alive) to be thrilled by my use and reuse. All these people, of course, had their own agendas and goals; if you want to see what they were thinking, read them.

Ideas germinated on airplanes, sprouted at meetings, vined over ruins, withered during tribal consultations. One idea crowded out another; pruning was as much a problem as weeding. And the result is still a tangle, a thick spiny hedge of concepts and facts. The presentation in this book reflects that unruly growth—as much a research program as an argument. It is, in fact, a very personal research program (no one crowds my bandwagon), so I insert my own experiences to illustrate particular points or quandaries. There are many side arguments and tangents, explaining reuse of old data and reworkings of old and new interpretations, and begging forgiveness. Be warned: It's messy in here.

Still, there are beginnings, middles, and ends. Chapter 2 begins with descriptions of Chaco and Mimbres. Chaco was, politically, the beginning—although, as we shall see in chapter 3, there may have been a run-up of pre-Chaco (ceremonial?) centers. Mimbres was Chaco's brilliant neighbor to the south, and Paquimé's precocious precursor—a key role, but Mimbres was less a protagonist than a chorus. Chaco has long been the *bête noir*, *deus ex machina*, eight-hundred-pound gorilla, and in-room elephant of Southwestern archaeology (to mix Bob Euler's metaphors with a few of my own). What was Chaco? Archaeologists despair, pronounce Chaco an unsolvable mystery.

In chapter 3, I solve that mystery—and it's not that big a deal, as it turns out. Most of chapter 3 looks at Chaco, Aztec, and Paquimé, and a few other sites on the same meridian. Chaco and Paquimé framed the seminal archaeological problem first posed forty years ago by Charles Di Peso, Paquimé's excavator. Di Peso suggested that Chaco and Paquimé were historically linked, the latter prime moving the former: Paquimé caused Chaco. Di Peso was right—Chaco and Pa-quimé were chapters of the same story—but his plot was flawed (Paquimé came after Chaco). Aztec Ruins provides the missing link, as it were, in that narrative. Aztec Ruins was excavated by Earl Morris (whose job I now have) in the 1910s, but several key aspects of the site were described much later by John Stein and Peter McKenna (1988), and Gary Brown, Thomas Windes, and Peter McKenna (2008). Aztec was the chronological and historical bridge between Chaco and Paquimé, but it surfaced in my thinking long after I had concluded that Di Peso was probably right: Chaco and Paquimé meant more together than apart. Thus, chapter 3 emphasizes Chaco and Paquimé, and brings in Aztec as a key—even critical—afterthought. And chapter 3 extends the story. We have Chaco-Aztec-Paquimé in sequence: What came before? What came after? As it turns out, the five centuries of Chaco-Aztec-Paquimé were preceded by a four-century run-up and a century denouement: from 500 to the arrival of conquistadors—a millennium on the meridian. Before Chaco, there were two earlier, sequential centers—each the largest sites of their times—on the very same meridian, the backstory to Chaco-Aztec-Paquimé. And after those three, things slide south to the fifteenth-century city of Culiacán, also on the Chaco Meridian—the princi-pal city of northernmost Mesoamerican polity, with implications to and from Paquimé (according to eighteenth-century savants). I'm not making this up, folks: the key sites of each epoch of Southwestern prehistory all line up, on the Chaco Meridian.

Chapter 4 focuses sharply on the meridian alignment of Chaco, Aztec, and Paquimé: the long thin line linking the capitals. Some people have problems with that part of my argument, and a few of their problems are real and merit consid-eration. Chapter 4 presents the evidence and anticipates a few challenges.

Chapter 5 summarizes the argument in narrative, and ends with admonish-ments and recommendations about how we might better know and understand the ancient Southwest—and North America. To archaeologists of a certain age (say, one to one hundred), my argument may seem outré, even outrageous. But it's not. Not at all—if you understand the contexts of those ancient times, and the contexts of today's American archaeology. In the ancient contexts, capitals and polities and geopolitics should be expected; the continent was awash in states and empires, and had been for many centuries before anything interesting happened in the Southwest. The extraordinary claim would be that state-level shenanigans were absolutely and completely absent north of the international border. Yet that is the position of modern American archaeology: no states north of Mexico. That is doctrine, dogma inherited from nineteenth- and early twentieth-century scholars, who had a colonial and even racist agenda (Lekson 2010). The facts say otherwise, and we've known these facts for many decades. American archaeology is my field and I love it dearly, but it's broken. Chapter 5 suggests some remedies.

IT'S COMPLICATED . . .

"State-level shenanigans" are glossed in the Southwest as *complexity*—an unfortunate word, but one we're stuck with. "Complexity in the Pueblo Southwest"—an idea whose time has come . . . and gone, and come and gone, and come and gone. We've danced too many rounds with the beast, the devil hound that drives otherwise pleasant, sober scholars to apoplectic sputtering. Something about "complexity"—the idea of political hierarchy in the Pueblo region—brings out our worst. Through cycles of heated argument and frustrated truce, it's the topic we love to hate.

Archaeologists of a certain age (say, sixty to one hundred) will remember the Grasshopper–Chavez Pass "debates," which rivaled Ali-Frazier and Hatfield-McCoy for endless bloodletting. (Archaeologists of uncertain ages may or may not want to review that "debate"; see Cordell 1984:346–351 and 1997:421–423.) At issue: Was there or was there not "complexity" at two fourteenth-century pueblos in central Arizona? A simple question, with dire and dreadful results. Single combat pitted professor against professor; platoons of students rushed in; surrounding regions were engulfed; battle became general. Journals filled with invective essays. Meetings crackled with jabs and insults. Those of us not caught in the mangle looked on, appalled. We hoped the combatants would wear themselves out before something awful happened. "Can't we all just get along?" more or less summed it up.

You have to choose your battles. Why quibble over complexity at PIV pueblos when there's Chaco Canyon? Chaco is not a cause worth dying for, exactly, but if any Pueblo place was a "complex" political capital, it was Chaco. As discussed in chapter 2 and appendix A, archaeological interpretations of Chaco span a spectrum from a sort of mystical "rituality" to the grim headquarters of a Toltec thug empire. I'm somewhere toward the middle of that range: Chaco was a small somewhat centralized state (a "polity"), derivative of common Mesoamerican models. I make the argument for your consideration, but the book assumes Chaco was "complex" in those antique terms: it had classes, governments, capitals, and regions.

How Chaco got that way is another story, one focus of chapter 2. Archaeologists have offered a range of models and theories about how Chaco got weird, but most suffer from a shared shortcoming: they assume Chaco evolved locally, that Chaco was making it up as it stumbled along. But there were states and empires galore to the south, in Mesoamerica, for two millennia before Chaco was a twinkle in anyone's eye. Mesoamerica had done all the heavy lifting: inventing villages, evolving polities, forming states and empires. Chaco was a "secondary state"—that's what we call tiny bubbles of political complexity out on the edges of older, bigger, long-boiling states and empires. That simple concept is essential to resolving the problem of Chaco, if not all Chaco's problems. We go over all that in chapter 2.

Political hierarchy is a constant question—in general, because most farmers we know had it; and specifically in the Southwest, because the Pueblos are so famous for avoiding it, at least in our stereotypes of Pueblos as peaceful, communal, ritual, independent farming villages. There was much more to Southwestern prehistory than that (Lekson 2009). This book defines one axis of history—mostly political—over 1,000 km and one thousand years. You will also find themes of hopefully larger interest, scattered here and there. Live dangerously, turn the page.

2

Mondo Chaco

All I say is, kings is kings, and you got to make allowances. Take them all around, they're a mighty ornery lot. It's the way they're raised.

—*Huck Finn*

It all starts with Chaco. Chaco was the first stable, strong polity in the Pueblo Southwest. For centuries before, Pueblo developments had been impressive but evanescent: villages, prior to Chaco, were grown and gone in a generation, popping up again in the next valley, a pattern repeated over and over. At Chaco, traditions took root (Lekson 1989b, 2006c, 2009). Chaco transformed Pueblo life—for better or worse, depending on your social status—and set the trajectory for all that followed.

In this chapter, I present my view of Chaco: what it was, where it came from, how it worked. The question of "where it went" occupies succeeding chapters; but the answer to that question almost certainly involves Mimbres, Chaco's brilliant contemporary; so I devote the last sections of this chapter to Chaco and Mimbres—an interesting if uneasy relationship.

Chaco Canyon contains a dozen "Great Houses"—large sandstone masonry buildings, remarkable for their scale, formality, and craftsmanship (figure 2.1). Building began as early as 850 (Windes and Ford 1996; Plog and Heitman 2010). Construction peaked in the late eleventh and early twelfth centuries. At its height—about 1020 to 1125—Chaco was unique in the Pueblo Southwest (Lekson, Stein, Windes, and Judge 1988; Lekson ed. 2006). Most eleventh-century Pueblo people lived in scattered single-family homes: five or six stone masonry rooms and a "kiva" (figure 2.2). Their walls were simple single-stone-wide

(a)

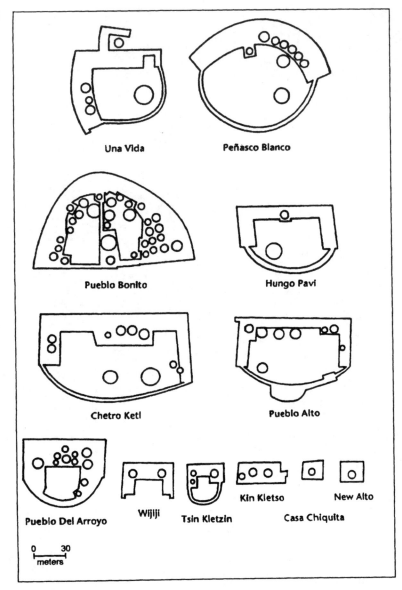

Una Vida

Peñasco Blanco

Pueblo Bonito

Hungo Pavi

Chetro Ketl

Pueblo Alto

Pueblo Del Arroyo

Wijiji

Tsin Kletzin

Kin Kletso

Casa Chiquita

New Alto

0   30
meters

FIGURE 2.1
Chaco Canyon Great Houses (a) and San Juan Basin outliers (b). All at
scale, but north varies. The difference in size between the big Bonito-class
cruisers in Chaco Canyon and typical outliers is obvious; but smaller Chaco
Canyon buildings aren't much bigger than the big outliers. Note also the
variation in ground plans; Chaco buildings don't all look exactly alike, a fact

(b)

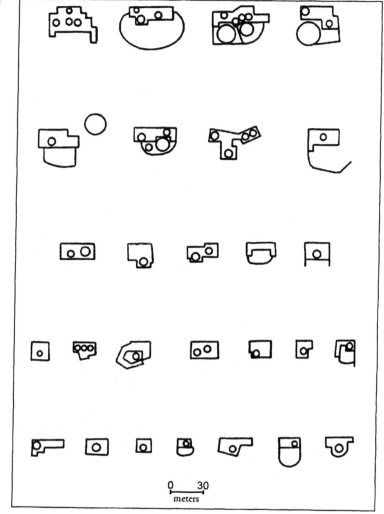

0 ___ 30
meters

used by outlier deniers to argue that these buildings are really local. Seeing differences is easy; seeing patterns is difficult—and far more interesting. The similarities are formal, structural, to a degree relational—and
more significant than petty differences. It's a small world after all. (After
Stephen H. Lekson, "Settlement Patterns and the Chacon Region," 1991;
courtesy the School of American Research Press.)

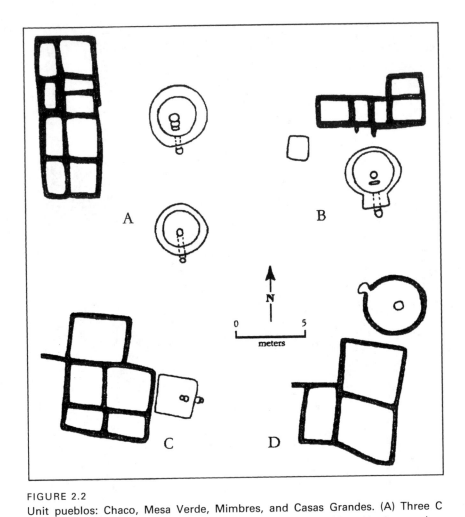

FIGURE 2.2

Unit pueblos: Chaco, Mesa Verde, Mimbres, and Casas Grandes. (A) Three C
site at Chaco Canyon (ca. 1050); (B) Yellow Jacket in the Mesa Verde area (ca.
1250); (C) Dinwiddie in the Mimbres area (ca. 1100); (D) Convento site in the Rio
Casas Grandes valley (ca. 1150)—the only late Viejo (pre-Paquimé) period site
excavated to date. "Unit pueblo" refers to the six-rooms-and-a-kiva module common throughout the Anasazi region (e.g., Chaco, Mesa Verde). It's also found
elsewhere, over a huge area that could be loosely called "Pueblo"— including the
Mimbres and the Casas Grandes regions (Kantner 2004). A number of unit pueblos
are known from Mimbres; the Casas Grandes sample is exactly one, and it may
prove to be an aberration. Some are made of rock, some of mud; some "kivas"
are below-grade, others aboveground. Those facts are important, played against
the shared basic pattern.

masonry and mud, not the massive finely finished walls of Pueblo Bonito. The layouts of those homes (often called "unit pueblos") were informal and organic, continually modified in small increments. The rigid geometries of Chaco Great Houses could be altered only at great cost—yet that too happened, occasionally.

Great Houses are the principal fact, the central matter of Chaco (Lekson 1986a, ed. 2007; Lekson, Windes, and McKenna 2006). Take away Great Houses, and Chaco would not be a national park. Take away Great Houses, and a vast literature—Chaco books, dissertations, articles—would vanish from library shelves. (Would we miss it?) Great Houses were architecture, by any standard, designed by one (or a few) to be seen by many. Some of the canons and geometries governing Chacoan building have been discovered (e.g., Sofaer 1997; Stein, Suiter, and Ford 1997); the control and organization of construction has been described (e.g., Lekson 1986a; Metcalf 2003); the larger architectonics of the Chacoan built environment are at least partially known (e.g., Fritz 1978). Chaco Canyon was an ensemble, but each building was a separate composition, with multistoried room blocks massed around open plazas. Many, and perhaps most, of the rooms were not residential; rather, they were nondomestic storage, transient lodging, or simple massing—but not homes.

A small number of people—hundreds, at most—lived in each Chaco Canyon Great House, and those people were of very high status. They were elites, who lived (and were buried) differently and more expensively than their lower-status contemporaries. The total population of Chaco was probably about 2,500 to 3,000 (Lekson 1986a, 1988c), of whom about half lived in Great Houses; the other half lived in unit pueblos, mostly clustered on the south side of the canyon, the wrong side of the tracks. That's a pretty top-heavy society: 50 percent elites, 50 percent non-elites. But the elites of Chaco had wider spans of control, bigger fish to fry: Chaco was the center or capital of a much larger region, taking in quarters of the Four Corners states. The total population of the San Juan Basin—the area immediately around Chaco in northwestern New Mexico—was at least 50,000 people (Dean et al. 1994 say 55,000 for the whole basin; a recent study of the Chuska Valley estimated 10,625 to 17,000 people in that rich subregion, Heilen and Leckman 2014—which suggests Dean's earlier estimate was reasonable). Various estimates have been made for the Mesa Verde area of southwestern Colorado; during late Chacoan times, a large chunk (perhaps one-half?) of the core Mesa Verde area had perhaps 12,000 people (Kohler, Varien, and Wright 2010:16). The San Juan Basin is about one-third of Chaco's region, and ranged from (relatively) empty space to densely populated districts, like the Chuska Valley. The Chuska Valley and central Mesa Verde were two of the most heavily populated districts in the Chaco region. Extrapolating from the figures for the San Juan Basin, the Chuska Valley, and the central Mesa Verde, I estimate—that is, I guess—that the population of Chaco's larger region was perhaps even twice that of the San Juan Basin; that is, something under 100,000 people. (I offer these estimates—for that's all they are—simply to indicate the approximate scales of Chaco and its region that frame my argument.)

Great House elites probably did not build their own homes; at least, the disparity between the labor required (Lekson 1986a) and the probable number of residents at each Great House (Bernardini 1999; Windes 1984) strongly suggests that architect, builder, and user were three very distinct social roles (Stein and Lekson 1992). Great House residents probably did not make their own pottery: over 50 percent of the pottery at Pueblo Alto at its height was made 80 km away, in the Chuska Valley and elsewhere (Toll 1991). They may not even have cooked their own meals: archaeologists search in vain for domestic cooking hearths, our customary index of the household (Windes 1984; Lekson 1986a). But there were elaborate, bathtub-sized cooking pits in plazas of every Great House—for example, the kitchen excavated in the plaza of Pueblo Alto (Plaza Feature 1 in Windes 1987b:410–445)—which suggest centralized cooking and cooks.

These, and other evidence, make a strong case for an elite class at Chaco (e.g., Lekson 2009; Schelberg 1984; Sebastian 1992). The people who lived in Chacoan Great Houses were not like the people who lived at Cliff Palace, or Alkali Ridge, or any of the thousands of hamlets, homes, and unit pueblos that housed the vast majority of ancient Pueblo people.

Chaco was so unlike ordinary Pueblo villages that archaeologists in the early 1970s thought that its inspiration must have come from the high civilizations of Mexico (Hayes 1981; Di Peso 1974). Mexican claims of the 1970s offended Southwesternists. The Chaco Project—a National Park Service research program of the New Archaeology 1970s and 1980s—reclaimed Chaco for the Southwest, denying historical Mexican involvement and deriving Chaco from an adaptation to local ecological conditions (Judge 1979, 1989). The pendulum swings, and today we are groping toward a new understanding of Chaco that incorporates both history and environment, on much larger scales—even looking south, to Mexico.

Not quite that far south was Mimbres, an archaeological region in southwestern New Mexico, famed for its black-on-white pottery (figure 2.3). Most pots were decorated with intricate geometric designs, but a considerable number show images and scenes of great artistic merit and compelling intrinsic interest: quotidian affairs and esoteric rituals, people of this world and spiritual beings of another (e.g., Brody 1977).

Mimbres architecture did not equal its ceramic art. Villages of considerable size were constructed of crude masonry in haphazard arrangements. Kivas—a key element of Anasazi villages—were present (figure 2.2), generally one to each room block (Anyon and LeBlanc 1980). The stone masonry, kivas, and black-on-white pottery suggested to early researchers that Mimbres was, in essence, Anasazi (e.g., Haury 1986). Another unwanted outside "influence": New Archaeologists of the 1970s denied any Anasazi involvement, asserting local origins, (again) in a local adaptive setting (e.g., LeBlanc 1983; Shafer 1995). Again, the pendulum swings:

FIGURE 2.3

Some famous pottery types. Top row from left to right: Gallup Black-on-white (UCM 9463), Mimbres Black-on-white (UCM 3268), Reserve Smudged-polished (UCM 13305); bottom row from left to right: Mesa Verde Black-on-white (UCM 492), Ramos Poly-chrome (UCM 9363). Regional entities had ceramic signatures, at least for archaeologi-cal pigeonholing. To various degrees, those signatures may have meant something to the ancients. Gallup Black-on-white is associated with the Chaco region (or rather, its distinctive designs, like those shown here). Mimbres Black-on-white was specific to its region. We cherish the pictorial designs (like the fish, here), but Mimbres's contem-poraries had no use for it. When Mimbres ended, the post-Mimbres peoples rejected it entirely, opting for the antidesigns of smudged-polished bowls. Mesa Verde Black-on-white was named for the landform and National Park, but it was made in great quantities from southeastern Utah on the east to Aztec Ruins on the west—the Mesa Verde region, which greatly exceeds the boundaries of the National Park. Ramos Poly-chrome was the calling card of Paquimé, although like most of the types named here, it was probably made over a much larger (Casas Grandes) region, and exchanged well beyond that area. (Photos by Erin Baxter; courtesy the University of Colorado Museum of Natural History.)

Mimbres may rejoin the larger Pueblo world—one theme of this chapter, important for later arguments—and at the same time cross the border, into old Mexico.

THE EMERALD CITY?

Most archaeologists would agree that Chaco was a seminal event in Southwestern prehistory (e.g., Cordell 1994, 1997; Cordell and McBrinn 2012; Kantner 2004; Plog 2008; Sebastian 1992; Ware 2014; Vivian 1990). (Other archaeologists think Chaco is just so much hype, but let us ignore those nugatory contrarians.)

We know it was important, but we don't know what Chaco was, exactly. For many archaeologists and public providers of archaeological knowledge, Chaco has been declared a mystery: something never seen before, something we will never fully understand. If I had a dollar for every time I've heard a Chaco ranger say, "Archaeology can never really know . . . ," I'd have retired a long time ago.

What was Chaco? For thirty years I weaseled out of a direct answer to that question and finally laid a few of the cards on the table in *A History of the Ancient Southwest* (Lekson 2009)—I'll show the full hand, below. There are some evident facts: Chaco was big. It was showy. It was expensive. Its architecture was clearly stratified (in the social sense): "Great Houses" were high-status buildings on one side of the canyon, and small, modest, lower-status "unit pueblos" huddled on the other. Not many people lived in the Great Houses, and those who did were buried with pomp, circumstance, and possibly retainers, or, more likely, descendants in a family crypt (Akins and Schelberg 1984; Neitzel 1989b:536–537; Plog and Heitman 2010). Much of each Great House was designed for functions other than gracious living: warehouses, offices, ritual, maybe even barracks. Anywhere else, Chaco Great Houses would be called "palaces," but that term seems incongruous—even indecorous—in the Pueblo region (Lekson 2006b). Get used to it: they were palaces.

Chaco Canyon, taken as a unit, was several orders of magnitude larger than any contemporary settlements in its region. The dense architectural core was monumental, built to scales far larger than other eleventh- and early twelfth-century Pueblo homes and villages. Chaco was built to impress, even awe. "Downtown Chaco" was a city, in the sense of a center that transforms and services a region (of which, more below). A vast network of roads and "outliers" surrounded the center and radiated out into a heavily populated hinterland—the Chacoan "regional system" 450 km across (of which, much more below).

THE (SOCIAL) DYNAMICS OF CHACO PREHISTORY

Those are the facts, sort of, more or less. We've been a long time getting to those sort-of facts, and the story of the research is almost as important as the facts themselves.

It's been clear for a long while that Chaco was not a happy, hippy-dippy commune. It was larger, less pleasant, more ominous. Back when my twig was bent,[1] a textbook complained that it was too bad we knew so little about Chaco, because it almost certainly was important (Martin and Plog 1973:108). The National Park Service's Chaco Project (1969 to 1986) gathered a great deal of information about Chaco—shelves and shelves of reports—and effectively "normalized" Chaco. It was more than a happy green valley of pueblos, but less than Caesar's Rome. The Chaco Project offered a Chaco reality check (for summaries: Lekson ed. 2006 and Mathien 2005).

Still, Chaco knocked Mesa Verde off the charts, and scores of other underpublicized Southwestern districts faded that much further into obscurity.[2] It must have been annoying for someone working on a really neat Rio Grande site to open the morning paper and read Chaco this, Chaco that. The extravagant claims made for the canyon (the Chaco Empire!) were bad enough, but "outliers" really drove the Southwest wild. "Outliers"—Chaco-like sites at considerable distances from the canyon—unleashed Chaco and delivered it right to everyone else's front door.

My experiences, of course, shaped my views on Chaco. The Chaco Project was already in progress when I realized I wanted to work there, presumably with that project. I snuck up on Chaco from Salmon Ruins (Reed 2006, 2008). Salmon Ruins is a Chacoan site 70 km north of Chaco Canyon, a fact that prompted Cynthia Irwin-Williams (1972) to coin the term "Chaco Phenomenon." (Cynthia knew she'd tangled with something extraordinary.) Salmon was an "outlier." "Outliers" were . . . well, we didn't know exactly what outliers were (but we'll dispense with the scare quotes). Outliers seemed to be Chaco-style buildings built at impossible distances from Chaco Canyon. There were precedents excavated in the early days of Southwestern archaeology: odd places like Lowry, Village of the Great Kivas, and a few other far-flung sites corrupted by bad Chacoan "influences" (those scare quotes are appropriate). In the mid-1970s, we suspected there might be more out in the great wide open, waiting to be discovered.

Cynthia thought so. She told a story on herself: When she first visited Salmon Ruins, her guides led her up a steep hill and then stopped. She asked, "Where's the ruin?" She was standing on it. Salmon Ruins was so big you couldn't even see it. I thought that there might be more Salmon Ruins out there—huge buildings! (In odd corners of the Southwest, there still are major sites, unknown to science; I've found a few myself, and it's a blast.) Maybe we could find big Salmon-sized outliers. That was heady stuff: fun, cheap, nondestructive, and a potentially big return for the money.

Bob Powers, Bill Gillespie, and I were given time and a Park Service truck, and we rocketed around the San Juan Basin looking for great big ruins. We had a great time—but we didn't find great big ruins. There *are* a few more Salmon-sized behemoths (in the Aztec area, as we shall see), but the outliers we found were all rather small—at least compared with Pueblo Bonito. And we found these little fellows everywhere: a few right next to the highway and many more in places known but to goats.

While we loosened bolts and dented fenders on an ill-fated string of government Suburbans, another project was busy depreciating vehicles purchased by New Mexico ratepayers. The Public Service Company of New Mexico, in the electricity business, lived up to its name and sponsored an outlier survey with an all-star crew: Rich Loose, Mike Marshall, and John Stein. They found what we found, but more (Marshall, Stein, Loose, and Novotny 1979). The Public Service gang really covered the ground, and the San Juan Basin map began to look measled: red-dotted outliers popped up on our maps faster than a bad rash. Then the Bureau of Land Management joined in, fielding crews to study roads that crossed potential coalfields. Some of the names changed (Kincaid 1983; Nials, Stein, and Roney 1987), but the story stayed the same: lots of little outliers, in likely and unlikely places. Scholars began "collecting" outliers, keeping lists and dotting maps (e.g., Kantner 2003; LeBlanc 1986b; Wilcox 1993; chapters in Lekson ed. 2006). It became competitive: Great Houses were traded like baseball cards, and outlier lists were compared and contrasted. At the time, this was controversial.

Older, more sober archaeologists denied that there were any Chaco outliers on Mesa Verde, in northeastern Arizona, in southeastern Utah, in . . . name your area. It was all turf stuff, and in retrospect rather silly; the outliers were there, and now there are something like 150 of them, once a matter of heated debate but today an archaeological fact.

THE REGIONAL SYSTEM

The "regional system"—scare quotes again, to a purpose—is perhaps the single most difficult sell for Chacoan archaeology (Lekson 1991, 1996a). The ruins at the Chaco Culture National Historical Park were generally accepted to be, well, odd; but Chacoan regional archaeology—its outliers and its alarming size—challenged and exceeded our methods at the time. We weren't used to archaeological entities that large in the Southwest, and denial was a common reaction. The regional archaeology of Chaco sets the stage for subsequent prehistory and for the rest of this book: Chaco is the ground floor of my house of cards. So it is important the reader understand my take on Chaco, even if we agree to disagree.

What were all these little outliers? Typically, it was nothing more, and nothing less, than a rounded mound about 40 m long and 25 m wide and 4 m tall (dimensions taken at Peach Springs, a garden-variety outlier Great House). In a couple of places, some sad fool had dug for treasure and found only rubble. A few courses of Chaco-like masonry were visible in those melancholy potholes. An archaeologist, of course, could tell it was a building, but I've taken the interested laity to outliers, and they had the Cynthia reaction: where's the site?

If we cleaned it out and cleaned it up, landscaped it, and trailed it, this outlier would be a nice little ruin. Nothing special, mind you: twenty-five rooms and a kiva, tops. Every cow town in east-central Arizona has a ruin that big or bigger. Mesa Verde is littered with twenty-five-room pueblos. What's the big deal? The outlier, thus described, sounds like a big little site—and it was, sort of.

My old friend and colleague John Stein described outlier discovery as an "aha experience." When you're on an outlier, things tingle. Scramble up the masonry talus of a steep-sloped mound and reach the top: look down on a Great Kiva and a plain dotted with dozens of conspicuously smaller rubble mounds and odd earthen berms, all looking back up at you, and you will realize that archaeology's current observational language is insufficient to record, describe, communicate, and analyze what you've just seen.

I am neither portraying nor advocating a mystical, transcendent New Age experience, nor a "phenomenological" epiphany. All the concrete knowable elements of "Chaco-ness" are open to Southwestern archaeology, but we are unaccustomed to recording, presenting, and understanding them. It is the combination of "usual suspects" architectural traits (massive masonry, multiple stories, elevated kivas, etc.), commanding height, nearby Great Kivas, extensive berms, roads, and the relative mass of the Great House ("big bumps"; Lekson 1991) contrasted to unit pueblos that causes the well-tempered antennae to hum. Put them all together and they spell . . . trouble. For Chacoan outliers, the unit of observation cannot be the Great House outlier itself, but the landscape of which it is the principal visual focus (John Stein figured this out: Fowler and Stein 1992; see also Lekson 1991; Stein and Lekson 1992; chapters in Lekson ed. 2006).

We had attribute lists for Chacoan buildings: formal ground plans, core-and-veneer masonry, a particular type of kiva, and so forth. Landscapes were more difficult to communicate—and remain so. Old reports and site files offer variations on this theme: "One of the pueblos in the cluster, at the upper end of the terrace, was somewhat bigger, perhaps of two stories. Nearby was a large circular reservoir, and numerous middens." Hey, mister: that's not a buffed-up, that's a Great House. But you'd never know it from the observational language used in old articles or many more recent site survey forms.[3]

Outliers are an empirical pattern, no less (and no more) valid than Dogoszhi Black-on-white or *tchamahias* or trough metates. Chacoan outliers are (almost) everywhere. Claims to the contrary—and they persist—are special pleading, stylite pillarism, selectionist sophistry, or—in a very few cases—really interesting exceptions to the rule.

The reality of outliers and a Chacoan region are now widely accepted. Old provincialisms and turf defenses fell under the weight of brute data. A degree of local dignity, of territorial pride, comes from arguments about whether a particular outlier is an "import" (that is, built by people from Chaco) or an "emulation" (that is, local people copying the big-city styles). I'm not sure we can know—the

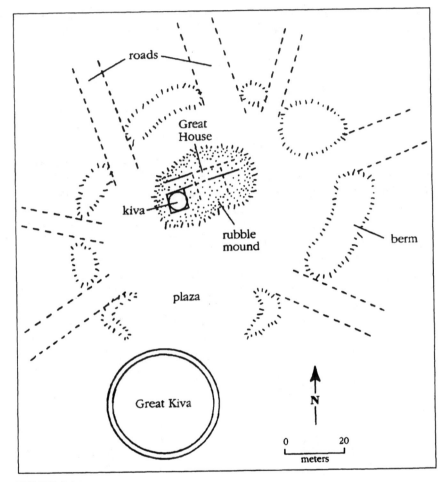

FIGURE 2.4
Outlier landscape (after Kintigh, Howell, and Duff 1996; and see Fowler and Stein 1992). An idealized outlier Great House encircled by low earthen berms, which were cut by radiating roads. Somewhere in the neighborhood was a Great Kiva and (not shown here) scores of unit pueblos (see figure 2.2) scattered in a loose "community." See also figure 2.8.

elites of Chaco didn't build their buildings; they had people to do that. If a Chaco noble told the locals out in the sticks to build a Great House, what would it look like? In form, a Chaco building; in fabric, more like local patterns upgraded for grander purposes.

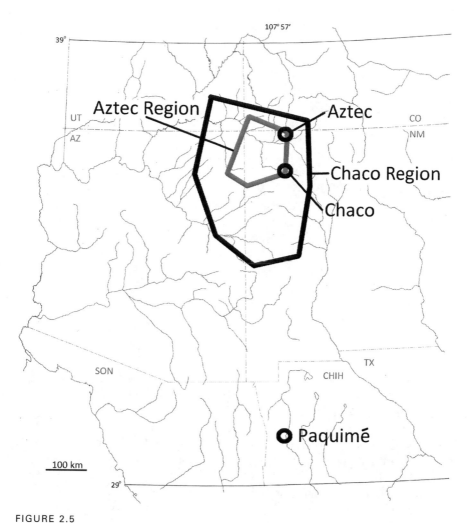

FIGURE 2.5
The Chaco region defined by eleventh-century outliers, and Aztec's reduced region defined by bi- and tri-walled structures (see figure 3.12). Chaco region based on Kantner (2003); Aztec region based on Glowacki (2006)—each with my modifications, interpretations, and additions.

Given that the pattern is real, what *were* outliers? In the past, when outliers were largely limited to the San Juan Basin, I would have dodged that question by responding, "Well, what was Chaco?" The center should define the periphery, so the meaning of outlier depended entirely on the nature of Chaco Canyon. Then

I would hint at the staggering range of conflicting views of Chaco Canyon and change the subject.

That evasion nearly cost me my faith. The explosive expansion of outliers outdistanced our abilities to render them believable, understandable. Our first schemata for outliers posited a system of subsistence redistribution across the San Juan Basin, mediated by Chaco (see below). Redistribution imploded under the density of far-distant outliers, far beyond the economic radius of Chacoan food transport. Outliers at Hopi, outliers at Tularosa, and finally outliers in the Mimbres (my idea—and no one else's—discussed below) violated the laws of time and space, or at least the conventions for our archaeological world. I began to think of outliers as "Great Houses," somehow a ubiquitous element of ancient Pueblo life, like "kivas." Much as Great Kivas formed community foci long before and long after Chaco, perhaps Great Houses were a temporally restricted, near-universal element of eleventh-century Pueblo villages. A village without a Great House was like a western town without a liquor store: not really a town. Perhaps Great Houses were effectively background noise: a constant pattern within which Chaco developed, possibly as an unhealthy aberration. Those timid, retro ideas emerged mainly in conversations and conference presentations, but they were shared by others. Outliers outlay nothing; each Great House was entire of itself but common to some grand shared Weltanschauung-like black-on-white pottery. "The community structure, identified here as Chacoan, could instead have been a nonspecific, pan-Anasazi pattern" (Lekson 1991:48). Outliers? Outliars!

Those doubts passed. I saw the light and returned to the fold (Lekson 2006c, 2009; and thus I use "outlier" rather than "Chacoan structure" or "Great House"). I reconsidered the consequences of my actions when the increasing specificity of outlier attributes (berms, roads, and the like; Fowler and Stein 1992) collided with the deep implausibility of a pan-Anasazi model. How would things as elaborate and standardized as Great Houses be a local condition, repeated again and again over a huge area?

Great Houses stand out against a variegated Anasazi background. Archaeologists subdivide Anasazi into a dozen local traditions or districts, but Great Houses—while not identical—are sufficiently similar to form an identifiable class, against that crazy quilt of local difference. If Great Houses weren't imposed or inspired by a central source, then they must be independent inventions or developments or adaptations. As Great House after Great House was explained (in forgettable conference papers, unsung and uncited) as local evolutionary developments, I was struck by the miracle of 150 cases of simultaneous equifinality. Miraculous? Ridiculous!

It was, of course, ridiculous: taken to its logical conclusion, a pan-Anasazi model required a nearly mystical faith in the powers of parallel evolution or, failing that, a near-complete ignorance of the empirical record. One hundred and fifty local evolutions might make sense one at a time, valley by valley, but together they defy belief. There must have been central control, or a central idea, the Big Idea (Stein and Lekson 1992). Yet I still encounter researchers who want to localize outliers and make them the end product of a local sequence, specific to their valley.

Roads and line-of-sight signaling networks did the trick, broke the back, nailed the coffin: they demonstrated a centrality to Chaco (if that was ever in doubt) and established that the regional system was an interconnected whole: indeed, a system. The smoke-and-mirrors line-of-sight system, as we know it from Chimney Rock and Far View, requires "repeater stations" to get the message into Chaco (appendix C). Someone had to sit atop a lonely butte (in this case, Huerfano Butte) to see and resend the message. That's a system, with interdependent moving parts.

And there's Chaco itself: a "prime object," in George Kubler's (1962) terms. Chaco was the center of the eleventh-century Pueblo world. That is not an assertion: it's as close to a fact as archaeology can hope to produce. After a century of work, we know Chaco and we know the Southwest. There may be a few more big sites lurking out in the bush yet to be discovered, but—in the eleventh century—there was no other Chaco. Chaco was a political and economic center, unique in its time and place. It was a city (a term I define and defend in chapter 3), a palace culture built around the homes of noble families. We will meet them again.

OUT ON THE EDGES

To escape the light-bending gravity of Pueblo Bonito and downtown Chaco, we can seek answers out at frontiers of the Chaco world. Instead of looking out from Chaco, look in from the edges. The periphery may help us define the center. The east and north boundaries seem sharply defined; the west is fuzziest; and the south is problematic—does Chaco reach into Mimbres, or not?—discussed below.

This is archaeology, after all; so let us go counterclockwise, beginning in the east. The site of Guadalupe sits atop the second-most spectacular setting of any outlier, a narrow high mesa overlooking the Puerco River, about 100 km from Chaco (Pippin 1987). There are a few candidate Great Kivas but no Great Houses beyond Guadalupe: the Rio Grande has been declared a Chaco-free zone. (The only likely exception is a small "mining camp" at the Cerrillos turquoise mines, south of Santa Fe; Wiseman and Darling 1986.)

Due north of Guadalupe and a bit over 140 km from Chaco, at the extreme northeast corner of the Chaco world, Chimney Rock sits in splendid isolation, atop the most spectacular setting of any Chacoan site (figure 2.6; Eddy 1977; Malville 2004; Todd and Lekson 2011). In the context of its local archaeology, Chimney Rock sticks out like a sore thumb. Chimney Rock is crisply geometric, quite large, and very Chacoan; the community looks like somebody stepped in a

FIGURE 2.6
Chimney Rock near Pagosa Springs, Colorado (150 km from Chaco). A textbook Chaco outlier that stands out from (and stands high above) its surrounding community of very local unit pueblos (see figure 2.7). One of the most magnificent sites/sights in the Four Corners, and since 2012 a national monument.

unit pueblo and tracked it all over Stollsteimer Mesa (figure 2.7). If ever there was a smoking-gun outlier, it's Chimney Rock. It's the holotype of the species, and it's out at the very edge: beyond Chimney Rock, the next stop is Cahokia. Chimney Rock is important, too, because it's one of several outliers that suggest Chaco was heavily invested north of the San Juan River by 1020 or earlier—a century before the move to Aztec (appendix C); that is, this area was well known to Chaco, and the move north was not into strange lands.

From Chimney Rock, at the northeast, an arc of outliers runs westward across southwestern Colorado; along the base of the Rocky Mountains (the San Juan and La Plata Mountains, in fact); as far north as Dove Creek, Colorado, and Blanding, Utah; and a bit beyond that at Carhart Pueblo, the northernmost of the species (about latitude 37°45'), 200 km from Chaco. From there, the frontier curves back through southeastern Utah to approximately the area of the Bluff Great House (figure 2.8) in the small town of that name, 200 km from Chaco (Cameron 2008).

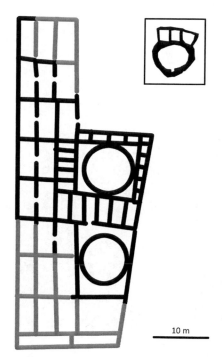

FIGURE 2.7
Chimney Rock and a local unit pueblo (inset) to the same scale, based on University of Colorado excavations in 1970 and 2009. While stylized in this figure, the differences in both fabric and form are indeed stark and unmistakable.

10 m

There are several outliers beyond Bluff to the northwest; the furthest out is Owen's site—250 km from Chaco—which stretches the Chaco world to the very edges of the canyons of the Colorado River. We are (reasonably) certain that no outliers lie below Lake Powell.

East and north seem firmly fixed. The west is problematic in part because it is Indian country: the Navajo Nation and the Hopi reservation. The tribes are good stewards, more protective of sites and ruins than many government agencies or private landowners. Understandably, they discourage digging. While many outliers have been reported on Indian lands, few have been investigated in recent times. White House, a classic Great House in Canyon de Chelly National Monument (figure 2.9), was partially excavated by Earl Morris in the 1920s (but never reported). But for several outliers further west at the Hopi mesas, we have only maps. Good maps, convincing maps, but still, maps. This dearth of work has led to doctrinaire pronouncements that there are no outliers in the Kayenta country, which is simply wrong.

West beyond the Nations we reach the Little Colorado River and Wupatki National Monument. Wupatki has long been the subject of Chacoan speculation (Stanislawski 1963; Downum 2004), but most archaeologists rejected those

FIGURE 2.8
Bluff Great House, at Bluff, Utah (200 km from Chaco), a typical outlier with outlier features (see figure 2.4) of berms, roads, and a Great Kiva. University of Colorado professor Catherine M. Cameron excavated parts of the site in 1995–2004 (Cameron 2009).

claims on distance alone: Wupatki is more than 300 km from Chaco. I reject that rejection: distance is no barrier. But Wupatki, as it turns out, was built between 1135 and 1195 (Downum 2004), after building ceased at Chaco Canyon. Wupatki played its role in the post-Chaco world, perhaps as a rival to Chaco's heir apparent, Aztec Ruins (Lekson 2009). Further west still, the Flagstaff area has not been friendly to Chaco, but wise men from the east have anointed a few candidate Chaco-era outliers (most notably, Ridge Ruin: Fowler and Stein 1992: figure 9.1; Fowler, Stein, and Anyon 1987:213).

A conservative reading of the west would draw a line from the Bluff area south through consensus Great Houses at Hopi, on through Holbrook (with its Great Kiva; Gumerman and Olson 1968), and ending at a cluster of round Great Kivas on the Mogollon Rim (Herr 2001) (figure 2.5). That's the "safe" western boundary, but given the case for possible outliers around Flagstaff and Great Kivas

FIGURE 2.9

White House in Canyon de Chelly National Monument near Chinle, Arizona (140 km from Chaco). Not the "White House" of Pueblo traditions, this Great House is one of the larger outliers. It was partially excavated by Earl H. Morris, later of the University of Colorado Museum of Natural History. The Upper Ruin (in the alcove high above the Chaco building) is a later cliff dwelling.

near Page, Arizona, the line may someday shift westward. (But whose outliers? Chaco's? Aztec's? Wupatki's?)

While the west is neither as fixed nor as firm as the east and north, the south is worse—far worse, a matter central to this book. My map places the south edge of the Chacoan world about 50 km south of the quirky little town of Quemado, New Mexico, and just north of the equally quirky town of Magdalena, or about 250 and 220 km, respectively, from Chaco (figure 2.5).

The site south of Quemado is called "Aragon" after an almost vanishingly small village, nearby—not quite, but close to Gondor's king (add an "r"). It was found and described by Walter Hough (in Hough 1907, it's site "No. 111"). Hough (1907: plate 8) gives us a picture of the ruin, its walls, and its large kiva. The setting atop a prominent hill is archetypically Chacoan, the walls are remarkably well coursed (not bad for Chaco, astonishing for the Mogollon uplands), and the kiva is big, round, and masonry-walled: in a word, Great Kiva-ish. We don't have a ground plan, and we never will: the site was bulldozed in the early 1980s.

The Great House north of Magdalena is the southeasternmost of the breed, not quite so far south as Aragon but still a respectable 220 km from Chaco. It, too, has an interesting faux medieval name: "Camelot." Discovered by a survey crew in the early 1960s, its massive tall walls, impressively deep Great Kivas, and setting atop a low hill, brooding over a surrounding community of unit pueblos, reminded the field crew of King Arthur's castle—then a Broadway musical and a Kennedy motif. They named the site "Camelot on the San Augustin" and left cryptic notes in the site files in Santa Fe. After years of petitions and pleas, I was able to visit the site (well protected on private land). Later it was formally recorded by Michael Marshall (Marshall and Marshall 2008). Mike and I agree: it's a Great House, but possibly post-Chaco.[4] Camelot: A fleeting wisp of glory, or just a silly place?

There's more argument over—and less direct research on—Chaco's south than any other compass point. The south's fuzziness results, in part, from taxonomic turbulence where Anasazi (north) meets Mogollon (south). But, more significantly, the southern conundrum reflects an archaeological circumstance of real importance. We find it hard to agree on a southern boundary, because the southern boundary of the old Chacoan world was more porous or diffuse than east, north, or west. To the east, the Chacoan world confronts the Rio Grande and the Great Plains beyond; to the north, it butts up against the Rockies; to the west, it surely ends at the low deserts beyond Flagstaff (if not before) and at the Mogollon Rim. But to the south? To the south lies the plateau-like Mogollon uplands and very "Anasazi"-like Mimbres (discussed below). And beyond Mimbres, Mexico. I think the vagueness of Chaco's southern boundary reflects ancient realities: Chaco didn't stop heading south; it just kept going. We can't establish the closure of Chaco's north and east, and (within reason) west, because the south was *not closed*. Chaco blended into Mimbres, and knew the Mimbres region before the capital shifted south, after 1275 (below)—much as Chaco knew the north before Chaco moved to Aztec to Paquimé (appendix C). And that's why we will spend some quality time with Mimbres, later in this chapter.

So what does the periphery tell us about Chaco as a center? For one thing, *it's real*—that is, the center really was a center. Chaco was many times larger than any eleventh-century outlier. Chaco alone is simply an anomaly, a pathology, an aberration; as the center of a region, it becomes something like a capital. With the rise and fall of roads (Lekson et al. 1988; cf. Roney 1992), outliers best defined its region; but inlying outliers (as noted above) lack descriptive clarity and rhetorical force. It takes a blatant ringer way out on the edge, like Chimney Rock or Bluff or Aragon, to validate all the humdrum, cookie-cutter, big-bump outliers that fill our maps with dots. Stubborn advocates of local development might dig in their heels and deny some second-tier Great House in the middle of Zuni country, awash with ruins great and small, and thereby call into question the reality of all outliers. But it takes a perverse obstinacy to dismiss Chimney Rock or—even after it's gone—Aragon. Patterns show clearest against contrasting backgrounds. The far peripheries, where backgrounds contrast most, validate the center.

REDISTRIBUTION REVISITED

OK, it's real. So how did it work? The biggest problem with the Chacoan region is that it's so very big—an "outer limit" of 250 km distance from the center at Chaco (Lekson 2009:130–133) and a maximum edge-to-edge of about 450 km, Owen's on the northwest to Camelot on the southeast. And at the same time, so clearly centered: Chaco really stood alone, above the rest. There were no competing peer polities in Chaco's immediate area (but see Wilcox 1993, 1999b), with the sole possibility of distant Hohokam (500 km from Chaco—seemingly a long way but closer than Paquimé; wait for chapter 3). Chaco in the eleventh and early twelfth centuries was the figurative if not geometric center of the Anasazi/Pueblo region, the northern Southwest.

An outer limit of 250 km from the canyon encompasses a circular area of almost 200,000 sq km. Chaco did not occupy that entire area (figure 2.5); in fact, less than half. There was an "inner core" of no-doubt-about-it textbook outlier Great Houses (Chimney Rock, Far View, White House, etc.) whose radius of 150 km from Chaco defines, approximately, the area within which bulk transport of foodstuffs to and from Chaco was possible (Lekson 2009:130–133; Malville 2001)—just a bit larger than the San Juan Basin, the conventional but long outdated region for Chaco.[5]

Within the San Juan Basin/"inner core," Judge's old redistribution model proposed in the late 1970s still makes sense (to me). Judge began with the fact that rainfall was uneven and unpredictable within and around the San Juan Basin and argued that Chaco served as a central "food bank," storing and routing corn surpluses, as needed, among its surrounding ring of outliers, with the central administration skimming something off the top for their services (Judge 1979, 1984, 1989). Judge later recanted (Judge 1993), but my faith in redistribution—as an important dynamic in the Chaco inner core's early days—remains strong (Lekson 2009). Like a tree down by the water, I shall not be moved—even if my roots rot. Just because an idea is old and unfashionable does not mean it is not useful or even, perhaps, correct. I myself am old and unfashionable . . . and sometimes correct.

The Judge model faded not so much from compelling challenges as from a weak defense. The redistribution model was based on three sets of data: first, highly variable rainfall around the margins of the San Juan Basin; second, the vast volume of "empty" storage space at Chaco Canyon Great Houses; and third, Chaco's geographic centrality, *within the Chaco Basin* (but not within its larger region). None of those things have changed: the dendroclimatic data remain valid, the empty rooms at Great Houses are still empty, and Chaco remains at the center of the San Juan Basin/"inner core"—in a spot of no obvious merit, otherwise. Claims that Chaco was a decent place for agriculture (Vivian 1990; Wills and Dorshow 2012), or that Chaco produced big surpluses (Sebastian 1992) seem strained at best. Larry Benson notes that from 616 to 1990, fewer than 3 percent of all Chaco's years had sufficient moisture for successful agriculture (citing Dean and Funkhouser 2002; see also Benson 2010a, 2010b). Chaco may have been slightly better for farming than the area immediately around it—what is technically called "stinking desert"—but Chaco was no Garden of Eden. In fact, Chaco was no Chuska Valley—Chaco's real breadbasket about 75 km to the west, at the base of the Chuska Mountains.

What has changed is the distribution of outliers; the outer limits have reached 250 km from Chaco. Evaluating Judge's model, practical people pointed out that bulk transportation of corn has energetic limits; there is a cost-benefit radius beyond which porter transport simply isn't economically feasible, and it's about 150 km (Malville 2001; contra Lightfoot 1979). That encompasses the "inner core," but many outliers in Arizona, Utah, Colorado, and south-central New Mexico are well beyond that limit—as noted, up to 250 km distant. Redistribution models just won't work—at least, with any efficiency—for today's swollen, bloated Chacoan region. But they still work inside that 150 km limit—which was pretty much the Chaco world as we knew it in the mid-1970s.

There were zones or tiers of integration around Chaco, and different models work for different zones. First, there was the canyon itself, an elaborately planned ceremonial city some wag called "downtown Chaco" (figure 2.10). Immediately surrounding downtown Chaco, a zone of urban sprawl encircling the canyon has been called the "Chaco halo," a radius of about 5 km (Doyel, Breternitz, and Marshall 1984). Presumably, the Chaco halo was intensely engaged in whatever was happening in the canyon—daily interactions. The San Juan Basin—subsumed in my "inner core" of 150 km radius (figure 2.5)—figures prominently in the Chaco literature, but our use differs from the geological origins of the term; "San Juan Basin" is not precisely correct, nor is "Chaco Drainage." "Inner core" is also inelegant and smacks of abdominal and back strength, but what I have in mind is the world seen from the canyon's high points (e.g., Pueblo Alto, Peñasco Blanco, the crest of South Mesa): Lobo Mesa on the south, the Chuska Mountains on the west, the San Juan Valley on the north, and the Nacimiento Mountains on the east. A radius of 150 km more or less defines it. I think Judge's redistribution model works in the "inner core."

Outliers so far out as Aragon and Owen's made us rethink redistribution; corn won't travel that far, at least on any regular basis. The porters eat the product. But the empirical pattern remains: those are real outliers. Lynne Sebastian (1992:152) once asked, "Can sites halfway across Arizona, hundreds of miles from Chaco Canyon, be considered 'Chacoan' in any meaningful sense?" It was a darned good question.

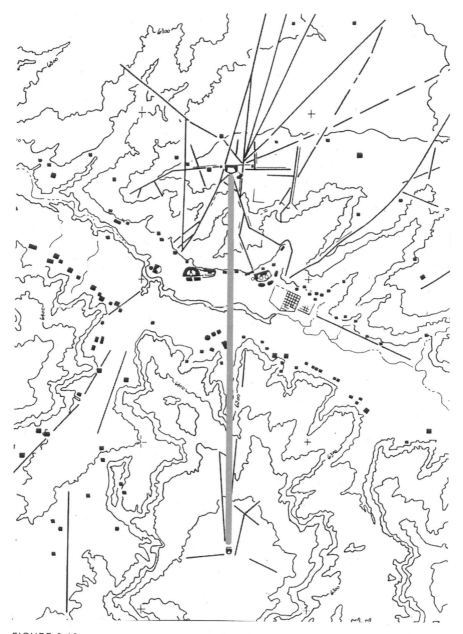

FIGURE 2.10
"Downtown Chaco": the center of Chaco Canyon, with Great Houses and unit pueblos (small rectangles), road alignments, and the central north-south axis from Pueblo Alto (top) to Tsin Kletsin (bottom)—the "Fritz line" first published by John Fritz (1978); it would be stretched and racked and distorted to become the Chaco Meridian. (After John Stein; Stein and Lekson 1992: figure 8.3, with modifications.)

CHACO HEGEMONY

Chaco's hegemony was more political than economic beyond 150 km—a key point, to which we will return. I'll sidestep the multivoiced, nuanced, contextualized usages of "hegemony" that clutter the literature and return to the dictionary definition: "preponderant influence or authority, particularly of one state over a confederacy."

For me, it's either hegemony or equifinality. Either there was a source, a "prime object" (sensu Kubler) that, through influence or authority, created the form we call outliers, or they all sprang up independently, the result of local pressures and processes and histories. But I cannot credit equifinality; the uniform architecture of 150 outliers *must mean something*. Within the 150 km "inner core," there was (I think) redistribution. For the out-there outliers, hegemony replaces redistribution. The organization of labor, the organization of space, and—of interest here—prestige or political economies of exotica all point to Chacoan influence or even authority over this huge region.

Goodies are good to think about. They are generally well represented in older reports and museum collections, and, for some questions, they are actually important. Copper bells, turquoise, bifurcate baskets, cylinder vases, jet frogs, macaws, parrots, cacao beans, and all the other *significata* of ancient Chaco may not be things we understand, exactly, but they are undeniably the things we save and show: we bring them back to museums, and we picture them in reports. (Odd that we try to normalize ringers in architecture and landscapes but celebrate rarity in artifacts; archaeologists must find baubles less threatening than buildings.)

Exotica, prestige goods, macaws: surely this is mere feather waving? Do not decry feathers. We think of feathers as lightweight fluff, but fluff counts too. Feathers marked status. As Cortés learned, feathers were more valuable than gold in Mesoamerica. (He asked for wealth; they brought him feathers. He had to clarify: gold, if you please, and pronto.) In ancient times, anyone caught wearing feathers above his rank would get a quick march to the top of the pyramid. There is nothing like good, fierce feather waving to wake up the congregation or to drive home a point. The display of exotic materials—feathers on a headdress or feathers on a spear—played a big part in the operation of low-octane polities.

The appeal of feathers and the rest of that bag of tricks may have been the same for them as it is for us: feathers, bells, shells, blue stones, and all the rest were striking and rare in color, texture, weight, or form (Clarke 1986). They are bright, shiny, and, above all, unusual. Turquoise was a rarity, but a macaw must have been a marvel. (Not, perhaps, to the parrot keepers of Chaco and Paquimé, who could have had no fanciful notions about squawking, biting, stinky birds—somewhere down the line, a bird is just a bird.) When macaws reached the northern Southwest, they were hotter than Hula-Hoops. They were big, astonishingly colorful, and they talked! (I imagine macaws as a sort of sibyl of the Crazy Eight-Ball variety: Should we plant? Should we go to war? Pieces of eight, pieces of eight: dead men tell no tales.) Pueblo histories, recounted in chapter 4, suggest that the political history of the Greater Southwest may have been a case of macaws and effects.

I use macaws, here, as a loose proxy for the whole panoply of rare and exotic goodies that marked Chaco's hegemony over its region. Over thirty were found at Chaco, more than at all excavated contemporary Anasazi/Pueblo sites combined. And, as we shall see, what we might call macaw products were distributed out to the very edges of Chaco's world.

Macaws and their company moved in a political economy, or, more specifically, a political-prestige economy. Here, as with "hegemony," I part company with the more ethereal configurations of "political economy"—another term variegated by anthropological usages (e.g., Cobb 1993; Hirth 1996). I mean a flow of relatively rare objects that create and maintain a political structure or hegemony. Macaw feathers were only one kind of exotica, presumably distributed from Chaco out to the edges of its hegemony, tying that huge area together in a network centered on the canyon. Turquoise was almost certainly another. Power relations cemented by exotica created a political economy (Brumfiel and Earle 1987). "The circulation and control of luxury items were crucial for developing, defining, and expanding both regional and supraregional political networks" (Hirth 1996:208), with or without concomitant economies of bulk or subsistence goods. Politically directed prestige economies (or "wealth finance") were critical to emerging elite leadership: "Control over the ideology of social ranking rested on control over the system of wealth finance" (Earle 1997:74).

Equally important, I think, is the power accrued by elites and nobles through the acquisition or control of distant things—objects and artifacts from faraway countries with strange-sounding names. That would be true for would-be nobles at distant outliers and the fabled capital at Chaco, and for the lords of Chaco Canyon and the equally fabulous cities of the south, Mesoamerica.

Mary Helms (1988, 1992) has written eloquently about this: would-be kings on the edges of great empires legitimize themselves to the commoners by traveling to the Emerald City of Oz, conversing with their fellow wizards, and bringing back an emerald or a horse of a different color, or whatever the big city offers. The key dimension is distance: "Local rulers are themselves drawn into more distant contact with a civilizational center, the allure including a hope that the ideological legitimacy of the center will become a distant *axis mundi* for local elites." Of particular relevance to Chaco, Aztec, and Paquimé are the roles of exotic materials, distant centers, and foreign visits to *emerging* elites, wannabe kings:

> Potential or hopeful local leaders may seek support from outside personages believed to be unusually powerful or may themselves seek to experience direct contact with the outside in order to derive exceptional powers by "walking in the wilderness" or by visiting distant lands and foreign sacred centers. Not only have leaders

sought experience with distant phenomena but they have also taken great pride in the acquisition of sea shells, copper bells, and a wide range of curious relics and other material goods from places beyond their realms. Similarly, both great kings and lesser tribal leaders, who are often believed to be the most ardent keepers of conservative ancestral traditions, may in fact be the first to receive representatives of new foreign faiths and customs, to accept new charms and protective amulets, to adopt foreign modes of personal deportment, official dress and regalia, and to accept foreign advisors, or even new political ideologies and models of rule. (Helms 1988:264)

Helms's model seems apt for Chaco, Aztec, and Paquimé (for Chaco, see Nelson 2006). Mexican objects doubtless found their way into the Southwest in different ways for different purposes, but the concentration of materials at Chaco and, later, Paquimé seems entirely congruent with Helms's description of local rulers on the make—big-men-who-would-be-kings, to mix anthropology with Kipling. The men buried with pomp and circumstance at Pueblo Bonito and at Paquimé (described in chapter 3) are clear candidates for those roles, and those rules. They used Mesoamerica just as chiefs and kings throughout the world used distant civilizations: to impress followers, to cement alliances, and to demonstrate their power.

My dichotomy of political-prestige economies (to 250 km) and subsistence economies (to 150 km) is probably false—the two were surely intertwined—but, like many fictions, it is a useful convention. It works, for example, for Chaco. Chaco began through subsistence economies: controlling and redistributing surpluses. Beyond the "inner core," a redistributive economy of bulk goods was probably impossible. Local networks presumably took care of the perennial local problem: What's for dinner? Roads cross-linking distant outliers may well define subregional redistribution, smaller copies of the Chaco Basin model. If a Chaco-centered economy operated out in the boonies, it was necessarily an economy of fluff, a political-prestige economy: rare, costly, symbolic, and above all portable. Macaws were all that. So were parrots, shells, turquoise, cacao, and copper bells.

Stunning direct evidence comes from the most impressive macaw artifact ever found in the Southwest (Borson et al. 1998). A wonderful macaw feather sash was found in 1954, in a cave in Lavender Canyon, Utah (about 270 km from Chaco and 80 km north of the Bluff Great House). It was an apron or sash, with buckskin belt straps attached to a squirrel pelt, from which dangled twelve scarlet macaw feather ropes, each about 1.2 m long. A picture is worth a thousand words: look at the color images in *National Geographic* (November 1982, vol. 162, no. 4:573) or *Archaeology* (January/February 1997, vol. 50, no. 1:55) or Utah State Parks (2014)—or just Google "macaw sash Blanding."

The sash was described by Hargrave (1979:5), who concluded that it "was manufactured outside the Southwest, probably in Mexico" in the twelfth century.

Later research (Borson et al. 1998) shows that the pelt was not a Mexican species, but instead a Southwestern subspecies of the tassel-eared squirrel, *Sciurus aberti*—native to New Mexico and Arizona, but not to southeastern Utah. The workmanship of the piece is more Southwestern than Mexican.

An AMS date on the pelt produced a date of 920±35 BP (Borson et al. 1998), which calibrates to about 1050–1150. During the eleventh century, there were only two main Southwestern centers of macaw keeping: Chaco and Mimbres (of which, more below). Chaco had the plateau monopoly on macaws and had tassel-eared squirrels—not a monopoly on squirrels (or squirrelly behavior), but an interesting fact. Archaeological tassel-eared squirrels (*Sciurus aberti*) were found at Pueblo Alto and Una Vida (Akins 1985:316). I think, but of course cannot prove, that the sash was made in Chaco and sent out to Chaco-allied elites, perhaps those at the Bluff Great House, and stored or retired in the nearby cave.

The north frontier provides other macaw-related (or at least fluffy) evidence for a Chacoan political-prestige economy. Less spectacular evidence comes from a group of artifacts termed "plume holders" or "feather holders" (figure 2.11): small ceramic bricks with quill-sized holes, presumed to presage Hopi feather holders (Judd 1954; Sullivan and Malville 1993). Only seventeen of these remarkable artifacts have been found in the northern Southwest: two from Pueblo Bonito; two from the Wallace Ruin outlier near Cortez, Colorado; two from the Chimney Rock area; and eleven from Chimney Rock itself (Sullivan and Malville

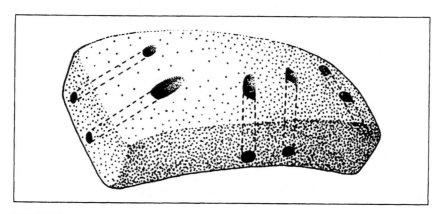

FIGURE 2.11
Feather holder from Chimney Rock (see figures 2.6 and 2.7). A rare, minor artifact class which, in the eleventh century, were found only at Chimney Rock and Chaco. Similar objects are known from historic and modern pueblos, where they are used in ritual. I usually work with massive buildings and expansive landscapes, but I also like rare, minor artifacts: easier to track and understand than potsherds or flakes.

1993:29–30). With all the digging that's gone on in the northern San Juan region, that restricted distribution seems real.

The most spectacular macaw artifact in the Southwest was found not at Chaco, but out on the extreme northwest edge of the Chaco world. Perhaps that was an accident of preservation: caves, like the Lavender Canyon site, have better preservation than rooms in ruins. But Bonito produced a wide range of perishable artifacts, as do most deep, dry Great Houses. Judd (1954:266) found—in addition to thirty birds—only four feathers in a single bundle (identified as macaw). The distribution points to a flow of prestige goods from the center out to the farthest periphery.

Of course, vast quantities of exotica stayed at Chaco. Abnegation was not a conspicuous Chacoan trait—at least for the upper class. There is more turquoise at Pueblo Bonito than all the other hundreds of excavated eleventh-century sites in the Southwest combined. But, at Chaco they had something more impressive than baubles: the power of the city itself to awe the populace and to affirm power.

PRESTIGE DEFLATED

Much ado about almost nothing: feather boas, blue baubles, tinkle bells. Political prestige or mere frippery? More than a few archaeologists have thought about exotic goodies and prestige economies in the Southwest with varying conclusions. Some see political-prestige economies; some don't. What interests me is not so much the predictable range of interpretations as the underlying assumptions about scale and process. Exotics are often bundled with craft goods (pottery, for example) into single all-purpose economic models. Pottery was probably not a prestige item—every village could make its own, whether it did or not. (Certain forms were interesting: think cylinder jars.) Yet gallons of ink have been spilled on the relative aristocracy of redwares and the political significance of Chaco Black-on-white (does typology confer status?). The real rarities become almost an afterthought.[6]

Southwestern archaeology has a strong populist penchant, and workaday pottery seems more honest than baubles of a would-be elite. As it turns out, good honest pottery (and obsidian) are showing us that Southwestern interactions—the daily grind working beneath elite networks—were surprisingly extensive (Mills et al. 2013), a subject to which we will return in chapter 3.

One class of economic models make sense for the San Juan Basin or the inner core (150 km radius)—an area I believe was crisscrossed by regular bulk-goods transport. Outliers over in Arizona or down by Quemadao probably did not participate in those bulk-goods economies. But far-flung outliers may well have been involved in a political-prestige economy of rare and wonderful things: macaws, bells, and the like. Trinkets defined Chaco's hegemony? There must have been something more . . .

PAX CHACO: PEACE WITH AN EDGE AND A BITE

An iron fist in the feather boa—to muddle sartorial metaphors. Whatever language they spoke, Chaco's nobles carried big sticks.[7]

The northern Southwest—Chaco's region—has become notorious for instances of horrible violence: whole communities—grandparents, families, kids, everyone—executed, chopped to bits, occasionally eaten, and then tossed *en masse* into a kiva or a room (Turner and Turner 1999). Isolated events like this may have happened as early as the sixth century (or perhaps not; see the discussion in Kohler et al. 2014:445), but they happened repeatedly—perhaps even frequently—during Chaco's time, especially between 1020 and 1180 (Kohler et al. 2014:449), and particularly during the latter decades of that span, when power was shifting from Chaco to Aztec. From 1180 to 1260, things calmed down; perhaps Aztec sorted things out. But with the final demise of the Chaco-Aztec polity, village-on-village violence—more like war than executions—escalated from 1260 to 1280 (Kohler et al. 2014; see also LeBlanc 1999).

How to kill a village? There were no weapons of mass destruction, no machine guns, no modern miracles for murder. Mass executions required numbers and organization. Organized groups—men who knew what they were about, with leaders to order the doing—did these things. Pueblos could organize one-off massacres, as at Awatovi in 1700. But the repeated group executions of Chaco's era suggest a level of organization beyond mob violence. Soldiers? If so, whose? Christie Turner, who first highlighted this doleful chapter of Southwestern history, suggested thugs from Tula (Turner and Turner 1999) but we don't need to go that far: Chaco and Aztec had the power and the organizational abilities to do wonderful things . . . and terrible things. I think these executions were done in the service of the state, keeping the commoners properly cowed.[8]

For those not under the harrow, a sort of "Pax Chaco" prevailed. This may seem like a contradictory term, but during Chaco's time, families could live in small houses scattered around a Great House or even far away from the centers, scattered over the land. They had, it seems, no fear of anarchic violence or thuggery; apparently you were safe from the massacres if you followed the rules.

In the Mesa Verde area, two-thirds of traumas observed on burials came from massacres/executions (Timothy Kohler, personal communication, August 12, 2014)—filter out those state-sponsored events, and evidence for Chaco-era violence falls to sort of "normal" background noise. Accidents will happen, and people got hurt accidently or on purpose (feuds). But settlement patterns show that—compared to earlier and later time periods—defense was not a primary concern. In the century before Chaco and the century after Chaco, big villages were the rule; only during the Chacoan era was the great majority of the population able to live in scattered single-family homes. That came to an end after about 1250. War returned, and single-family homes aggregated into the big Mesa Verde villages and cliff dwellings: circle the wagons, safety in numbers.

LORDS OF THE GREAT HOUSE

We have a lot of facts, but we can't agree on what Chaco was. It's a mystery. The mystery of Chaco: a carefully cultivated conundrum, celebrated in videos and coffee-table books. It's true: there are a truly staggering range of interpretations of Chaco, some of them mutually exclusive—and I won't review them all here (see Mills 2002—or, less authoritatively, the "literature review" chapter of any recent dissertation on Chaco). But something of an embarrassment: we've been digging up Chaco for over a century, and we have plenty of data, so we should be able to solve that mystery. As archaeologists, that's what we are paid to do.

The default view of Chaco comes through the lens of Pueblo ethnology—not always a one-to-one mapping but readings that conform to our stereotypes of Pueblos, or somehow lead to modern Pueblos. That's probably not a useful tactic. Pueblo societies developed, historically, in reaction to and rejection of Chaco, after 1300 (Lekson 2009). If that is true—and it is—then we need other, independent, non-Puebloan "triangulation points" to define, delimit, and understand Chaco's (and the Southwest's) ancient past.

Rather than looking to accounts of Pueblos written in the nineteenth and twentieth centuries, I think Chaco should be considered from the context of its contemporary world, specifically Mesoamerica in the tenth through fourteenth centuries (Early and Middle Postclassic periods). We should look at what was happening in ancient North America in that era. That was the world that Chaco knew; they had no idea that five centuries later they'd be Zuni or Hopi or Acoma.

In *A History of the Ancient Southwest* (2009), I tried to build Southwestern histories within continental contexts—constructing new frames of reference, so to speak. It seems clear that Chaco wanted to be Mesoamerican, but the Mesoamerican models I considered didn't work: I was aiming too high. I was reading about great cities and empires—Teotihuacan, the Toltecs, and so forth. But nothing I was reading seemed useful for Chaco and the Southwest. My error was thinking too big—not about Chaco, but about Mesoamerica. All politics are local, and the biggest empires were made up of local, smaller polities. I was introduced to the *altepetl* (described below) by my esteemed colleague at the University of Colorado, Dr. Gerardo Gutiérrez, an expert on the subject. (Dr. Gutiérrez is not responsible for my mistakes and errors here and should be absolved of all culpability.) After my redirection away from empires and down to the smaller scales of the *altepetl*, I have consulted many other works and scholars—see appendix A for references and details, which are many and cumbersome, and omitted in the following summary.

In brief: the ubiquitous local polity in Postclassic Mesoamerica was a small unit—often called city-states—termed, in Nahua, *altepetl* (plural *altepeme*; hereafter not italicized). This political formation was also common among many non-Nahua groups. The altepetl form probably began in the Late Classic period, and perhaps even earlier, and was widespread across Mesoamerica. That is, it was both antecedent and contemporary with Chaco. It surely would have been known to Chaco and the larger Southwest.

The altepetl was *not* a great empire like those of the Aztecs and Tarascans. Those empires encompassed scores of altepeme. An altepetl was, in fact, rather small. The population of altepeme averaged about 12,000 people and ranged from as few as 2,000 to as many as 40,000 people. Altepetl territory was also small: typically about 75 sq km. We will return to the matter of size—size matters!

Our knowledge of altepeme comes from both codices and archaeology. In brief, an altepetl consisted of a ruling class of multiple (ideally, about a half dozen) noble families and their associated commoners, within a defined agricultural territory. The whole was a unit, city and countryside. It was a tributary system, in which commoners owed goods or labor to their noble families, and minor nobles to major nobles, and so forth. Tribute typically was not oppressive: a few bushels of corn, a few weeks' labor, occasional military service, and so forth. Nobles ruled their own commoners, who might (or might not) be localized within a spatial segment of the altepetl. Rulership of the altepetl itself revolved through the leading noble families. There was a king, but the office didn't descend in a kingly line. When the king needed replacement—old, inept, dead—the half-dozen highest noble families decided on a successor, usually from a noble house other than the outgoing officeholder. Thus no one house achieved dominance over the others: governance was shared—at least among the upper class.

By the time of the codices, numerological and cosmological rules defined the ideal altepetl form. Theoretically, an ideal altepetl would have eight major noble families; but of course this varied in practice. If the numerological rules codified the existing reality, eight could be considered a reasonable "modal" (or ideal) number of major noble families, with the same number of social segments among commoners. Noble families were distinguished (in life and in archaeology) by their palaces: noble houses, elite residences. Secondary noble houses could be located in the countryside among commoner farmsteads, but palaces of the major noble families clustered within a tight central zone, often at a place notable in the altepetl's history. This "central cluster" could be considered urban, in a smallish way. Some archaeologists call them city-states; others deny that the central cluster was fully urban. The center/city—notably boasting a half-dozen noble houses—certainly had urban aspects, but typically it was rather small: median population was about 4,750 people (with a range of 600 to 23,000 people). One-third of Aztec altepeme central clusters, for example, had fewer than 3,000 people—much like Chaco's 2,500 to 3,000.[9]

Chaco Canyon was perhaps one of the most obvious examples of "stratified housing" in archaeology, a palace civilization almost Cretan in its clarity. The major Great Houses were so very markedly different from normal houses, the ubiquitous unit pueblo. Not subtle, not nuanced: the archaeology gods gave us a softball to hit. Great Houses and unit pueblos almost certainly demonstrated two social divisions, two strata, two classes. The passing years have added more and more data supporting that conclusion. The evidence as it now stands seems, to me, overwhelming. Great Houses were *not* pueblos; nor were they temples; nor were they hotels. Great Houses were elite residences, noble houses: in a word, palaces.

If one accepts that Chaco Great Houses were palaces, the similarities to the altepetl form become (almost) obvious. The cluster of major Great Houses in Chaco Canyon is remarkably similar to the central cluster of altepeme (see figure A.2). The Chaco central cluster was there, I think, because Chaco Canyon itself was important. Centuries before the first Great House, Chaco Canyon had seen truly remarkable developments in the sixth and seventh centuries (discussed in chapter 3). This recalls foundation myths of altepeme centers, built at historically significant places. The six or seven major Great Houses in Chaco, in this model, represent the altepetl's half-dozen major noble families. Other smaller Great Houses represent cadet branches, minor nobility, priesthoods, and so forth.

The radial divisions of Chaco's region, marked by the major roads, parallel the (idealized) radial spatial subdivisions of many altepetl, with each noble family controlling its piece of the pie (see figure A.2). Commoner residences were built within the central cluster and (of course) throughout the region, with secondary Great Houses (i.e., "outliers") taking care of business out in the boonies. Like the altepetl, there is no useful separation of center and countryside: the ensemble constitutes the polity, by happy accident termed as the Chaco regional system.

There were, of course, differences. Most altepeme central clusters had a pyramid, and many had markets. Chaco lacked pyramids and, perhaps, lacked markets. John Stein and his colleagues (2007) argue for pyramids at Chaco; the jury is out. I argue below that Chaco's inner region—the San Juan Basin—was of a scale suitable for transportation of bulk goods and perhaps had markets, but the jury's out on that, too. It is worth noting that half of the Aztec atlepeme centers also lacked markets. Markets, it seems, were not essential.

Chaco, of course, had features and building types not seen in altepeme; for example, Great Kivas—although Great Kivas may represent, at least in part, "schools" sometimes found in altepetl centers. Domestic architecture (a cultural bedrock!) differed enormously. Houses in north and west Mesoamerica generally comprised three or four freestanding small buildings centered tightly around a patio. Chaco people—noble and commoner—lived in nicely built pithouses (often called "kivas") with a suite of aboveground masonry rooms to the rear. Chaco palaces do not look like Mesoamerican palaces—Chaco palaces are much bigger!

Material culture, social systems, and (presumably) ideologies of Chacoan and Mesoamerican societies were quite distinct. But altepeme and Chacoan political structures were very similar because Chaco elites imported or imposed that sort of thing, top down. (Archaeology currently favors bottom-up models; but don't try that populist stuff on an ornery king.) Chaco translated Mesoamerican forms into local idioms of architecture, ideology, and cosmology.[10]

The biggest differences between Chaco and altepeme were in scales: demographic and spatial. Chaco had a lot more people over a much bigger area.

The average altepetl was about 12,000 people, with a maximum of 40,000. I estimated over twice that for Chaco's region (above). But consider: the altepetl was an economic unit; for Chaco, the economic region was within a 150 km radius. The population of Chaco's "inner core" was something in excess of 50,000—more than the altepetl maximum of 40,000, but not orders of magnitude bigger. More people than the Mesoamerican model, but not a lot more. The population in the 150 km to 250 km zone was big, but they were not engaged in a bulk-transport economy—the "outer limit" was a political economy of fluff and feathers. The lack of "peer polities" may have something to do with Chaco's unseemly size: it kept expanding because no peers pushed back.

Chaco's region (perhaps 100,000 sq km) is enormously larger than the altepetl average, 75 sq km. That's a big difference, a *big* difference. The alarming disparity in spatial scales, I think, reflects dramatic differences in productivity between Chaco and Mesoamerica. Mesoamerican altepeme enjoyed very happy environments for corn agriculture. High productivity supported dense populations in small areas. Chaco's region, in very stark contrast, was bleak. Prime arable lands were scarce and patchy, scattered far and wide. Overall population density was consequently quite low—pockets of settlement separated by stretches of empty desert.

Chaco, I think, stretched the altepetl political form to its elastic limits, over very difficult terrain. Chaco solved its scale problems with technology and ideology: roads and line-of-sight signaling systems held its over-large domain together.

For a while. In the end, Chaco failed. Perhaps the altepetl political form was ill suited for Chaco's difficult environment and inflated spatial scale. Perhaps as likely, Chaco's altepetl failed because it stood alone. Mesoamerican altepeme were peer polities, city-states jammed shoulder to shoulder into central Mesoamerica. Altepeme and city-states thrived on competition. That was the altepetl's proper context, the social and political environment in which it evolved. While the political form could be copied, transplanted, or coevolved in the Southwest, the altepetl's larger context—highly productive agriculture and scores of peer polities—could not. Chaco had no peers, unless it were Hohokam.[11]

Chaco was altepetl-like. Is this an outrageous interpretation? Novel, but hardly outrageous if we recognize the Southwest as a place on North America—not as a political subdivision of the United States—and accept that modern Pueblo societies rose, at least in part, as a rejection of Chaco. Chaco as altepetl should not alarm us. Indeed, the altepetl has much to recommend it, above competing interpretations of Chaco. The altepetl is not a sodality or curing society or kachina cult, plucked from ethnographic Pueblos and forced into the distant past (e.g., Ware

2014). Nor is it a novel construct, something we invented—ritualities, pilgrimage centers, et cetera—papering over an ancient polity that was clearly non- or un-Puebloan (e.g., Yoffee 2001). Nor is it an abstract anthropological theory, like "chiefdom" (a term used in American archaeology to keep ancient Natives down; see Pauketat 2007), or an anthropological case study, abstracted from societies distant in time and space, like sub-Saharan chiefdoms without chiefs (e.g., Sebastian 2006). The altepetl was a real Native political form of Chaco's time and place. We can be sure that Chaco *knew about* altepeme. (They didn't know about Hopi or Zuni; they didn't know about "acephalous chiefdoms.") There are demonstrable historical connections between Chaco and altepetl societies—all those Mesoamerican things at Chaco. If Chaco wanted to create or evolve into a (secondary) state, the altepetl would be the obvious way to go: not too big, not too small, just right. It was the political form that Chaco knew.

We are told that "no ethnographic models seem to fit Chaco" (Hays-Gilpin 2011, speaking for many; see appendix A). Thus, Chaco becomes a mystery. Because we are hoodwinked by the national boundary between the United States and Mexico, we haven't looked quite far enough for ethnographic models. Altepetl is an ethnographic model from Chaco's time and place, a form of society that Chaco knew. It's homegrown and historically appropriate. It fits Chaco like a glove. Mystery solved?

CHACO AND MIMBRES

In appendix C, I make the case that Chaco knew the north (the northern San Juan) from the early eleventh century on—long before the first shift from Chaco to Aztec Ruins. Here I argue that Chaco (and its successor Aztec) knew the south and the region of the post-Aztec capital Paquimé through Paquimé's predecessor, Mimbres. Mimbres and Chaco were exactly contemporary—Mimbres's peak was about 1000 to 1130—and the Mimbres Valley was pretty much exactly south of Chaco Canyon (figure 2.12).[12]

Famous for its pottery (figure 2.3), Mimbres was more than just a pretty vase. Sprawling one-story masonry Mimbres settlements were, perhaps, the first real pueblos in the Southwest (Lekson 1992, 1993, 2009).

Mimbres's genius did not extend to architecture. Masonry was haphazard, and layouts were irregular, compared to Four Corners ruins, and positively regrettable compared to Chaco's ponderous formality. Chaco loved right angles; Mimbres didn't. Artists' visions of Pueblo Bonito aren't exactly warm and welcoming, but they are impressive. Artists' visions of Mimbres villages call for massive FEMA-scale influxes of disaster relief.

But they were really big, and there were a lot of them. About a score of Mimbres sites represent large villages of up to 500 residents each. Most were in the Mimbres Valley, but large Mimbres villages were found all along the desert-facing

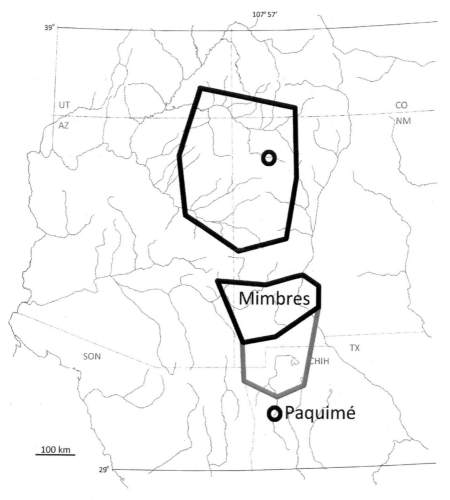

FIGURE 2.12

The Mimbres region, in southwestern New Mexico and northernmost Chihuahua. The big Mimbres towns (see figure 2.13) were mostly in a latitudinal band along rivers from the Gila on the west (under the "M" in "Mimbres") to the Mimbres Valley (between "m" and "b") and the Rio Grande on the east (under the "e"), and several other small creeks flowing out of the well-watered Mogollon highlands into the Chihuahuan Desert. The gap between northernmost Mimbres and southernmost Chaco in the late eleventh and early twelfth centuries is real, but not large. The extension sagging south from Mimbres proper into Chihuahua represents a well-attested but poorly understood distribution of Mimbres Black-on-white, in varying quantities. Isolated sherds are found well south of Casas Grandes. Assuming that rodomontade follows the sag, Mimbres people presumably chatted up the south and knew quite a bit about the southern extension, including the future site of Paquimé.

slopes of the Mogollon uplands in a 200 km long, 50 km wide band from the Arizona border to the Rio Grande. The two very largest towns were on the Gila River—but the bulk of the Mimbres population lived along the Mimbres River.

Fueled and tethered by large-scale canal irrigation systems (Herrington 1982; Lekson 1986c), Mimbres villages were truly permanent, fixed over many generations—unlike contemporary Anasazi villages, which typically lasted a generation or two. Several grew to remarkable size (figure 2.13). The largest Mimbres village sites had up to four hundred rooms, and—unlike Pueblo Bonito and other Great Houses—most Mimbres rooms were homes. People lived in Mimbres villages in Pueblo-like densities. Evidences of village life are everywhere, as are the remains of the occupants, buried beneath the rooms. Swarts Ruin alone produced about one thousand burials. Mimbres villages were, I think, the first real "pueblos": densely packed apartment-like villages, held together with ceremony more than government.

To cope with high densities and deep sedentism, Mimbres developed the earliest forms of kachina ceremonialism (Schaafsma 1994) and sorted out how to keep a big town together without kings or nobles. These were remarkable achievements.

Mimbres was a moiré of Anasazi lifestyles over Hohokam infrastructure (Lekson 1993, 2009:134–137). Mimbres pueblos, kivas, and black-and-white and indented corrugated pottery were Anasazi; elaborate ditch systems and consequent deep sedentism (they were tethered to their infrastructure) were Hohokam. The "Anasazi-ness" of Mimbres is a long and bitterly contested research theme (LeBlanc 1986a). Wiser heads than mine have looked at Mimbres and thought: Anasazi (Haury 1936, 1988). I say, where there's smoke, there's fire. Mimbres hooked up with Anasazi, after 1000. "Hohokam-ness" has been mooted for earlier Mimbres figurative pottery, Mimbres cremation cemeteries—cremation being the preferred Hohokam practice—and above all Mimbres canal irrigation technologies (Creel 1989; Shafer 2003; see also Hegmon and Nelson 2007, which lists the similarities but discounts their importance). I've argued that Mimbres was like a weather vane: when Hohokam was going strong, up to about 1000, Mimbres looked west and paid attention to Hohokam. When Hohokam waned and Chaco exploded, after 1000, Mimbres suddenly began to look very Anasazi (Lekson 1993, 2006a, 2009). Moiré may be more than mere metaphor.

Hohokam exceeds the scope of this chapter (this argument is laid out more fully in Lekson 2009). Our principal concern here is Chaco and its world. The "Anasazi-ness" of Mimbres in the tenth and eleventh centuries cannot be separated from Chaco, because to a large extent Anasazi at that time *was* Chaco. Chaco encompassed almost but not quite all of the Anasazi region.

Mimbres, we have been told, is properly Mogollon, not Anasazi; what did Mimbres have to do with Chaco? Well, Mimbres after 1000 shifted from Hohokam-ish pithouses to Anasazi unit pueblos with indented corrugated jars

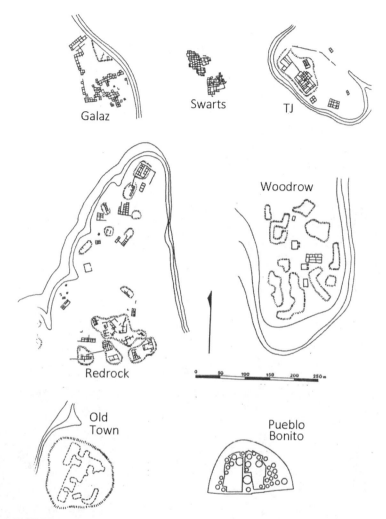

FIGURE 2.13

Mimbres sites, at their peak around 1100, and Pueblo Bonito at Chaco about the same time. Mimbres towns could be large, with up to 500 people—at a guess—in Pueblo-like densities, unlike the scattered plans of contemporary Chaco communities. (Pueblo Bonito is not a community—it is a palace.) Galaz and Old Town are two of the very largest of a score of sizable towns in the Mimbres Valley. Swarts is a smaller Mimbres Valley site; it was extensively excavated and produced over 1,000 burials (suggesting a population in the hundreds). TJ is at the Gila Cliff Dwellings National Monument and is therefore exceptionally well preserved. Redrock and Woodrow are on the Gila, where towns were much larger but far fewer; these are the only two big towns known from that river valley.

and fabulous black-on-white pottery—that's Anasazi. But the Chaco part of the picture comes from two now-familiar classes of data: prestige goods and architecture.

I used macaws as a proxy for prestige goods in the Chaco world. Mimbres, alone in the eleventh-century Pueblo region, rivaled Chaco in its aviary interests. There were lots of Mimbres macaws and parrots on pots and in the flesh (Creel and McKusick 1994). Thirty-one macaws were found at Pueblo Bonito, and several more at other Chaco Canyon sites; more than seventeen have been found at Mimbres sites, and images of macaws are conspicuous on Mimbres pottery (figure 2.14). Mimbres sites also produce copper bells in Chacoan numbers

FIGURE 2.14
Mimbres macaws. A score of macaws have been found in Mimbres sites, and they appear on many Mimbres bowls (Creel and McKusick 1994). A Mimbres Black-on-white bowl (UCM 3238) showing two macaws with a tailed anthropomorphic figure—a monkey? Monkeys flourished in some of the same forests as macaws. While the artist probably had a live macaw to model, the anthropomorphized monkey might reflect travelers' tales. So far, no one has found a monkey in a Mimbres site. No one's found bones from deep ocean fish, either, but the Mimbres painted them (Jett and Moyle 1986). (Courtesy the University of Colorado Museum of Natural History.)

(Vargas 1995). In the eleventh and early twelfth centuries, Mimbres rivals Chaco for exotica. There may be more of one at Mimbres or more of another at Chaco but other Anasazi districts in the eleventh century are not even in the running.[13]

And there are disturbing hints of architectural connections. Perhaps literal connections: Chaco-style roads are now being found in the Mimbres Valley (Creel 2006). How far north or south those roads extend is unknown; Mimbres road studies are only just beginning.[14] And off road: parallels in commoner housing and—perhaps—elite residences. I have argued that the basic element of Mimbres settlement was an Anasazi-like unit pueblo (five rooms and a square kiva) (figure 2.2), jammed together in the larger Mimbres towns but scattered in Chaco-style communities where landforms allowed (Lekson 1988a, but see Shafer 1995). Most Mimbres communities centered on a Great Kiva—square, but no less. In the most densely aggregated towns, the Great Kiva may have been replaced by plazas (Anyon and LeBlanc 1980) in a sequence familiar from other parts of the southern Pueblo world (Adams 1991; Haury 1950).

All that's missing is the Great House, and Mimbres may have had those too. Not textbook Chaco Great Houses with multiple stories, blocked-in kivas, enclosed plazas, berms, and all the rest, but something sorta maybe like them. Emulations, perhaps. What's an emulation? A key question dogging the Chaco regional system, far to the north, concerns "export" versus "emulation": Are outliers planned and built by Chaco architects ("exports"), or are they local copies ("emulation")? Well, what would an emulation look like? It might lack many of the interior details, the checklist features, the Chaco-specific attributes. But it would, presumably, be bigger, more massive, and more formal than the surrounding houses of the people. That is, it would *look like* a Great House, built on a local fabric—not just local materials, but local technologies and even local floor plans. I think there are a few "emulation" Great Houses in the Mimbres area.

I'll offer two, one on the Gila River and one on the Mimbres. At the very large Woodrow Ruin in the Gila Valley (Sedig 2015), a central room block rises conspicuously above the surrounding community of typical Mimbres room blocks—today, low hummocks (figure 2.13). Two huge Great Kivas are immediately adjacent. This central room block was excavated by a youth group in the 1960s; there is no report, but we can still see the interior walls and arrangements. Unlike other Mimbres sites, the walls are thick and straight. The room block forms a crisp rectangle with all angles right (more or less). Large front rooms were backed by pairs of smaller rear rooms—a Chaco/Anasazi plan, not a Mimbres room suite. The walls, like most Mimbres walls, are river cobbles set in mud, but well coursed and massive. The walls are Mimbres, but the form is not. This could be emulation, a Great House in Mimbres fabrics and technologies.

My second example is frustrating, archaeologically, but important nevertheless. The Baca site, in the Mimbres Valley, was excavated by amateurs and reported by an aficionado (Evans, Ross, and Ross 1985). Baca was later bulldozed, so, like Aragon, there's no looking back; the report is all we have. The maps and photos are less than we might wish, but what they show is remarkable (figure 2.15). The tall walls of Baca were of coursed ashlar masonry, not river cobbles; the rooms are trim rectangles, and the ground plan was a very Chacoan D, with a rectangular room block 25 to 30 m long and 10 to 15 m wide and a plaza-enclosing arc of rooms. The excavators noted a broad road-like feature running along the north edge of the building: "well-packed [and] treated like the Mimbres did their floors . . . water applied to the 'caliche' and rubbed to a smooth surface . . . it was in step-like layers that were lengthy and not very deep" (R. Evelyn Ross, personal communication, 1987). Sound like a Chaco road? At one time, that might have seemed absurd, but similar road segments have been found at Old Town, one of the longest Mimbres Valley sites (Creel 2006), and more are turning up in the Mimbres area.

Was Baca a Great House? Was Woodrow? Mimbres archaeologists deny that possibility with the same fervor Colorado archaeologists used to deny Great Houses at Mesa Verde. No Mimbres site will display the unmistakable singularity of Chimney Rock or even Bluff; geology denied access to the fine tabular sandstones that made distinctively Chacoan masonry possible. And indeed I would not suggest that Mimbres candidate Great Houses were built by Chaco masons or designed by Chacoan leaders. They are examples of what we might seek as Great House "emulations"—Great House forms on local fabrics, adapted to local social and political situations.

Mimbres was probably not submerged or encompassed politically within the Chaco regional system, but it was linked historically to that great center. Macaws

FIGURE 2.15
The Baca site, in the Mimbres Valley (Evans, Ross, and Ross 1985). The Baca site map has been dismissed as the inaccurate work of amateurs who excavated the site, before it was bulldozed and destroyed. The map is sketchy, but the compact rectangular block with a D arc of rooms is unlike any other Mimbres site, as was the well-coursed masonry. Moreover, their discovery of a broad "road" anticipated the confirmation of roads in the Mimbres Valley (Creel 2006). I think Baca was a Mimbres version of a Chaco Great House. The site's gone now, so outlier deniers can say: "We'll never know." We can't know everything, but we can know something, if we can read a map.

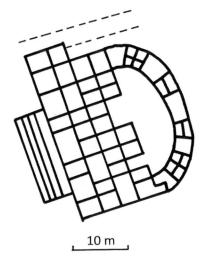

10 m

and architecture show that linkage. In the eleventh- and twelfth-century Pueblo world, macaws and copper and other prestige items are notably concentrated in Mimbres and Chaco—almost exclusively in those two areas.

We might object that very little Mimbres pottery was found at Chaco, and only slightly more Chaco pottery was found in the Mimbres Valley. We put prodigious faith in pottery, but as noted above, prestige economies were not about pottery. In any event, Mimbres decorated pottery was probably specific to Mimbres society or ritual. Mimbres bugs and birds look cute to us, but Mimbres art also depicted decapitations and scary monsters. The art was highly charged—even the bugs and birds. The cult did not travel well, especially the later figurative pottery we prize so highly. That stuff stayed in the Mimbres area: you had to be Mimbres to appreciate it. Chaco could have had anything it wanted, and it didn't want Mimbres pottery. And, of course, the majority of later Chaco pottery was not actually made at Chaco. Pottery exchange between those two may or may not provide a useful index of interaction.

All the same, Mimbres and Chaco pottery were part of a larger tradition, what archaeological hipsters call "communities of practice." Two examples: black-on-white bowls and indented corrugated jars. The designs differ, but the techniques of manufacture on Chaco and Mimbres decorated bowls are strikingly similar. For both, all effort went into interiors: slipping, polishing, painting, and so forth. Bowl exteriors were roughly smoothed but not particularly well finished, and in both Chaco and Mimbres, a very distinctive spillover of thin white slip forms a ragged dribbled band along the exterior rim—what archaeological not-so-hipsters call "slip-slop." It's quite distinctive for both Chaco and Mimbres black-on-white bowls—and not on black-on-white bowls from other areas.

The nonpainted pottery—cooking and storage jars, mostly—from both areas are sufficiently different that we can tell them apart, yet they developed over time in lockstep, perfectly parallel sequences from plain, to neck-banded, to shoulder corrugated, to all-over corrugated, to—finally and my favorite—indented corrugated. Indented corrugated is perhaps unique to the American Southwest, globally; I can't find anything like it in other times and places. It's strikingly distinctive. And it's the final form at both Chaco (and its region) and in Mimbres. Somehow, I can't convince myself that we are seeing two independent inventions of indented corrugated pottery. Chaco and Mimbres, I think, were linked by history. At some very basic level—attested by pottery—they shared a common culture.

When Chaco exploded in the eleventh century, the shock waves reached Mimbres. I think Mimbres Great Houses emulate Chaco's; who knows what other areas of Mimbres society were affected. Specific events are lost to us, but architecture and exotica tell the story. There was no great divide between Mimbres and Chaco, only distance: a short distance. Events in one must soon have been known in the other, traveling over the trails (road?) that carried macaws, bells, turquoise, and who knows what else. Separate societies, but, at least after 1000, part of the same larger "culture area"—if I may be allowed an archaism. The dramatic events at Chaco reached Mimbres—and Mimbres managed, somehow, to remain separate if not entirely equal. Perhaps the vivid Mimbres cosmology—expressed in those beautiful, terrible bowls—was a reaction to Chaco, a reinvention of Mimbres to avoid whatever cosmologies Chaco was selling. In the end, a political chain linked local groups from the Rocky Mountains on the north to the Chihuahua basins on the south. And when Chaco's boom times ended, in the early twelfth century, Mimbres was both a cause and an effect of what followed a century later at Paquimé—a story hinted at below and told in chapter 3. It's important to note that from the earliest days of Mimbres studies, maps showing "Mimbres" dip very deep into Chihuahua. Not the big villages, perhaps, but sites with lots of Mimbres pottery pop up well south on the Rio Casas Grandes. If pottery tells us anything, it tells us that Mimbres knew that valley and the future site of Paquimé.

Major construction ceased at Chaco about 1125; at exactly the same time, Mimbres ends. What happened next to Chaco is the problem addressed in the remainder of this book. What happened to Mimbres?

LIFE AFTER MIMBRES

Mimbres at 1100 consisted of a score of very large villages and many smaller settlements in the Mimbres Valley, the Gila Valley, and along a stretch of the Rio Grande. Total population was probably between 5,000 and 10,000—say 7,000, or that order of magnitude. Mimbres villages have already been described: stone masonry pueblos and kivas. Ceramic decoration had reached an artistic peak, collected by museums and celebrated in coffee-table books.

At about 1125, Mimbres quit building stone masonry pueblos and quit building small kivas. They also quit painting pottery. It was like someone flipped a switch. So quick and complete was this change that for decades, archaeologists spoke of a Mimbres "collapse," with populations vanishing or migrating out to who knows where (Blake, LeBlanc, and Minnis 1986; LeBlanc 1983; Shafer 1999). This, we now think, was not entirely the case (Nelson 1999; Hegmon et al. 1999; Lekson 2006a). Mimbres people did not vanish; they changed clothes. A remnant remained in the Mimbres Valley (Creel 1997); others headed for the hills (Nelson 1999; Hegmon, Nelson, and Ruth 1998); and still others moved downstream and out into lower, desert reaches of river valleys (Lekson 2006a).

It is true that most of the big Mimbres towns on the Gila and the Mimbres were deserted, and it is likely that population diminished, perhaps even halved after a generation or two. And it's true that population shifted up to the hills and out into the deserts. Moreover, architecture shifted from stone masonry to puddled adobe—much harder to see on a survey. And the brilliant Mimbres painted pottery traditions abruptly ceased, replaced mostly by unpainted ceramics (figure

2.3). For decades, that ceramic change ensured archaeological invisibility: in an area famed for its painted pottery, plain pottery simply disappears.

Not only was there a geographic shift (small, by Plateau standards) and a dramatic change in material culture, but also a watershed in ideology. Mimbres painted pottery was a primary locus for the expression of Mimbres ideology and cosmology (e.g., Brody 1977; Shafer 1995). Remarkable creative energies were invested in cosmological imagery on the interior of bowls. After 1125, the bowl-interior field of design was completely rejected; bowls were not only not painted, but their interiors were smudged a deep black and then highly burnished, creating a dark black mirror effect. In the course of about one generation, bowl interiors transformed from one of the most celebrated fields for Southwestern expressive art to a black, blank antidesign. Whether Mimbres potters made these black bowls or obtained them from other makers, that's what was on the breakfast table. Grandpa ate his gruel from a bowl showing the warrior twins; grandson ate his from a bowl that showed absolutely nothing at all. Something big had happened, something that inverted the old ideological order. People turned their backs on the old ways and built new villages with new fabrics out in the deserts of southern New Mexico and the Jornada region. These post-Mimbres villages, called El Paso phase or Animas phase or—most importantly—Black Mountain phase (Lekson 2006; Hegmon et al. 1999), are the likely base population for Paquimé, one century later. Art and physical anthropology link Mimbres and Paquimé populations (Moulard 2005; Turner 1993)—a tale told in chapter 3.

It's difficult to imagine that the simultaneous end of both Chaco and Mimbres were not related: an event, or a response to a mutual cataclysm, real or imagined. The cultural linkages of Chaco and Mimbres, their exact contemporaneity, and— to anticipate later chapters—their positional relationships all point to profound historical connections. After 1125, all vestiges of the Chacoan system were gone from the old Mimbres region. Chaco was gone and not forgotten—gone, but *not* never to return.

NOTES

1. Many people assume that I champion Chaco simply because I once worked there. Fieldwork happens out in the field, and it's difficult—maybe impossible—to separate site data from place sense. There's a cornfield in Tennessee I still detest, forty years after a particular summer from hell, so don't ask me about the Cumberland Valley Archaic. I freely confess to a deep fondness (approaching bias) for the Cliff Valley of the upper Gila, vis-à-vis the Mimbres Valley. I misspent a part of my youth around Cliff, shooting pool and having fun, so I like the place. But I'm fairly neutral about Chaco Canyon. Chaco was an entertaining place to work, but Chaco was, first and foremost, work. I do not think Chaco was important because I worked there; I worked there because I thought Chaco was important.

2. More than a few just wanted Chaco to go away. In the early days of the Chaco Project, when Chaco was getting a lot of ink and media attention, a University of Colorado crew working at the huge Mesa Verde site of Yellow Jacket produced a bumper sticker that announced, in big red letters, "Chaco Is a Dairy Queen Outlier." It must have seemed funnier around a campfire (most things are better around a campfire). Even out of context, it has a pleasant Dada spin. I mailed a half dozen out to Chaco with a bogus Park Service memo on park privatization.

3. Until fairly recently, few people had the chance to see many outliers, to see the pattern; you have to go looking for outliers. There are over 150 outliers out there, which seems like a lot until you realize that those outliers are sprinkled over a huge area among many tens of thousands of eleventh- and twelfth-century unit pueblo sites. Outliers are actually rare birds. Assume 150 Great Houses evenly sprinkled over 100,000 sq km (40,000 sq miles); that's one outlier per 775 sq km (267 sq miles). At the industry standard of 20 acres a day, it would take an inquiring-minded archaeologist three decades just to find one of these things. How many would you have to see before a pattern began to emerge? Three? Five? Twenty?

It's no wonder people had problems with outliers. Those of us who, through happy opportunity or alarming obsession, have seen many outliers still lack the language to effectively describe the pattern. Most of our colleagues have only seen a few, usually the excavated, spruced-up, set-piece exhibits such as Lowry Ruin or Far View House. Small samples do not forge strong patterns, and it's hard to connect excavated and restored Far View House to an undistinguished lump like Peach Springs. You can't, until you see a whole series of Peach Springs–like lumps, in a wide range of settings and states—"states" of both condition and constitution.

4. Many outlier Great Houses were originally built in Chacoan times and used/occupied through the post-Chacoan twelfth and thirteenth centuries, so the surface sherds look late; I'd say there's a fair chance Camelot began in the eleventh or twelfth century.

5. The 250 km limit is an empirical observation: that's how far out the farthest out are. Interestingly, that's true for Hohokam ball courts from Phoenix (the epicenter for Hohokam) and Chacoan outliers. The 150 km inner core began as an observation: that's about how far out the slam-dunk, no-doubt-about-it outliers are from Chaco. But far more importantly, it's also the practical limits for bulk transport by porters and tumpline economies.

We've been hobbled by falsely short distance thresholds. David Wilcox, in many intriguing bull's-eye maps, used radii increments of 36 km—a day's walk; and many archaeologists have there-and-back-again ideas about half a day's walk: to preview chapter 3, Whalen and Minnis (2001) limit Paquimé's hard-core polity to about 15 km or a half day's walk, or a zone of daily interaction. Kent Lightfoot (1979) set a 50 km limit for "prehistoric food redistribution at Chaco," and his limit has been quite influential. But it's probably wrong. Nancy Malville, who studies porters in cultures where porters matter, concludes, "Foot transport of foodstuffs and durable goods would have been feasible in the pre-Hispanic Southwest on a regular basis over distances of at least 100 to 150 km and on an occasional basis over much longer distances" (Malville 2001:230). 150

km limits have been independently suggested for Postclassic "trafficking in bulky goods" (Santley and Alexander 1992:44).

6. For Southwestern goodies, for example: Bradley 1993; Crown and Hurst 2009; Doyel 1991 (and citations therein); Hudson 1978; Mathien 1986; Neitzel 1989a; Nelson 1986; Vargas 1995; and of course the old guard: J. Charles Kelley 1986; Charles Di Peso 1974; Joseph Whitecotton and Richard Pailes 1986; and Phil Weigand (and Harbottle) 1993. For prestige economies in the Southwest: Crown 1994; Di Peso 1974; Douglas 1990; Doyel 1991; Kelley 1995; Mathien 1993; Neitzel 1989a; Nelson 1981; and Toll 1991.

But in the rush to refute *pochteca*, bells, shells, birds, and trinkets were swept under the rug. Toll (1991:86) describes exotics as "extremely small quantities," "minuscule." Mathien also minimizes and concludes that "Chacoan control of critical goods or trade routes is unlikely," principally because of "the absence of a scarce resource," for example, turquoise, at Chaco Canyon (Mathien 1993:55, 56). In Vivian's (1990) *Chacoan Prehistory of the San Juan Basin*, macaws and bells didn't even merit index entries. "Exotics," in *Chacoan Prehistory*, refers to chipped stone and pottery; we look in vain for a macaw. "Luxury goods" (Sebastian 1992) and "exotica" (Saitta 1997), while important, are largely subordinate to agricultural surplus and surplus labor, respectively. Turquoise, ornaments, and other "long-distance imports" suffer from near-fatal "problems of differential sample size, depositional context, and differential excavation and recording techniques," but "further examination . . . would be warranted" (Sebastian 1991:117). With this faint praise, exotica are buried under other labor and food, at the epicenter of all oddities: Chaco had more weird stuff than the Santa Fe flea market.

7. Long wooden swords, actually. Variously misidentified as canoe paddles and digging sticks, hardwood swords with baseball-bat handles and single-edged blades show damage and wear consistent with whacking, not tilling.

8. And perhaps taking women. There are imbalances in the ratios of young men to young women: too many women at Great Houses and too few women in the countryside (Harrod 2012; Kohler and Turner 2006). It seems likely that the extra women at Great Houses were slaves (Cameron 2013). If it were possible to determine the genders of the massacre victims, it would be interesting if young women were underrepresented: a thesis topic for someone other than me.

9. Mesoamerican urban centers were not necessarily large in size nor densely populated. Michael Smith (2000; see also his *Aztec City-State Capitals*, 2008) offers the most useful information: most Aztec cities ranged in size from 10 ha to 90 ha. For the metrically challenged (like me), 10 ha is a football field, squared; 90 ha is slightly more than 220 acres, about one-third of a square mile. The populations of these urban centers were as small as 600 to a median value of about 10,000 (and of course a few much larger), and they fell far short of 1,000 people/ha or even "several hundred" people/ha. Smith (2008) notes two density classes: low from 10 to 38 persons/ha, and a higher density class of 44 to 72 persons/ha (and a third density particular to Teotihuacan: 157/ha). Look at the lower (but not the lowest!) end of those ranges: those are Southwestern numbers!

10. Or—to make things more palatable—Chaco could have coevolved an altepetl structure with significant knowledge of and interplay with Mesoamerican systems.

11. Chaco knew about Hohokam—someone at Chetro Ketl wore a very distinctive Hohokam shirt on Casual Fridays (Maxwell Museum 2011)—but the nature of that interaction is not yet understood. (Ouch!—what a typical archaeological cop-out.)

12. I have an inclusive view of Mimbres (Lekson 1986b): my Mimbres ranged from west of the Arizona line to east of the Rio Grande—from longitude 107° to 109°. In fact, the largest Mimbres sites are not on the Mimbres River, but in the upper Gila River Valley, at Redrock and Cliff, New Mexico (Lekson 1984b). However, when pothunters attacked the big Gila sites, those ruins did not produce the anticipated numbers of Mimbres pots: Was my valley "different"? I thought there might be a hopscotch intervalley sequence (a model more fully developed by Nelson and Anyon 1996), but the surface archaeologies of the Mimbres and the Gila were nearly identical (Lekson 2006a).

But I admit: there *is* something special about the Mimbres Valley. Unquestionably, the Mimbres was the epicenter of the eponymous art style. Better suited than the Gila or Rio Grande for small-scale, preconcrete canal irrigation, the Mimbres Valley could support denser occupations then those neighboring, larger river valleys. Population density is important (see chapter 5), and Mimbres Valley populations also were probably more aggregated and certainly more circumscribed than Gila and Rio Grande peoples. Those differences, together, suggest that new social and ritual organizations (i.e., kachina ceremonialism) probably developed in the Mimbres Valley—adapting elements of southern cosmologies and pantheons to purely local needs.

Which brings us back to the Mimbres Valley's longitude. Most of the Mimbres Valley—the length of the river below the confluence of its upper forks and above Deming—is due south of Chaco—the canyon from Fajada to the Escavada. Both are circumscribed, oasis-like (the Mimbres Valley was an oasis; Chaco was at best oasis-ish), and both saw unparalleled social and architectural developments during the eleventh and early twelfth centuries. Both were and are the obvious major concentration of Mesoamerican things, east of the Continental Divide. All this fits together, somehow, in some vast conspiracy theory . . .

13. Mimbres ruins produced considerable amounts of turquoise, but not Chacoan quantities (e.g., Cosgrove and Cosgrove 1932:64). An exception: Over 3,000 pieces of turquoise (mostly "residual" or "waste" fragments) were recovered from a single Mimbres context at the West Baker site (McCluney 1968). The West Baker site is located near (but not at) the turquoise mines at Old Hachita, which rival Cerillos in scale, with twenty chambered mines (Phil Weigand, personal communication, 1989; Weigand and Harbottle 1993:163). "An unknown polity(s) was involved in the development of the Azure-Old Hachita areas" (Weigand and Harbottle 1993:173). Mimbres? Paquimé? Both? The Old Hachita mines were the same distance from Paquimé as the Cerillos mines were from Chaco. If Paquimé politicos were responsible, turquoise did not stick to their hands. Only 1.2 kg of turquoise was recovered at Casas Grandes, mostly from architectural, dedicatory deposits (Di Peso, Rinaldo, and Fenner 1974e:187).

14. And now we have roads in the Hohokam! Wilcox (Wilcox, McGuire, and Sternberg 1981) identified road-like features at the margins of Snaketown. Motsinger (1998) traces one of these roads almost 6 km, to another site (and conspicuous landscape feature) at Gila Butte. I hope that Hohokam archaeologists heed the mistakes we made (and continue to make) with Chacoan roads (presented, with tact, in Vivian 1997a, 1997b). There's a joke here, about reinventing wheels, which I will leave to the reader.

3

Meridian Nexus

This here's a p'inter. Right up there is our line for the Pole Star and the jolly dollars.

—*Long John Silver*

DOWN THE YELLOW BRICK ROAD

The eleventh century set the stage for a political history of the Pueblo Southwest which ended, in the fifteenth century, at Paquimé. There were prequels and sequels, discussed later in this chapter: things happened before and after, on the meridian. Not all were political, and not all were in the Southwest. The history of Southwestern *political power* is the story of these three sites: Chaco, Aztec, and Paquimé.

Chaco emerged in the eleventh century as the political center of the northern Southwest. Something happened at Chaco that had not happened before in the Pueblo world: a permanent center—a capital city—organized and controlled a sizable region. There were large villages before Chaco, but none were regional centers, at least political centers. Chaco was monumental, permanent, and very central—something new under the Southwestern sun.

So, too, was Mimbres: permanent and different, at least. New ways of living—social and ritual—developed in the eleventh-century Mimbres world, which would ultimately overshadow Chaco's political heritage in the formation of modern Pueblo cultures. Large Mimbres pueblos were both cause and effect of canal irrigation—technology borrowed from the Hohokam. Large, permanent, high-density Mimbres villages functioned largely without the complex political structures of Chaco. The Mimbres region carried Chacoan ideas far into the Chihuahuan Desert, to the site of future Paquimé.

Such was the Pueblo world of the mid-eleventh century: Chaco in the north, Mimbres in the south. A few generations later, in about 1125, large-scale construction ended at Chaco. Mimbres suddenly and completely transformed itself. Chaco's end around 1125 (when Great House construction ceased) has been presented as a collapse of monumental proportions—an event that got the attention of thinkers and policy makers (e.g., Diamond 2005). But, like Mimbres, Chaco didn't die; it moved.

The political principles (and, perhaps, principals) that ruled Chaco were perpetuated in two subsequent, sequential centers—first at Aztec and then Paquimé. In this and the next chapter, we trace that political history, from Chaco to Aztec to Paquimé, and wave briefly at the "before" and "after" meridian sites.

Chaco-Aztec-Paquimé was hot stuff when it was originally proposed fifteen years ago. Chaco alone was difficult: the idea of Chaco as a political capital disturbed many Southwestern archaeologists—and still does. Nothing like Chaco appears in Pueblo ethnohistory, where we conventionally look for the proper limits of the prehistoric past. Even worse, the Chaco regional system jumped the carefully tended taxonomic walls built around our research areas. It violated personal and professional space. Good fences make good neighbors, so megaChaco, Chaco *uber alles*, was not a happy notion.

One way of dealing with the problem of Chaco is to keep it short and then forget it: Chaco was a short-lived anomaly, a flash in the pan, an aberration with few lasting effects. I don't think so: Chaco-Aztec spanned almost four centuries from 850 to 1275, quite a bit longer than the United States' run, so far.

To return to my personal misadventures: the political history of the Pueblo Southwest first revealed itself in a tiny bit of data—two dots on a map. It's hard for data to be more bit-like than that. The dots were Chaco and Paquimé, two late prehistoric sites in the American Southwest. Chaco Canyon (850–1125) and Paquimé (1250–1450) were the largest, most important sites of their respective eras and regions. They were soon be joined by a third dot: Aztec Ruins (1110–1275), the largest site of *its* time and place. But the archaeological historiography begins with Chaco and Paquimé.

Chaco and Paquimé have been the subject of nervous speculation for years: Charles Di Peso first hinted that Chaco and Paquimé were an item (Di Peso 1974)—his ideas will be explored a bit more below. I scoffed (e.g., Lekson 1983b, 1984a), and so did many others. A liaison between Chaco and Paquimé seemed unlikely, impossible. The two were from different worlds: 630 km apart in space and further apart in time. Chaco was too old, Paquimé too young. We looked at their ages, we looked at the maps, and we knew it would never work.

However, some peculiar and particular architectural things linked the two, discussed below. And something cartographic caught my eye. Chaco and Paquimé were on the same meridian. That is, they were more or less exactly north-south of each other: Chaco-Paquimé might be May-December, but they made a striking pair. I initially dismissed their alignment (already, the "A" word) as an unpleasant coincidence, as would most of my readers, but independent data made me reconsider. Those independent data were primarily from Aztec Ruins, which I and others discounted as a Chaco outlier—a knockoff or, at best, a spin-off. Aztec, as it turns out, matches Chaco and Paquimé in size and historical importance—an insight noted many years ago by John Stein and Peter McKenna (1988). Aztec was the third major center in Pueblo prehistory; it, too, was also almost exactly on the Chaco-Paquimé meridian (figure 1.1). And the dates worked: Aztec filled the chronological gap between Chaco and Paquimé.

Two dots become three: Chaco (850–1125), Aztec (1110–1275), and Paquimé (1250–1450). And that *ménage à trois*, of the three sequential centers of the Pueblo Southwest, were alarmingly aligned. Perhaps the Chaco-Paquimé meridian alignment was not a fluke.

The argument is long and, I fear, complicated. There are so many side issues that every archaeologist will disagree with something. Since my conclusions suggest major revisions for Southwestern archaeology, the argument is particularly susceptible to "false in this, false in all" rejection. Resist that temptation; suspend, for now, disbelief. The basic data of the argument are simple, straightforward, and sound: tree-ring datings of Chaco, Aztec, and Paquimé; unique architectural elements shared among only those three sites; the Great North Road; and a set of geographic coordinates.

The following sections of this chapter begin with the methodological problems of unique events. The alignment of Chaco, Aztec, and Paquimé, if nothing else, is unique in the Southwest; and archaeologists have difficulty with uniquity. After that methodological preamble, the chapter gets down to cases, describing Chaco, Aztec, and Paquimé and the remarkable archaeological parallels between and among those three celebrated sites.

UNIQUITY AND MÖBIUS LOGIC

In this section, I admit and lament the tactical difficulties of promoting an interpretation that many archaeologists would cross the street to avoid. The Chaco-Aztec-Paquimé meridian is a mighty hard sell. There is a tale told of Leonard Woolley, when he proposed that flood deposits at Ur represented the biblical deluge: "'We all agree that your theory is mad,' one colleague commented, 'The problem which divides us is this: Is it sufficiently crazy to be right?'" As it turns out, Woolley *was* wrong—but he wasn't crazy.

Chaco-Aztec-Paquimé is rhetorically challenging because it is unique. It cannot be shown to be part of a class, a group, or a pattern, and that makes my colleagues (and me!) uneasy. Uniquity is unsettling.[1] American archaeology is much more comfortable with redundancy, repetition, patterns, and processes.

The first and highest hurdle for unique past phenomena is establishing their reality. Some unique events announce themselves in the archaeological record with unmistakable clarity: the eruptions of Vesuvius, for instance. Events less dramatically attested are more liable to doubt. The Chaco-Aztec-Paquimé alignment is surely one of the latter. It was important but left no smoking craters. This leads to a necessarily circular rhetoric: if the alignment was *not* by chance, then interesting conclusions can be posited; and those conclusions support the original but tenuous assertion that the alignment was not chance. That Möbius-strip circularity seems necessary, since mainstream archaeology has no developed rhetoric (or statistic!) for dealing with uniquity, for dealing with events, with history. (I take up the shortcomings—indeed, the absence—of an effective archaeological historicity elsewhere; Lekson forthcoming.)

The unique history that I ask you to consider is this: a series of three major centers sequentially dominated their respective areas of the Southwest—first, Chaco (850–1125) in northwest New Mexico; second, Aztec (1110–1275) in the Mesa Verde region; and third, Paquimé (1250–1450) in northern Chihuahua. A ruling class of noble families emerged at Chaco and perpetuated itself by moving their capital city along Chaco's meridian. Position legitimized or perhaps reflected five centuries of political continuity. Local populations were variably integrated into regional systems by both subsistence/craft bulk economies and political-prestige economies of Mesoamerican and regional exotics—birds, bells, shells, turquoise.

That summary shows us where we are going, but to get there we will follow twisted paths and side roads. The following sections briefly describe Chaco, Aztec, and Paquimé and present data from architecture, minor artifacts, extraregional interactions, and regional organization. These aspects strongly suggest that the Chaco-Aztec-Paquimé alignment was not a coincidence, but rather the result of something like history.

THREE SOUTHWESTERN CITIES

Chaco and Paquimé are generally recognized as the two largest regional centers in Pueblo prehistory; Aztec had the size and scale, but its role as a regional center is only beginning to be appreciated. I call them cities. "City" is not a word you see attached to Southwestern sites.

It is my impression that many (most?) Southwestern archaeologists share a vision of "city" that harks back to classic definitions of Weber: densely packed, large, hustling, bustling, and—importantly—*integral to states*. (And we don't want states in the Southwest.) The conventional definition of "city"—large population and high density—remains influential in recent urban studies; for example, *The Ancient City* lists seven criteria (Marcus and Sabloff 2008:12–13), mostly familiar, and *Urbanism in the Preindustrial World* (Storey 2006) offers a telling rule of thumb: "I have always thought that a true urban center needed to have a population density of at least 1,000 persons per sq km. However, I now think that the density need not be that high. A true city . . . can have a population density even in the low hundreds of persons per square kilometer, as long as the overall site is in the tens of square kilometers" (Storey 2006:22–23). We don't see those densities and areas at Southwestern sites! (But see note 9, chapter 2.) It's true: we have no Londons, no Tenochtitlans, no Romes.

But not all roads lead to Rome. It has become abundantly clear that ancient cities were not circumscribed by Western models of urbanism and their attendant criteria of density and size. Indeed, as Michael Smith notes, if we use the standard criteria for urbanism, there were only two cities in all of ancient North America: Teotihuacan and Tenochtitlan. Joyce Marcus nailed the problem: "trying to define the city so as to satisfy Western social scientists, not Mesoamerican Indians" (cited in Hirth 2003:59).

North American urban centers (with those two notable exceptions) did not look like Rome. Nor did many cities on other continents and in other eras. What to do with thousands of urban centers disenfranchised by the old Weber/Wirth/Sanders criteria? A new definition of "city" appeared in recent years, which avoids density/area criteria and focuses instead on *relations* or *functions* between center and hinterland. Bruce Trigger (1972, 2003) was perhaps the first archaeologist to formally state this new definition of city: "The key defining feature of an urban center is that it performs specialized functions in relation to a broader hinterland."[2] What "specialized functions"? More on this later.

Introducing the Principals

We've spent a lot of time with Chaco already, but there are some aspects of Chaco that haven't been broached, or that need repeating. To begin, there are important differences in our knowledge of each of the three cities, Chaco, Aztec, and Paquimé. A century of sustained research gives us a huge set of data from Chaco and its region (Frazier 2005; Lister and Lister 1987; see also Lekson ed. 2006; Mathien 2005; and Chaco Research Archive 2010). We know a *lot* about Chaco.

We know less about Aztec. Earl H. Morris excavated one of three major and Great Houses in the early years of the twentieth century (Morris 1919, 1921, 1924a, 1924b, 1928). The National Park Service excavated one tri-walled structure (Vivian 1959). There have been the occasional ad hoc excavations (more recently, a major program of excavations in West Ruin, as yet largely unreported; Brown, Windes, and McKenna 2008) and surveys in the immediate surroundings (Stein and McKenna 1988). A recent project based at Salmon Ruins, but encompassing Aztec too, has added much to our understanding (e.g., Reed 2004, 2008).

For the first edition of this book, Paquimé was known almost exclusively from a single research program, that of Charles Di Peso, who excavated about one-half of the site in the 1960s (Di Peso 1974), and a few early reconnaissance surveys of the region (e.g., Brand 1935). Since then, there has been an explosion of research in the Casas Grandes area (e.g., Whalen and Minnis 2001, 2009; Stewart et al. 2005). "Explosion" is relative: compared to Chaco and Aztec, we still have much to learn about Paquimé and the Casas Grandes region. But now we know more than we did in 1999.

So much for the centers; what of their regions? Seemingly endless work has defined and refined Chaco's region (e.g., Kantner 2003; chapters in Lekson ed. 2006). Our knowledge of Aztec's region is also extensive and highly detailed (largely the work of Crow Canyon and the Village Ecodynamics Project: e.g., Varien and Wilshusen 2002; Kohler, Varien, and Wright 2010); unfortunately, the region has not yet realized that it was Aztec's. I refer to what archaeologists conventionally call the "Mesa Verde" area—most of which was Aztec's in the twelfth and thirteenth centuries. We'll return to this identity crisis below. Since Di Peso, there has been little work at Paquimé itself (beyond innumerable critiques and reinterpretations of Di Peso's magnificent report; Di Peso 1974), but important work (cited above) has been done in the Casas Grandes region—that is, Paquimé's region.

We met Chaco in chapter 2. A précis: Chaco Canyon (850–1125) was a monumental capital city, a palace civilization. Huge masonry palaces and other buildings defined a central precinct of several square kilometers—"downtown Chaco." Chaco was the center—the capital—of a region that incorporated most of the southern Colorado Plateau. Planning was rigid, formal, and geometric: precise symmetries, solar and cardinal orientations, and dramatic use of natural features all operated on scales far above the individual building, encompassing city, landscape, and region.

Aztec (1110–1275) (figure 3.1) had long been considered a late, last-gasp Chacoan center—perhaps a colony of refugees leaving a failing Chaco. The West Ruin at Aztec, excavated by Earl Morris, is only one of perhaps six Great Houses in the complex. The equally large East Ruin remains largely unexcavated (Richert 1964), and, incredibly, the other Great Houses remained, until the 1980s, largely unknown. Survey and mapping revealed an urban complex comparable to Chaco's, as formal if smaller (Brown, Windes, and McKenna 2008; Stein and McKenna 1988; McKenna and Toll 1992; Reed 2008).

Aztec's Great Houses were among the very largest Chacoan construction projects ever attempted—West Ruin, built in less than a decade, was the single largest construction event ever completed in the Chacoan tradition (figure 3.1). The cityscape was pinned to tri-wall structures and Great Kivas, and a remarkable array of roads, mounds, and berms (Stein and McKenna 1988) (figure 3.2). Aztec was all about the tri-wall (figure 3.12, below), a building of unknown function but obvious importance. The first tri-wall was built at Chaco, behind Pueblo del Arroyo. It was either never completed, or razed. In either event, it was a squib. What

FIGURE 3.1

Aztec West. Model at Aztec Ruins National Monument. Aztec West was excavated by Earl H. Morris (a series of monographs: Morris 1919–1928). The model, like all such models, tries to turn it into a pueblo; it was a palace and governmental building. Note the Hubbard tri-walled structure upper left (see also figure 3.12) and the tri-walled structure upper right; these were key elements in the Aztec cityscape (figure 3.2). (Courtesy Aztec Ruins National Monument.)

didn't work at Chaco worked very well indeed at Aztec Ruins: the whole cityscape is pinned to the central tri-wall, which in fact was a quadri-wall, the mother of all tri-walls. Tri-walls were the hubs or pivots of the Aztec cityscape.

There was an intermediate between Chaco and Aztec: Salmon Ruins (figure 3.3) (Reed 2006, 2008). There were many Chaco outliers in the San Juan Valley, but Salmon was more than a garden-variety outlier: it was a huge building, as big as the major Chaco Canyon Great Houses. Built in about a decade from 1095 to 1105, Salmon Ruins was the original terminus of the Great North Road (discussed below) and perhaps the first site selected for the New Chaco. But Salmon Ruins was a squib. It never developed into a city—washed out by an unruly San Juan River?—and that role shifted almost immediately to Aztec. We will return to Salmon later in this and other chapters.

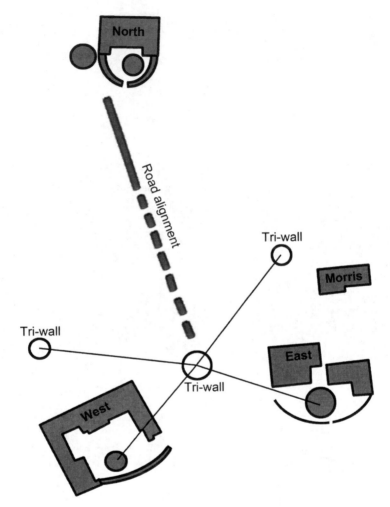

FIGURE 3.2
Aztec Ruins complex (after Stein and McKenna 1988) showing Aztec
West, Aztec East, Aztec North, and other major buildings of the city—
one of which is named for Earl Morris, who excavated Aztec West.
None of the other buildings have been excavated, but there are tree-
ring dates from intact rooms in Aztec East.

From about 1300 to perhaps 1450, Paquimé was the premier city in the
Southwest, with a five-story, poured-adobe, Puebloesque core of residences,
workshops, and warehouses (figures 3.4 and 3.5). That does not mean it was necessarily the largest site of its time—sprawling Classic Hohokam towns covered

FIGURE 3.3
Salmon Ruins, near Bloomfield, New Mexico, during its excavation by Cynthia Irwin-Williams (Eastern New Mexico University) from 1972 to 1980. (I lived in the third building from the left—"temporary" structures that still stand.) Salmon was a major construction project, but it was soon superseded by Aztec Ruins. It seems likely the flooding by the unruly San Juan River suggested a location on the comparatively calm and manageable Rio Animas, about 15 km due north. (Courtesy Cynthia Irwin-Williams.)

more area, and a few Rio Grande and Hopi sites were almost as big. Hohokam is interesting but beyond the purposes of this book. In brief: Hohokam may have been Paquimé's "peer polity," a rival that fueled Paquimé's rise; Hohokam declined while Paquimé ascended (Lekson 2009).

Paquimé's central buildings were surrounded by a remarkable mix of Mesoamerican and Southwestern public and ceremonial monuments: I-shaped ball courts (figure 3.6), Great Kivas (unit 11, room 38), pyramids (sort of), and effigy mounds. Paquimé's planning and formality rivals and—in my opinion—surpasses Chaco's and Aztec's.

Like Chaco and Aztec, Paquimé was the largest site of its time and place. Its "place"—its region—extended over much of the deserts and mountains of northern Chihuahua and southern New Mexico (among others, Di Peso, Rinaldo, and Fenner 1974a:1–7; Minnis 1989; Whalen and Minnis 1996b, 2001, 2009), and its influences were felt throughout the southern Southwest and well up the Rio Grande Valley (Schaafsma 1979). The city and its region were Chacoan in scale.

FIGURE 3.4
Paquimé. View with Cerro Moctezuma, a line-of-sight signaling tower, in the distance. This image was taken before stabilization efforts covered the walls with stucco: a needed remedy since adobe exposed does not survive very long, but a different look.

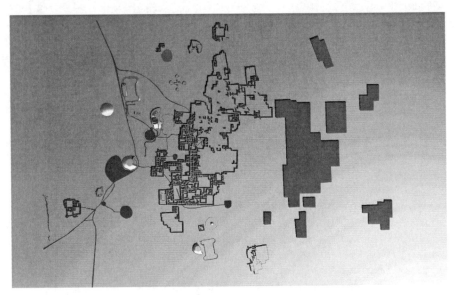

FIGURE 3.5
Paquimé plan. Based on the site map by Charles Di Peso (1974), showing the now-disputed eastern wing (Whalen, MacWilliams, and Pitezel 2010). Note two I-shaped ball courts northwest and south, and the Mound of the Cross at the north of the excavated area. (Courtesy Dennis Holloway.)

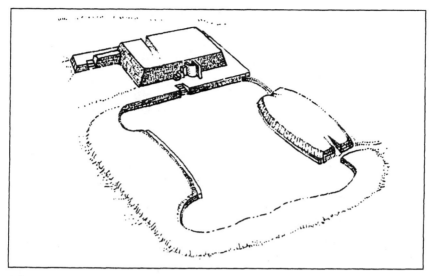

FIGURE 3.6

The north ball court at Paquimé. At least three and possibly four ball courts were discovered. This is the real Mesoamerican court, not the ovals of Hohokam. Presumably some version of the real Mesoamerican "game" was played here, if perhaps minor league. (After Di Peso, Rinaldo, and Fenner 1974a.)

Alarms and Intrusions, Immaculate Inceptions

Chaco, Aztec, and Paquimé all share singular beginnings: they all came from somewhere else, then lived long and prospered, and then went away to somewhere else. Coming and going was not that unusual: towns and villages opened and closed with alarming frequency in the northern Southwest (less so in the southern Southwest). Typically a village lasted a generation or two. Chaco, Aztec, and Paquimé lasted many generations, perhaps three centuries at Chaco, one and a half centuries (or more) at Aztec and Paquimé.

All three effectively rose *de novo*. Nonlocality starts with Chaco. For the Chaco of our title, the ninth- to early twelfth-century city, the canyon was occupied before Chaco's rise, but the key features arrived at Chaco only after developing elsewhere: Great Houses. The first proto–Great Houses rose north of the San Juan River—in the Dolores River Valley, to be precise, in the centuries before Chaco (Wilshusen and Van Dyke 2006). For proto–Great Houses, impermanence was the rule. Those early Great Houses, like the communities that surrounded them, were short-lived: a generation or two, and then on to . . . somewhere. One of the "somewheres" was up the Chaco River to Chaco Canyon (Windes 2007) where, for some reason, the form "took root": the three earliest Great Houses at Chaco

(Peñasco Blanco, Pueblo Bonito, and Una Vida) were not abandoned after a generation, but were maintained and expanded for well over two centuries—in Bonito's case, almost three.

Why? What was it about Chaco? As noted in chapter 2, it was a rough place for agriculture. Dramatic events in the 500s and 600s—discussed later in this chapter—established a history at Chaco, with the largest site complex of its time. That history, remembered, was probably appropriated by the Great House elites, much as the urban centers of altepetl (chapter 2) were often claimed to be a historically charged spot. Prior to the rapid and monumental construction of Aztec Ruins, there were few earlier settlements of any size at Aztec (McKenna 1998). To be sure, small earlier sites were scattered along the fertile Animas River—how not? But at Aztec's location, there was nothing earlier of consequence. It was just another spot along the Rio Animas, and in fact miles away from the sandstone quarried for the Great Houses. And when it was abandoned around 1280, nothing followed: the entire region was abandoned, with tens of thousands of people relocating to the southwest, southeast, and south.

Far south indeed: I argue that several hundreds of elites or nobles from Aztec and/or Chaco went all the way to Paquimé. That city too rose *de novo*. Evidence is thin for pre-Paquimé populations in the Casas Grandes Valley, and so—probably—was settlement. (This is a matter of considerable controversy, and we will return to an extended discussion in chapter 4.) At the site of Paquimé itself, however, no significant prior occupation was exposed in Di Peso's extensive excavations (Di Peso 1974), nor—as far as he or we know—in the area immediately surrounding. Elsewhere in Chihuahua, yes; but not there, at the site of the last great Southwestern city—a subject to which we will return in chapter 4.

Chaco, Aztec, and Paquimé were conspicuously *planned* towns. Although each took decades to complete, their forms followed geometries and layouts so evident that even archaeologists can see them, many centuries later. They could be considered "new towns," as that term is used in modern urban studies—something like a planned urban center created in an undeveloped area with government sponsorship. Why was Chaco *there*, and Aztec *there*, and Paquimé *there*? The meridian had something to do with it, a matter to which we will return.

Size and Scale

Consider scale and population. The central precinct at Chaco (downtown Chaco, figure 2.10) encompassed over 6 sq km, including open space (Lekson 1986a). Aztec covers about 1.5 sq km (the park boundaries, pulled up tight around the site). Di Peso estimated the area of urban Paquimé at about 0.35 sq km (Di Peso 1974:370). For comparison, Taos Pueblo today encloses about 0.05 sq km, and Sapawe, perhaps the largest of the protohistoric Rio Grande pueblos, covers about 0.12 sq km (cf. plans of other pueblos, ancient and modern, in Morgan 1994).

The total roofed areas for the eight major structures in downtown Chaco (not including scores of known smaller buildings) is about 67,500 sq m (Powers, Gillespie, and Lekson 1983: table 41). We don't have this information for Aztec, but my estimate would be less than half of Chaco's total. The total for Paquimé, including both central and peripheral ("ranch" style) architecture, is 33,500 sq m (Di Peso, Rinaldo, and Fenner 1974a: figure 127.4),[3] again, about half Chaco's total. (Note that in a rush to downsize Paquimé, the existence of the unexcavated half has been questioned: Whalen, MacWilliams, and Pitezel 2010; of which, more below.) Thus, downtown Chaco included about twice the roofed areas of Aztec and Paquimé. Put another way, Chaco = Aztec + Paquimé, an interesting (approximate) fact we will consider later.

Chaco was larger than Aztec and Paquimé, but architectural density was higher at Aztec and higher still at Paquimé. That is, through time the cities got smaller, denser, and noticeably more compact. Chaco used space, a great deal of space; there was distance between the Great Houses of downtown Chaco. Chaco was probably more unbuilt than built space—a real sprawling, sunbelt city! At Aztec, Great Houses and tri-walls were much more densely packed in the city's core; built and unbuilt spaces are more nearly equal in area. Paquimé reached very high densities of construction, with open space limited (and delimited) by a central plaza and a narrow outer zone of ball courts and "pyramids." Paquimé was massed like a modern pueblo, but Di Peso et al. (1974; see also Wilcox 1999a) saw Paquimé as an aggregate of contiguous or nearly contiguous "houses," separated by small interior plazas, alleyways, or unfenestrated walls. It is tempting to see Paquimé as multiple Great Houses (Di Peso counted about a dozen) jammed into a single, contiguous city—the formal culmination of decreasing spacing and increasing density of noble palaces from Chaco to Aztec to Paquimé.

Population estimates for all of Chaco Canyon range as high as 5,600 (Hayes 1981:50). The most conservative (or would that be most radical?) estimates place the core population at less than 1,000 (Windes 1984, 1987a). I calculated that downtown Chaco had between 2,500 and 3,000 people (Lekson 1986a, 1988c; see also Bernardini 1999). Based on the same assumptions I made for Chaco, Aztec comes out with about half of Chaco's total; that is, Aztec had around 1,000 people. Paquimé may have been bigger: Di Peso estimated the population of Paquimé at about 3,000 (Di Peso, Rinaldo, and Fenner 1974a: figure 127.4), and I argued that Paquimé may have approached 5,000 (Lekson 1989c). But, as noted above, some archaeologists would halve those figures; if we take Di Peso's estimates and accept the halving, Paquimé falls to 1,500. The exact figures we will never know, but by that reading Chaco was bigger than either Aztec or Paquimé. Roughly, Chaco = Aztec + Paquimé, again.

Form

Differences in area and cityscape between Chaco, Aztec, and Paquimé reflect—or, perhaps, predict—larger historical trends in Puebloan building. Each exemplified the architectural "rules" of its time. Pueblo villages of Chaco and Aztec's era (eleventh through thirteenth centuries) consisted of discrete single- or extended-family homes: five rooms and a kiva, so consistent we call them "unit pueblos." Unit pueblos were often scattered around or at least in the vicinity of a Great Kiva and—in Chaco—a Great House overlooking it all from high atop a hill (Lekson 1991): a Chacoan landscape! With the end of order and disruption of the Pax Chaco, villages of Aztec's time became much larger, aggregations of "unit pueblos," shoulder to shoulder as row houses along streets, or jammed higgledy-piggledy into caves and alcoves, like Mesa Verdes cliff dwellings. Aztec, too, pulled inward, with less open space than Chaco.

The trajectory of pueblo history and architecture hit a rough patch around 1300. More than a rough patch: more like a brick wall, or Alice's looking glass, or Calvin's transmogrifier. Everything changed. Before 1300, every family house, the unit pueblo, had a kiva (actually a pithouse, Lekson 1988b) and every village a Great Kiva. After 1300, the family "kivas" disappear, and villages had one or a few real kivas, presumably an evolution (descent with modification) of the Great Kiva tradition. Before 1300, the unit pueblo was one story and shallow: a half-dozen rooms at most, two rooms deep. After 1300, the front narrowed to one room, five or even six or seven rooms deep, with rooms stacked in up to four stories—many more rooms per household—built as row houses or apartments. To recapitulate: before 1300, family homes were freestanding, and villages were loosely dispersed, at least until the hard times of the late thirteenth century. After 1300, pueblos became compact apartment buildings.

Paquimé paralleled contemporary fourteenth-century Pueblo town planning (figure 3.5). As mapped by Di Peso, Paquimé was a massive, terraced, U-shaped pueblo-style building surrounding a central plaza (Di Peso's "east plaza"; Di Peso, Rinaldo, and Fenner 1974a: figure 125.4). Many fourteenth- and fifteenth-century pueblos looked like that. If Di Peso was right, the view from the central plaza would have been much like Taos Pueblo today: terraced adobe room blocks surrounding a large, well-defined plaza. Like Taos, ceremonial architecture and mounds are located around the outside of the building. I do not mean to imply a direct historic linkage between Paquimé and Taos, but to show that Paquimé's fourteenth-century architecture resembled contemporary fourteenth-century and later Pueblo traditions.

As noted above, several archaeologists recently have argued that Paquimé did not really look like that: Di Peso got it wrong (Whalen, MacWilliams, and Pitezel 2010). In their view, Paquimé had no central plaza. It was long but not skinny, along the terrace edge above the Rio Casas Grandes floodplain.[4]

Whatever. Paquimé may or may not have looked like a fourteenth- or fifteenth-century Pueblo site, but neither did it look like Chaco or Aztec. Should that disturb us? No. Nothing in the fourteenth or fifteenth century looked like Chaco—or any other twelfth- or thirteenth-century towns and villages. Again: everything changed at 1300. And Chihuahua, of course, had its own history and traditions.

Paquimé didn't look like Chaco, and it may not have looked like Taos, but Paquimé still looked far more Puebloan than any Mesoamerican architectural tradition of which we are aware. Domestic architecture in ancient northern and western Mexico typically consisted of three or four freestanding single-room structures tightly clustered around a small patio, a pattern we know from Hohokam in southern Arizona but not from Paquimé or the Pueblo region to its north.[5] Formally Puebloan: but neither Chaco, Aztec, nor Paquimé were "pueblos," in the sense of farming villages. They were palaces.[6]

Cardinal Knowledge

All three cities were formally planned, with internal geometries and canons of design (Di Peso 1974:370ff.; Fowler and Stein 1992; Fritz 1978; McKenna and Toll 1992; Sofaer 1997; Stein and Lekson 1992). The meridian played a role at each, but in three different ways.

Cardinality was unusual in Southwestern architecture (Morgan 1994) and in prehistoric North America generally (see, for example, Aveni 1977; but see also Ashmore 1991). The scarcity of cardinal orientations may reflect the unimportance of north for calendars, which in farming societies track farming schedules. Agricultural economies follow the sun, not the stars—and north is nothing but the point around which the stars revolve. North is a very real but relatively useless direction; it doesn't help you plant. Indeed, for many years it was assumed by White scholars that the cardinal orientations so evident today in Pueblo ritual and worldview were borrowed from Spanish and American maps and compasses. Thus the appearance of meridian alignments in antiquity is interesting.

The cardinality of Chaco Canyon and its architectural organization around a meridian were noted almost four decades ago by John Fritz (1978; see also Van Dyke 2004). The exact north-south siting of Pueblo Alto and Tsin Kletsin—both conspicuous mesa-top buildings (figure 2.10)—is a matter of public record, so familiar that it now evokes little comment in the vast Chacoan literature.[7]

Pueblo Alto was built in the very early eleventh century (see appendix C) directly above a small but massive early to mid-tenth-century building, which had been razed to its foundations (Windes 1987b:15–25). We don't know what's under Tsin Kletsin, but I would not be surprised to find a tenth-century building or monument of some sort.

Variously esoteric equinoctial, lunar, and other astronomical alignments have been suggested for Chaco (e.g., Sofaer 1997). They initially met with resistance and objections (e.g., Zeilik 1987), but today they are at least provisionally accepted. Clearly, most buildings (noble and commoner) were noncardinal; they were usually to the south-southeast (think of Chetro Ketl and early Pueblo Bonito).[8] The south-southeast orientation was typical of pre-Chacoan building, and indeed all commoner houses of Chaco's time; I think it was a traditional Anasazi orientation before Chaco, supplanted by the cardinal for Chaco's purposes.

Chaco and Paquimé employed the meridian as the major axis of planning; Aztec did not. Aztec was planned around a central axis (figure 3.2), much like Chaco's meridian; but Aztec's axis orientation was to the south-southeast (an azimuth of about 150°), manifest as a road running northwest from the Aztec complex to Aztec North and then on in the general direction of Great Houses on the La Plata River and Mesa Verde (Stein and McKenna 1988; McKenna and Toll 1992). The major sandstone buildings at Aztec (East and West Ruins) face south-southeast. Aztec North sits on the bluffs above East and West Ruins, marking the "upper" (northwest) end of Aztec's central axis. Aztec North, however, does not face south-southeast; it looks conspicuously but not precisely to the south (an azimuth of about 185°; Lekson 2004).

Thus, Aztec followed the "solsticial" or south-southeastern orientation and arrayed its formal cityscape around it—much like Chaco's use of the Alto–Tsin Kletsin meridian, dialed back to the older order. But the Aztec complex itself—its location—was fundamentally cardinal: it was built at the north end of the Great North Road, the meridian out of Chaco—a situation to which we will return below. Once north marked the spot, Aztec opted for the older solsticial direction. A compromise which pleased no one?

At Paquimé, the cardinals were markedly important—much more so than at Chaco. So pervasive that Di Peso called Paquimé a "cardinal city." The Mound of the Cross (figures 3.5 and 3.7) was a cardinal monument at the north end of the city (Di Peso, Rinaldo, and Fenner 1974a:287–288). Di Peso thought the Mound of the Cross "served as a cardinal direction datum for the builders who aligned the city in terms of its orientation" (Di Peso 1974:409).[9] One of Paquimé's more impressive monuments was a football-field-long effigy mound of a horned serpent on the west edge of the city; it runs very much north-south, with the creature's head facing north. (Horned serpents show another strong connection to the Pueblo north.)

The city itself was cardinal, as if designed on graph paper. Major plaza-defining walls were north-south, east-west (figure 3.5). Room walls at Paquimé followed suit, with less accuracy. They vary from the cardinals to minor degrees, but the basic cardinality of the pueblo's underlying scheme is obvious (see plans in Di Peso 1974 and Di Peso, Rinaldo, and Fenner 1974a, 1974b). The place looks like it was designed on an Etch-a-Sketch, turning one dial at a time, up and over,

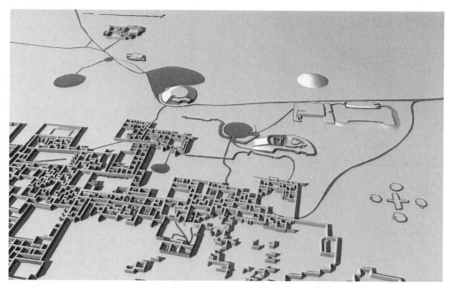

FIGURE 3.7
Paquimé rooms and Mound of the Cross. The rigidly orthogonal plan of walls is evident. Rooms with many (right) angles may reflect the need to "fold" and strengthen three- or four-story poured-adobe walls. Adobe is not a good material for verticality, and the "folding" would effectively buttress walls that might otherwise fail as a long, straight wall. Note also the I-shaped ball court, Mound of the Cross, "pyramids" in the mid-distance, and the Horned Serpent effigy mound, running north-south in the far distance. (Courtesy Dennis Holloway.)

up and over (figure 3.7). Paquimé was a cardinal city, so much so that Di Peso used the Mound of the Cross as its symbol on his maps and charts.

The importance of cardinality was more strongly evidenced at Paquimé than at Chaco or Aztec, and more than at any individual buildings at Chaco Canyon (only Pueblo Alto comes close). Chaco grew around its meridian axis, while Paquimé incorporated the meridian as an axis of its orthogonal plan. Paquimé was on the grid.

Why cardinals? Cardinals orthogonalize north. The meridian is north's reverse (north-south), and east-west its perpendiculars. North was the only real direction. Sun, moon, planets, and stars were constantly wandering; those celestial orbs were anything but fixed. The sun moved overhead daily and yearly swung from north to south and back again. The moon came and went on its lunatic monthly cycle, and slid north and south on a strange quasi-generational rhythm. The planets were crazy, looping and arcing in peregrinations that defied logic until Copernicus and Galileo. (Ancient societies figured out their timetables, but not their physics.) The stars came and went with the seasons. But whichever of the numberless stars were overhead, they rotated lockstep around north. That never changed. Every night, everyone could see the stars spin around the one fixed point in the sky. North was set, permanent, fixed—although at 1100, that point was a void, Polaris was off the mark.

All the heavens revolved around north, and everyone saw it, every night. North was the only real direction—everything else in the skies moved. Pueblo people call north "the heart of the sky."[10] Celestial south, at Chaco's latitudes, was of course invisible, far below the horizon. South was only the reverse of north, a complement to the sky's heart. North played no practical calendrical role—but it was not arcane. If you wanted to start a new cosmology, north could be useful.

Fabrications

Chaco and Aztec look alike—the very earliest investigators noted that fact (Morgan 1881). But Paquimé looks . . . different. Chaco and Aztec were built of sandstone; Paquimé was built of adobe. Chaco and Aztec pottery was black on white; Paquimé pottery was polychrome. Chaco and Aztec had kivas; Paquimé had ball courts. Substantial differences, but inconsequential for my argument. Let us move past those bright, shiny, superficial differences and plunge into deeper, murkier similarities.

Why not, in our first reactions, be superficial, skin deep? Judge these books by their covers: Chaco and Aztec are postcard paragons of Anasazi sandstone masonry, while Paquimé used massive adobe to monumental effect (figure 3.8). Historically, Southwesternists set great store on wall fabric and style. Surely, the fundamental difference of sandstone versus adobe is fatal to my argument? Perhaps not: Aztec provides an intermediate condition, both stone and mud, for those who might be comforted by smooth transitions and synoptic series.

Chaco and Aztec were built of sandstone masonry; Paquimé's walls were poured adobe. Most construction at Aztec—both East and West Ruins—was of Chaco-style sandstone masonry and its derivatives. However, the third large Great House at Aztec, the North Ruin, was constructed of massive poured adobe (Brown, Windes, and McKenna 2008; Lekson 2004; McKenna and Toll 1992). North Ruin was a large building in a typical Great House D configuration—its footprint comparable to Wijiji at Chaco Canyon. Its adobe mound covers an area about 60 by 45 m and stands 2 m tall. North Ruin has never been excavated and has no tree-ring or other dates. It is tempting to think of it as late, a transition from Chaco's stone to Paquimé's mud. But a sack of sherds from a North Ruin pothole were early in Aztec's history, as if Aztec North was the first Great House there (Brown, Windes, and McKenna 2008; Lekson 2004). Either way, Aztec North is a Chaco Great House of considerable size, built of massive poured

(a)

(b)

(c)

FIGURE 3.8

Walls: (a) Chaco, (b) Aztec, and (c) Paquimé. Chaco used an excellent local
sandstone to create its impressively patterned masonry. Aztec did the best it
could with an inferior stone. Paquimé's valley offered only river cobbles and
basalt (at some distance; see figure 3.4); they chose adobe, poured or puddled in thick courses (visible here). The foolish youth is me, many years ago.

adobe—like Paquimé.[11] Puddled adobe was a familiar Anasazi technology, and post-Mimbres horizons built similar walls. The point is this: Massive poured-adobe walls were used at Aztec Ruins, and massive poured adobe was the principal technique at Paquimé. For those who recoil from immoderate change, here perhaps is continuity.[12]

God Dwells in the Details

Chaco, Aztec, and Paquimé shared remarkable parallels of detail: distinctive architectural elements found uniquely and conspicuously at Chaco and Paquimé, and—to a lesser degree—Aztec. Most of these parallels were originally noted by Charles Di Peso in "A Comparison of Casas Grandes and Chaco Canyon Architecture" (Di Peso, Rinaldo, and Fenner 1974a:208–211). My self-appointed job at the Chaco Project was to refute Di Peso's claims; and I did (Lekson 1983b). I argued that most of Di Peso's parallels could be dismissed, defused, or otherwise explained away; but a pesky residuum of unusual features, unique to Paquimé and Chaco, defied easy rejection. In fairness to myself, I noted those features (and added one more of my own; Lekson 1983b:189). But, having disposed of *almost* all of Di Peso's parallels, I thought my job was done, and I ignored the remainders. It was true: there were some fairly interesting features that were at Chaco, Paquimé, and nowhere else.

Specifically Di Peso noted colonnades and stone-disk "foundations"; I added room-wide platforms (I'll describe all these bizarre features presently). And more recently, I've come to think of two other architectural oddities that link Chaco, Aztec, and Paquimé in a somewhat different way: bi-/tri-walls and T-shaped doors. Thirty years ago, I found the first three—colonnades, disks, and platforms—disturbing (Lekson 1983b); now I find them compelling (Lekson forthcoming—from which I borrow and modify several paragraphs).

Colonnades, room-wide platforms, and disks were very different manifestations of architectural symbolism: public, private, and hidden, respectively. Colonnades are very public; they appear on exterior walls facing open, public spaces (plazas, courtyards, etc.). Room-wide platforms were installed within rooms; they would have been effectively private, affecting only those who had access to those rooms. Stone-disk foundations were invisible, hidden after construction. Only those involved in planning and construction would know that stone disks were in place. I'll tackle platforms and disks first and return to colonnades thereafter.

Room-wide platforms (figure 3.9) are well attested in quantity at Chaco, Aztec, and Paquimé (Di Peso, Rinaldo, and Fenner 1974a:238–246; Lekson 1983b:189, 1986a:38; Morris 1928) and nowhere else in the Southwest. They were very deep shelves—across almost half the width of the room, set midway between floor and ceiling in both ends of rectangular rooms or in room-sized alcoves. They appear to be original equipment (not later additions), and they would have defined completely the uses to which a room could or could not be put. In effect, a large rectangular room at Chaco became a narrow walkway from door to door between room-wide platforms filling both sides of the room. So too at Aztec. At Paquimé, they most often appear in alcoves off larger rooms. At Chaco and Aztec, they typically appear in rooms one room removed from the plaza; at Paquimé they are everywhere.

Their purpose is obscure. Di Peso (1974) thought they were for sleeping, while I thought that they were for storage, doubling the floor area available for non- or minimally stackable goods. Whalen and Minnis (2009) suggest that the key was "the enclosed spaces beneath them," which was about the same volume as a storage room, but "private, protected, and readily accessible" (Whalen and Minnis 2009:82). Their guess is as good as mine (or Di Peso's). Bed, shelf, wine cellar: pay your money and take your choice. In any event, they are distinctive private architectural elements, known only to those who actually used them—you can't see them from outside. If Di Peso was right and they were sleeping platforms, then they might communicate to visiting elites: we've made our bed properly and now we'll lie in it properly, like the princess and the pea.

Massive stone disks, 0.6 to 1.2 m in diameter and about 10 cm thick (figure 3.10), were stacked like pancakes under major roof-support posts in Chaco Great Kivas, the Aztec Great Kiva, and several important rooms at Paquimé (Di Peso 1974:214; Di Peso, Rinaldo, and Fenner 1974b:230–234; Lekson 1983b:189; Vivian and Reiter 1960:91). There are rumors of a stone disk at an outlier south of Gallup, New Mexico, but no others have been found—and they'd be pretty hard to miss. At Chaco and Aztec, these disks were four deep; at Paquimé, they were usually single, but in one case, two disks were "stacked" together. They may have functioned as foundations, but why four deep? Turquoise and shell offerings were placed on or below the disks at all three sites. Disks, in any event, were hidden; after installation, they were far beneath the floor level and could not be seen. My conclusion: hocus-pocus of importance to the elites and their architects.

Room-wide platforms and sandstone disks—private and hidden—are evidence, I think, of migration of nobles rather than diffusion of ideas. Colonnades, however, clearly communicate and demonstrate networks and histories and have long been a prime candidate for diffusion. Colonnades have long been identified as Mesoamerican forms, unique within the Southwest to two sites: Chaco and Paquimé (Di Peso, Rinaldo, and Fenner 1974a:211, 264–266; Ferdon 1955:4–5; Lekson 1983b:185–186; Lekson, Windes, and Fournier 2007) (figure 3.11). There are no known colonnades at Aztec Ruins. I used to excuse this absence as the product of too little excavation; now I think the absence of evidence is indeed evidence of absence. The guys at Aztec didn't want a colonnade; they weren't playing that game. (There may be a parallel with bi- and tri-walls, discussed below.)

(a)

(b)

(c)

FIGURE 3.9
Room-wide platforms: (a) Chaco, (b) Aztec, and (c) Paquimé. An inelegant term for an important feature. Di Peso called them "bed platforms," and he may have been right. In ruins, they might appear to be part of a collapsed roof (being built much the same way as a roof, with vigas and *latillas*, etc.). Recognition of the feature requires walls standing at least most of a story tall, so the beam sockets of the platforms are preserved. The current distribution is limited to Chaco, Aztec, and Paquimé.

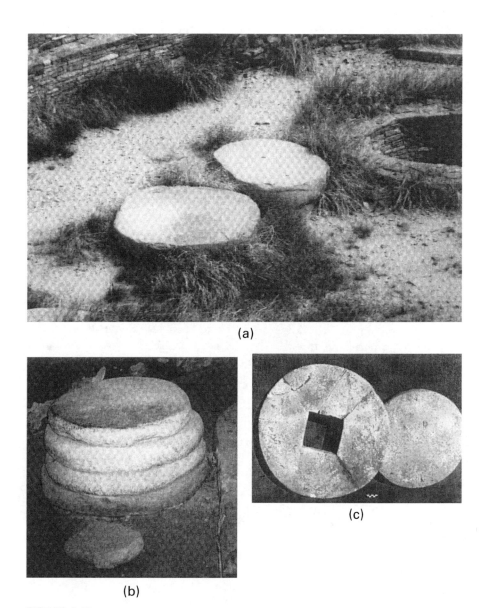

(a)

(b)

(c)

FIGURE 3.10
Sandstone disks: (a) Chaco, (b) Aztec, and (c) Paquimé. They were stacked like pancakes below floor, supporting major structural posts in important rooms. At Chaco
and Aztec, they were found in Great Kivas; at Paquimé, they were found in larger
rooms. No archaeologist could miss these massive, heavy objects; out of all the sites
in the Southwest, they occur only at these three sites.

At both Chaco and Paquimé, colonnades were plaza-facing (i.e., exterior), ground-level features. At Chaco, a remarkable thirteen-pillar colonnade occurs at Chetro Ketl, and a very problematic possibility has been identified at Bc 51; at Paquimé, there are seven monumental colonnades with from two to seven pillars. In the Chaco colonnades, the pillars were rectangular stone masonry and rose from a low base wall. With one exception, Paquimé colonnades had full-length floor-to-ceiling rectangular adobe pillars; one was a *portal*-like construction of wooden posts.

The Mexican provenance of colonnades has been gloated about elsewhere (Ferdon 1955; Di Peso, Rinaldo, and Fenner 1974a). Colonnades were a hallmark of the Postclassic period in central Mexico and the Yucatán. They marked important buildings—temples, palaces, and so forth—much the way we (and the Romans) put columns in front of churches, banks, government offices, and mansions. Intriguingly, some of the earliest known colonnades are not from central Mexico, but the northern frontiers: at La Quemada, a Classic period site (Nelson 1995, 1997; Trombold 1990), which has long been implicated in Southwestern business. Could it be that colonnades started in the north and diffused south to Mesoamerica and north to Chaco?

It had become my habit, when lecturing to captive audiences (students) or touring innocent civilians through Chaco Canyon, to use Chetro Ketl's colonnade as evidence that the Southwest—top to bottom—was well and fully integrated into the Mesoamerican world. Look, I said, everyone would have to understand the symbolism of the colonnade, or it would just look like a ridiculous wall with too many close-set windows—darn hard to heat in winter. People had to get the joke; they had to know that colonnades marked important buildings.

Now I'm not so sure. Chetro Ketl's colonnade was one of the last things built at that site, after the plaza level onto which it opened had been raised, artificially, over 1.75 m above the valley floor (Lekson, Windes, and Fournier 2007). That's taller than most people back then. No one outside the building could see the colonnade—from the opposite canyon rim, perhaps, but without binoculars, it wouldn't look like much. So you had to be a resident or a guest of Chetro Ketl to see the colonnade. My guess: resident elites and visiting elites. The colonnade was not a general pronouncement, a mass communication; it was built by elites to impress other elites. It may or may not be important that the colonnade was sealed at some point after construction: that is, the spaces between the columns were filled in with decent but not exceptional masonry. This could be a final closing of the site; it could also be a decommissioning of the colonnade, a hostile takeover. Of this, more below.

Public colonnades, private interior room-wide platforms, and hidden sandstone disks. There are two other architectural features of particular interest, but these are not limited to these three sites: multiwalled structures and T-doors.

(a)

FIGURE 3.11

Colonnades: (a) Chaco and (b) Paquimé. There is only one colonnade at Chaco, at Chetro Ketl (Lekson, Windes, and Fournier 2007): a second candidate at unit pueblo site Bc 51 fails to persuade. We know of no colonnades at Aztec Ruins, but only one major building there has been excavated. But for now, no colonnades at Aztec Ruins. There were seven colonnades at Paquimé. Colonnades in Postclassic Mesoamerica marked important buildings: palaces, temples, etc.

(b)

Multiwalled structures (shortened to "bi-wall," or "tri-" or "quadri-wall" as appropriate) were compact round buildings with one, two, or even three concentric rows of rooms tight around a central kiva. Bi- and tri-walls were the architectural signature of the Aztec region, comparable to Chaco's Great Houses and Hohokam ball courts—iconic structures that define their regions (figure 3.12).

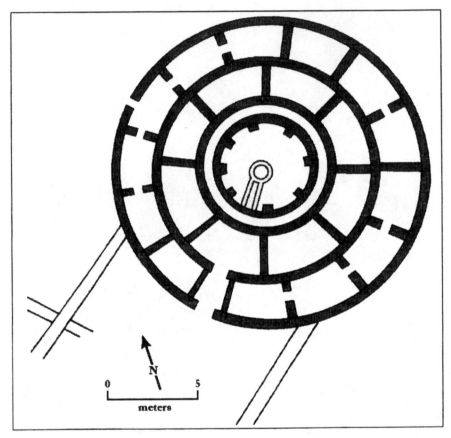

FIGURE 3.12
Hubbard tri-wall at Aztec Ruins. (After Vivian 1959.) Perhaps the last major structure built (and then razed) at Chaco Canyon was the tri-wall structure behind Pueblo del Arroyo. Apparently Chacoans didn't care for the form or what it meant. Bi-, tri-, and quadri-walled structures are central to the cityscape of Aztec Ruins (see figure 3.2). Whatever didn't work at Chaco worked just fine at Aztec. Multiwalled structures like this one are distinctive to Aztec and define its region shown in figure 2.5. There are no comparable structures in Mimbres or at Paquimé. Colonnades (figure 3.11) went south, tri-walls went north?

Only three bi- or tri-walls have been excavated: one at Chaco (Pueblo del Arroyo; Judd 1959), one at Aztec (Hubbard Mound; Vivian 1959), and one at Yellow Jacket (the Great Tower; Kuckelman 2003). The structure at Pueblo del Arroyo in Chaco Canyon was built and destroyed very late in the Chaco era. The other two were built in very late Chacoan or Aztec times and continued in use through the thirteenth century.

The earliest tri-wall (at Pueblo del Arroyo) was one of the last structures built at that site—perhaps comparable in time to Chetro Ketl's colonnade. The Pueblo del Arroyo tri-wall was either never finished, or more likely it was finished and then razed. Tri-walled structures apparently didn't fit Chaco's requirements.

They clicked at Aztec. Bi- and tri-walls were prominent indeed at Aztec Ruins, with a central quadri-walled structure (the mother of all bi-walls!) as the pivot of Aztec's four quarters, the linchpin of its cityscape (figure 3.2). Aztec was all about bi-, tri-, and quadri-walls.

Aztec's excavated Great House and reconstructed Great Kiva get our attention today, of course, but back then all roads led to the bi- and tri-walls. The bi- and tri-walls would have caught people's eyes, something new—they'd seen Great Houses before. Two dozen bi- and tri-walls were built in Aztec's region, usually at towns that had an earlier Chaco-era Great House. It's quite possible that Chacoan Great Houses continued in use during Aztec's era, but often they were repurposed: burial chambers, subdivisions for squatter-like intrusions, et cetera (Lekson and Cameron 1995). Bi-walls and tri-walls—symbols of Aztec Ruins—showed both commoners and nobles that there was a new sheriff in town.

This business of colonnades and bi-walls interests me strangely. At the very end of Chaco's run: one colonnade, sealed; one bi-wall, razed. Only one colonnade at Chaco, none at Aztec, and many at Paquimé. There's a story to be told here—a history—if we can read the ruins. I begin to wonder if Chaco's noble families parted ways when construction ceased there, around 1125: some to the bi-walled north (Aztec) and some to the colonnaded south (Paquimé). Did Aztec reject Mesoamerican ideologies, a return to a more locally based view, surrounding the deeply local "kiva" within multiwalled structures? And for Paquimé, the opposite: a move toward closer and thicker Mesoamerican entanglements? Remember: Chaco = Aztec + Paquimé in size and population. And remember: Aztec had almost no Mesoamerican exotics; Paquimé had tons. Of course, Paquimé follows Aztec in historical sequence: Aztec ended around 1280; Paquimé itself rose after 1300. But it must have taken a while—decades?—to get from Chaco to Chihuahua, and it's possible Casas Grandes (if not Paquimé itself) started well before 1300; see appendix B.

Bi-walls and tri-walls were part of a package of interesting things that were left behind when Aztec fell, and tens of thousands left the Four Corners for the Rio Grande and the western Pueblos. That was a watershed: the end of class societies (in the Pueblo north) and the conscious invention or reinvention of Pueblo societies as an alternative to centuries of royal rule.

Bill Lipe (2010) defined a suite of distinctive features and objects—he called it the "central Mesa Verde complex"; I'd call 'em Aztec *indicia*—that didn't make the trip: unit pueblos and "kivas," kiva jars, mugs, and deer-humerus scrapers. These things were redolent of the *ancien régime*; they had no place in the brave

FIGURE 3.13
T-shaped doors: (a) Chaco, (b) Aztec, and (c) Paquimé. T-shaped doors map the history of the Chaco Meridian: first at Chaco Canyon, then at Aztec and throughout its region, and finally in remarkable numbers at Paquimé and the Casas Grandes region.

new world.[13] To these, we could add bi- and tri-walls—and our final contestant: T-shaped doors.

"The T- or Tau-shaped door is an enigma," mused Neil Judd (1964:28); he found thirty-two at Pueblo Bonito (figure 3.13). Charles Di Peso listed T-shaped doors as one of twenty-three specific architectural details linking Casas Grandes and Chaco Canyon (Di Peso, Rinaldo, and Fenner 1974a:211); he found 335 at Paquimé. T-doors also appear in small Casas Grandes sites (Whalen and Minnis 2009:77–79) and very conspicuously in cliff dwellings of the Sierra Madre (Lazcano 1998).

The T shape was spectacularly manifest on two remarkable altar stones from Paquimé. The better-preserved example was a finely finished rectangle of felsite, 58 cm by 55 cm and 15 cm thick, with a perfectly proportioned T-shaped opening cut through its center (Di Peso 1974:558).

Di Peso was ambivalent about the T-shape's provenance. The Mexican connection for the T was not particularly strong: "Below the Tropic of Cancer, it was used both on the Chichen Itza friezes and as a window design, but apparently never as an entry [door] form" (Di Peso 1974:446). The T altar, in contrast, was seen as "vaguely analogous to those of the *kachinki* and the altar screens of the water serpent ceremonies of the modern Pueblo groups" (Di Peso 1974d:324); elsewhere he alludes to the T representing a rattlesnake's tail (Di Peso 1974:694, n. 44) or even the Mesoamerican Tlaloc (Di Peso, Rinaldo, and Fenner 1974a:236). Whatever its ultimate iconography, the T-door seemed to Di Peso to be a particularly potent symbol of Paquimé: "This was one of the diagnostic Casas Grandes architectural features which, like the raised hearth, helped to give identity to the Paquimé cultural tradition" (Di Peso, Rinaldo, and Fenner 1974a:236)—except that, as Di Peso noted, T-doors also appeared at Chaco and other Anasazi sites.

Four years after Di Peso's Casas Grandes report, Robert Lister (then director of the NPS Chaco Project) published a list of "traits noted in Chaco Canyon that are identified as, or presumed to be, Mesoamerican"; among these traits were T-shaped doorways (Lister 1978:236). This went a step beyond Di Peso, who would not finger a Mesoamerican source for Paquimé's T-doors. Lister was probably thinking of Paquimé itself as a "Mesoamerican" source for Chaco (for Lister, Paquimé was Mexican, which of course, legally speaking, is true).

Randall McGuire (1980) responded to this suggestion, negatively, in a journal article, and I added a conference paper in 1981 (Lekson 1983b). We reclaimed T-doors for the Southwest. McGuire (citing Love's 1975 survey of T-doors) noted that the "T-shaped doorway originated in the SW; not Mesoamerica" (McGuire 1980: table 1); and I couldn't have agreed more (Lekson 1983b:185). The T-door was an Anasazi leitmotif: we see T-doors everywhere, at Navajo Mountain, Arizona, ruins on the west to the La Plata Valley, New Mexico, on the east, from cliff dwellings near Moab, Utah, on the north to Paquimé and the Sierra Madres of Chihuahua on the south.

That ubiquity seemed to void Di Peso's claims for T-doors. If T-doors were everywhere, they could not support Di Peso's arguments for T-doors as a unique linkage between Paquimé and Chaco . . . or could they? Let's rethink this. At Chaco, T-doors originally were almost always exterior, often ground-floor entries, open to the outside world. Not all Chaco's T-doors today are exterior, but almost all *began* as exterior doors, later "interiorized" by additional construction. An informal analysis of other, later Anasazi T-doors suggests that they were predominately exterior features (Lekson 1986a). At Aztec, too, T-doors were exterior doors, opening onto the plaza. That changed at Paquimé: exterior doors were T shaped, but so were many interior T-doors that never saw the light of day (Di Peso 1974). T-doors were also conspicuous as exterior doors at cliff dwellings in the Sierra Madre (Lister 1958:58ff; Lazcano 1998) and a few contemporary cliff dwellings in southernmost New Mexico and Arizona (Gila Cliff Dwellings, Montezuma's Castle).

They catch our eye because they were *meant to be seen.* We can safely assume that exterior T-doors were intended to be visible to friends and strangers. Given the fact that T-doors were originally and later generally exterior doors—visible to the world—the message may well have been one of membership or inclusion. A T-door proclaimed that the building behind it was one of a larger set of buildings similarly demarked, denoting a set of people similarly demarked—the T-door people, whatever that meant. Archaeological explanations of this very unusual shape can be found in textbooks and National Park signage. The standard story: the T shape allowed burdens to be carried through the door, diminished winter drafts, and other simple solutions: pragmatic conjectures about portage and ambient temperatures. No. T-shaped doors were emblems. T-shaped holes cut in Mesa Verde mug handles and Paquimé's altars demonstrate that the shape meant something. A T shape on an exterior wall was a very conscious choice to send a very particular message.

They were everywhere, but they were not everywhere all at once. There's a chronology, a sequence, a history. The earliest T-doors I know of were in Great Houses at Chaco, from the eleventh century. There are, apparently, no earlier T-doors (Richard Wilshusen, personal communication, 1997; contra Love's 1975:296 report of a T-shaped door at Mesa Verde dated to 831). T-doors at Chaco all postdate 1020; that is, they were not part of Chaco's early days, but rather a feature of the Chaco florescence (Judd 1964:28; Lekson 1986a). They appear at many excavated outliers (e.g., Lowry, Guadalupe, Escalante)—but not, to the best of my knowledge, at eleventh-century unit pueblos (Love 1975; and my anecdotal queries of colleagues). Initially, at least, T-doors appear to have been exclusive to, and to have marked, Great Houses.

During Aztec's era, T-doors were a dominant feature at Aztec itself, but they were also democratized: T-shaped doors appeared at sites throughout the Four

Corners, particularly conspicuous in the Mesa Verde area—Aztec's would-be region. T-doors—like mugs, discussed below—also show up in the Kayenta district.

Most telling is the distribution in the fourteenth century—and beyond. After 1300, T-doors all but disappeared from the Pueblo region, and explode all over northern Chihuahua, like a bad rash. Di Peso rightly considered the T-shaped door a defining element of Paquimé and its region. About 60 percent of all doors at Paquimé were T shaped, and at the smaller sites investigated away from the big city, "the T-shaped doorways of the neighboring sites always outnumbered the rectangular ones" (Whalen and Minnis 2009:77; see also Di Peso, Rinaldo, and Fenner 1974a:236; Di Peso 1974:684 n. 43). They are harder to quantify, but nevertheless T-doors were everywhere in the many cliff dwellings of the Sierra Madres (Lazcano 1998).

A few fourteenth- and fifteenth-century examples are known from later sites on the Rio Grande (for example, Gran Quivira; Hayes 1981:39) and at least one Hopi ruin (Mindeleff 1891:190), perhaps at Acoma (Love 1975:300), and perhaps among the Piro Pueblos (Luxan's 1582 account: Hammond and Rey 1929:74); but they were very rare indeed. T-doors in the post-Chaco, post-Aztec northern Southwest have the feel of cultural detritus, remnants of an earlier symbolic system. The distribution of T-shaped doors dramatically shifted south after 1300. Marian Love, in the most complete survey of the subject concludes:

> That such a distinctive shape as the T-shaped doorway should have been concentrated in the Mesa Verde-Chaco and Casas Grandes regions, and thinly spread in other areas, suggests that the original idea diffused from a center through trade and/or via parties of migrants. At present, the few dates we have suggest such diffusion from north to south. Should this, in fact, be the case, the T-shaped doorway will be the only feature known to have diffused southward from the Southwest into Mexico. (Love 1975:303)

One thinks of the bow and arrow, of course; but the point here is not Love's conclusions but the pattern behind Love's age-area rhetoric: we now have the dates, and we can say with some confidence that T-shaped doors began at Chaco, proliferated across the Four Corners during Aztec's era, and all but disappeared from the northern Southwest at the same time they reappeared far to the south, at Paquimé and the Casas Grandes region. T-doors are, indeed, all over the map, but in sequence: T-doors followed the Chaco-Aztec-Paquimé meridian. If some enterprising graduate student crossed their eyes and dotted the Ts into a GIS with time periods, they would pop up first around Chaco and at a few of its outliers, then show strongly at Aztec and throughout its region, and finally all but vanish in the north and explode at Paquimé and all over northern Chihuahua.

Minor Artifacts and Major Dudes

But what about pottery? Isn't pottery the critical criterion in Southwestern archaeology? Chaco Black-on-white (the signature type of Chaco) doesn't look at all like Ramos Polychrome (the fossil type of Paquimé) (figure 2.3). OK: nor does Lino Black-on-gray look like Mesa Verde Black-on-white, or Mesa Verde Black-on-white look like Cieneguilla Glaze-on-yellow—but most of us believe they were made by ascending and descending generations of the same people. Some sort of simple emphatic continuity between Chaco and Paquimé would help; but if archaeology were that easy, anybody could do it. We seldom get easy clues: change was their constant, their reality. Following continuities across change is the challenge.

The Chaco-Aztec-Paquimé progression spans five centuries. That's a long time, and through those many years, material culture changed broadly across the greater Southwest. Changes were, cumulatively, marked and even dramatic: layer the fifteenth-century Southwest directly over the tenth-century Southwest, and we might think there was a total cultural replacement, complete discontinuity. (The striking differences between historic pueblos and ancient ruins led early explorers to suggest that Mesa Verde and Chaco were not Puebloan, but instead Aztec—as in Mexica Aztec.) Architecture evolved, more powerful bows were introduced, corn hybridized, and ceramics changed, dramatically. A lot can happen in five centuries.

We expect to see material continuities when a group moves from place A to place B. Pots, to a great degree, still equal people. It's great when Kayenta pottery shows up at strange sites in Hohokam country, but it's seldom that simple. Since midcentury, we've tried to anticipate and tabulate indicators—subtle or obvious—of postmigration culture (e.g., Haury 1958; Clark 2001; Cabana and Clark 2011). Sometimes the only way to track a migration is a demographic dip in the homelands, and a demographic bump in the new lands—with almost no continuity in material culture.

This is important: Chaco-Aztec-Paquimé was not a mass migration or a folk movement; it probably was an elaborately staged shift in the capital's location, directed by a small number of nobles and elites—perhaps a few hundred, maybe a thousand people. Nobles show themselves, archaeologically, in very different ways than non-elites. In this case, pottery is probably meaningless. Chaco elites did not make their own pottery (pottery did not equal people); their crockery may have been nicer, but it was basically the same wares as commoners'.[14] Ditto Aztec. And ditto Casas Grandes: its pottery came from long local traditions, combining Mimbres and Chihuahua arts and crafts.

The movement up and down the meridian was *not* a migration; it was a political statement—perhaps couched as a revelatory journey—by a small powerful elite. When the capital shifted first from Chaco to Aztec and then to Paquimé, nobles moved with a few commoners, possibly slaves. Or, as mooted above, perhaps half went north and half went south. In either case, should we expect major transformations in local traditions of pottery, metates, axes, and arrowheads when parasitic upper-class nonproducers arrive? Probably not.

Elites co-opted local popular symbols and imposed their own configurations of exotica and monumental building. That's where the action was. So we won't explore the minor artifacts—sherds and lithics—of Chaco, Aztec, and Paquimé, but a brief example from Chaco and Paquimé might suggest how such a survey should be framed—not with pottery tempers, motor habits, or motifs, but in contextual parallels. Thus: the parable of odd pots and Major Dudes.

At Pueblo Bonito at Chaco Canyon, a cache of 192 (of 210 known) "cylinder jars" (figure 3.14) were located in a complex of rooms that also housed the highly unusual crypts of the two most elaborate burials known from the canyon and the Southwest: the Major Dudes.

The Major Dudes were founding fathers: they've been dated to the early 800s, when Bonito itself was barely begun (Plog and Heitman 2010). It would be good to know if they grew up at Chaco or came from elsewhere (to presage: Ridges Basin?)—something we could know from analysis of trace elements in their teeth. They were both middle aged, buried with all the wealth in the world—turquoise capes and that sort of thing. Their crypt was reopened from time to time for the addition of new burials (retainers? descendants?)—the disarticulated remains of at least twelve additional individuals (Akins 1986; Akins and Schelberg 1984; Frisbie 1978; Plog and Heitman 2010)—and lots more stuff, as if they didn't already have enough.

The two-hundred-odd cylinder jars are just that: odd. They have a literature all their own (summarized in Toll 1990; see also Crown and Wills 2003), with Mesoamerican implications and refutations—the form is found all over Mesoamerica, but outside Chaco, nowhere else in the Southwest. They were (big surprise!) cylindrical in form, averaging 24 cm tall and 11 cm in opening diameter (Toll 1990:273). With a few red-slipped exceptions, all are black-on-white or plain white. Most are Gallup or Chaco Black-on-white, but painted decoration includes a range of styles (including Puerco and McElmo). For the longest time, we didn't know what cylinder jars were. They might be standard measures, but their volumes are too variable. Many have four or more lugs or small handles that could have secured skins for use as drums; but their bases are closed, not open as they presumably would be for drums. Turns out, they were cacao cups. Patricia Crown and Jeffrey Hurst (2009) discovered the chemical markers for cacao in Chaco's cylinder jars. In Mesoamerica, cylinder jars and cacao were high-value items, things nobles would have, but never commoners. The boys at Bonito had both the jars and the chocolate.

The cylinder jars came from the central warren of tiny, old rooms which also contained a remarkable inventory of wooden "canes" or "wands," turquoise jew-

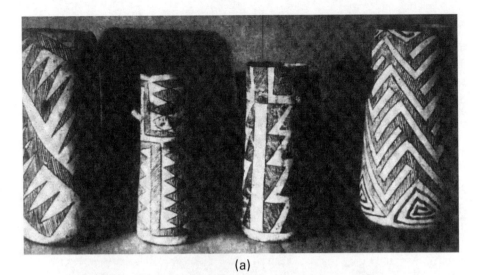

(a)

(b)

FIGURE 3.14
Chaco cylinder jars (a) and Paquimé hand drums (b). Two of the most distinctive ceramic forms in the Southwest, and the most restrictively distributed. Only a few hundred examples are known of each. Cylinder jars were for cacao—perhaps among other things—and almost all of them were found at Pueblo Bonito, most in a single room. Hand drums were for thumping and pounding, and almost all of them were found in a single room at Paquimé.

elry, arrows, and other items—including the Major Dudes, below the floors. Their crypt was below the room immediately adjacent to the cylinder jars.

Now look south to Paquimé. A similar situation involves odd vessels—"hand drums"—and elaborate burials. Hand drums (figure 3.14) were a ceramic form unique in the Greater Southwest to Paquimé (Di Peso, Rinaldo, and Fenner 1974c:356–365). They were roughly similar in size to cylinder jars (average height 17.6 cm, average opening diameter 11.7 cm), but with a marked "waist" and open bottoms. Presumably, skins were stretched over the larger end, although they lack lugs. A few were painted in several local styles (Babicora, Ramos), but most were plain or textured. Over 80 percent of the 109 known hand drums were found in a single cache on the floor of a room which, with an adjacent room, "contained two elaborate subfloor tombs with which a large number of ceramic hand drums were associated. These two subfloor tombs . . . were covered with board planking. . . . Both of these graves contained a large quantity and diversity of artifact accompaniments compared with burials from other architectural units" (Ravesloot 1988:32). One crypt burial contained a dozen individuals, five of whom were disarticulated above the principal internment: a middle-aged man with rich offerings. Another middle-aged man was buried in a similar crypt in the next room (Di Peso, Rinaldo, and Fenner 1974e: 387–396; Ravesloot 1988:34). Ravesloot (1988:70) and Di Peso (1974:419) suggested that the highest-status burials at Paquimé were three people whose bones were found in big Ramos jars in the Mound of the Offerings. After that group, the crypt burials of Unit 13 were judged the next highest status (Ravesloot 1988:69). I'm not sure we know who the Mound of the Offerings burials were. They may have been important, or they may have been trophies (all three lacked heads). But the two middle-aged men in the wooden crypts were, unquestionably, Major Dudes.

The striking similarities of odd, unique vessels with equally unique crypt burials at older parts of both Pueblo Bonito and Paquimé tell us more, I think, than the between black-on-white cylinders and polychrome hand drums—cacao cups versus bongos. (We have no comparable dudes-with-pots from Aztec, but, again, we have excavated much less of Aztec than Chaco and Paquimé.) To follow elites, we'll do better with uncommon contexts and *rarae aves* than with bulk crafts and quotidian objects. To repeat: rarities may well track one set of networks, pottery and lithics other networks.

Hecho en Mexico

Both Chaco and Paquimé had very obvious Mesoamerican "connections." Colonnades and ball courts are pretty convincing, and they both had actual Mexican stuff: copper bells and macaws, and lots of them. Aztec, despite its bold pioneer-days name, had only one copper bell and three macaws at Aztec West (and, as noted, no colonnades). We will return to Aztec's deficiencies below; the absence of evidence, in this case, may be evidence of a profound change in the Chaco-Aztec world.

More than any other Pueblo sites, Chaco and Paquimé have been explained by, or related to, or denied any Mesoamerican associations (see, among others, reviews by Di Peso, Rinaldo, and Fenner 1974a:208–211; Judge 1991:29–30; Lekson 1983b, 2009; Mathien 1986; Mathiowetz 2011; McGuire 1980, 1989, 1993a; Whalen and Minnis 2003). Why? Because Chaco and Paquimé appear so anomalous in the placid course of Pueblo prehistory, they invite intervention and *deus ex Mexica* explanations.

There is, of course, lots of evidence: macaws, parrots, copper objects, shells, and other artifacts originating far to the south. These were found in relative abundance at Chaco and absolute abundance at Paquimé. Indeed, Paquimé's metalwork makes central Mexican archaeologists jealous: Paquimé has more fancy tinware than Tula. What's all that stuff doing out on the wild frontier?

What do all those Mexican things mean? Were there Mesoamericans in the Southwest? Worse yet, Southwesterners in Mesoamerica? Third parties, *pochtecas* peddling trinkets to the rubes up north? Prevailing consensus denies a significant Mesoamerican presence or causal role at Chaco. Paul Reed (2004:45) summarizes the "moderate view of Mesoamerican-Chaco interaction": "Goods like copper bells and macaws were exchanged, perhaps directly or through intermediaries. Beyond this, it is possible that actual Mesoamerican, perhaps Toltec, traders visited Chaco from time to time. But the presence of these individuals is not believed to have dramatically affected the course of events at Chaco Canyon."

Paquimé, with its many Mexican details, is more frequently and less contentiously linked to the south. Of course, Paquimé is actually *in* Mexico, which helps Mesoamerican arguments; but, before 1848, so was Chaco. But even at Paquimé, current thinking runs against Di Peso's direct intervention (e.g., McGuire 1993a:38; Minnis 1989). Michael Whalen and Paul Minnis (2003:328) summarize what I believe is the current consensus among Casas Grandes researchers: "We do not seek to deny the importance of distant contacts and of borrowing from the outside. Mesoamerican elements clearly were critical parts of the ritual system and political-prestige economy that underlay power at Casas Grandes. Instead of being reflections of distant developmental stimuli, however, we interpret these elements as imports used to support and augment the power of local political entrepreneurs." Local trumps distant again.

I wouldn't necessarily disagree. That's probably true—for the commoners, who constituted most of the population. But not the nobles. All politics are local—except when they aren't. The scale of long-distance interactions for political elites and nobles greatly exceeded the reach of subsistence and craft economies. It's a matter of how we weigh the evidence, I suppose: by significance or by tonnage. Mexican exotica (as discussed above) are often dismissed as low-volume trinkets, vastly outweighed by tons of good honest Southwestern sherds. Bling and power float over the work-a-day world; the rich are different.

Copper bells and other copper artifacts, particularly abundant at Paquimé (Di Peso, Rinaldo, and Fenner 1974b:507–510), probably came from West Mexico (Vargas 1995; but see Hosler 1994:221 for a contrasting view). The bells certainly look West Mexican, but of course that's how they'd look if Paquimé imported West Mexican coppersmiths. (The Casas Grandes and Mimbres regions were rich in copper. A key question for Casas Grandes copper is metallurgy: was it made from local ores?) Scarlet macaws also originated in coastal Mexico—their natural range is at least 1,000 km south of the Southwest (Hargrave 1970). Cacao at Chaco came from farther still (Crown and Hurst 2009; see also Washburn et al. 2014); cacao has not yet been found at Paquimé, but nobody's looked.

For archaeologists intimidated by large scales, who want it all to go away, these Mesoamerican things can be minimized by invoking "down-the-line" trading— "through intermediaries"—with objects being passed from one hill tribe to another in a daisy-chain exchange. That wouldn't work for macaws, and I doubt very much it worked for the masses of high-end copper objects (and tons of shell) found at Paquimé.

There's been a fair amount of research on Southwestern macaws (Hargrave 1970; McKusick 2001). Many were brought up young, perhaps when they were more docile? The idea of hauling big, angry macaws over long distances makes one pity the porter—what a nasty job. (Mimbres pots show macaws peeking out of burden baskets on people's backs.) Live birds were carried north to Mimbres and on to Chaco. It is not impossible that attempts were made to breed birds in the Mimbres area—shell has been found—but probably without any great success.[15] Macaws were definitely bred, on commercial scales, at Paquimé, where more than 300 were found along with elaborate breeding pens (figure 3.15) (Di Peso 1974:598–601; Di Peso, Rinaldo, and Fenner 1974e:272; Minnis 1988; Whalen and Minnis 1996c; Somerville, Nelson, and Knudson 2010), which required importing and probably refreshing a breeding stock, and probably importing the expertise to keep tropical birds alive in the Chihuahuan Desert.

Chaco was a conspicuous eleventh-century consumer of macaws. Paquimé was a fourteenth-century producer. Aztec . . . well, Aztec had three macaws—two actual macaws (Lori Pendelton, personal communication, 1997) and one macaw feather (Morris 1919:64). Aztec Ruins and its region have not produced many foreign curios.[16]

But, of course, Aztec West is only one of the half a dozen large buildings at Aztec. What a different picture we would have of Chaco had only Chetro Ketl and not Pueblo Bonito been excavated! With the current data, however, it appears that long-range exchange—spectacularly evident at Chaco in the twelfth century and Paquimé in the fourteenth century—was greatly reduced at Aztec during the

FIGURE 3.15
Macaw pens at Paquimé. Macaws were bred at Paquimé, in startling quantities (Somerville, Nelson, and Knudson 2010). Macaws eat fruit when they are at home, but fruits are not abundant in the Chihuahuan Desert. They lived long enough to hatch eggs, but they probably were not happy birds. The stone rings and stone plugs seem excessive, but a crabby macaw is an unpleasant beast: sharp strong beaks, long talons, and evil dispositions.

thirteenth century. This parallels the marked decrease in all sorts of intraregional exchange in the northern San Juan and Mesa Verde area during Aztec's run. Things moved internally (Mesa Verde–style pottery, for example; see Glowacki 2006) but, compared to the rest of the Southwest, there was little pottery from beyond the Mesa Verde region, from the outside world south of the San Juan River. In this case, both quotidian and prestige networks seem to show the same thing: relative isolation during Aztec's era.

Marine shell was really important at Paquimé (and to the Hohokam of southern Arizona), less so at Chaco and Aztec. Most shell came from coastal Mexico and the Sea of Cortez; some came from California. I rely here on Ronna Bradley's (1993, 2000) excellent summaries. Based largely on species assemblages, she concluded that there were two major shell production and distribution systems in the Greater Southwest: a Hohokam system and a Paquimé system. These two systems were largely sequential, with the Hohokam system dominating prior to about

1275, and Paquimé replacing the Hohokam system thereafter: Hohokam down, Paquimé up (Lekson 2009). Hohokam shell reached Chaco in significant quantities—but it's possible it came through Mimbres "intermediaries." Aztec and Wupatki—both post-1125, pre-1275 centers—were also in this network, but they produced far less shell than Chaco. Paquimé's shell production was phenomenal. Di Peso found one and a half *tons* of shell at Paquimé. It supplied Pueblo villages far to the north and northwest during the fourteenth and fifteenth centuries.

Mimbres complicates the picture: Mimbres had lots of shell and close ties to both Hohokam (early) and Chaco (late) (Lekson 2009), as demonstrated by Bradley's (2000) analysis: pre-Mimbres ("Late Pithouse period") sites shared species with Hohokam shell assemblages, but later Mimbres phase (contemporary with Chaco) shell more closely resemble Paquimé patterns. Mimbres (1000–1130) was substantially earlier than Paquimé (1300–1450; see appendix B). Thus Mimbres shell initially aligned with Hohokam, but by Chacoan times Mimbres apparently developed an independent industry, an end run around Hohokam. We know Mimbres went to the beach: depictions of Sea of Cortez fish appear on Mimbres pots (Jett and Moyle 1986). The similarity of the shell species involved suggests that shell networks pioneered in Mimbres times were continued (on greatly expanded levels) by Paquimé. Coincidence? Probably not.

The Grin Remained After the Rest Had Gone

Teeth tell the tale. The peculiarities and details of teeth are genetically linked— my teeth look like my parents', and their parents', and so forth (good thing, because my family was blessed with fairly solid teeth). So dental characteristics can be used to define and track closely related groups. As it turns out, teeth show a strong link between Pueblo Bonito and Aztec Ruins, and both Bonito and Aztec teeth don't look very much like the local northern San Juan teeth. It's worth quoting Kathy Roler Durand and her colleagues' results from their wide-ranging analysis, because I love it when I'm right:

> Our analysis revealed a close connection between the Pueblo Bonito and Aztec Ruin great houses, supporting Lekson's model of migration from Pueblo Bonito to Aztec Ruin at the end of the Pueblo II period [that is, the era of Chaco]. The dentition of the inhabitants of Aztec Ruin clearly did not have the same trait frequencies as the local Middle San Juan Region population. (Durand et al. 2010:126)

Further south, I argued in the first edition of this book that Mimbres constituted a major portion of Casas Grandes' commoners, who built and supported Paquimé. Who were the Mimbres? Christy Turner (1993) asked that very question and decided that Mimbres teeth, at least, were more southern than northern: Mimbres clustered with (were more like) ancient people in Coahuila, Chihuahua, Sonora, and Sinaloa and much less with Southwestern populations. DNA analysis from the Mimbres Valley confirms that some of people at Mimbres sites came from down south, sharing genetic markers with Cora, Huichol, and Nahua—haplotypes which were rare in other Southwestern groups (Snow, Shafer, and Smith 2011).

What about Paquimé and Casas Grandes? We don't have DNA (yet), but the teeth suggest that Casas Grandes had more in common with Mimbres than with locals. Indeed, for Turner (1999), Casas Grandes was a problem:

> What is to me most unexpected about this analysis is the relatively great dissimilarity the Casas Grandes dental sample has with the other sample of teeth from Chihuahua. . . . In sum, dental crown morphology suggests the population of Casas Grandes had close epigenetic connections with people living in Sinaloa and in the Mimbres area. These relationships are closer than that between Casas Grandes and another sample of Chihuahuan dentition. (Turner 1999:232)

That makes sense if Mimbres shifted south into the Casas Grandes Valley—which, of course, is what I say happened. While this is all very satisfactory, what's missing are (1) analysis that separates populations into classes—nobles and commoners—which could be done; and of course (2) the final link in the chain, comparing elite burials at Chaco and Aztec and elite burials at Paquimé—Founding Fathers and Major Dudes. There's work to be done.

REGIONAL INTEGRATION

The regional structures of Chaco, Aztec, and Paquimé were not identical—how could they be?—but there were intriguing parallels. Chaco, Aztec, and Paquimé were each, in their respective times and places, the regional center: the largest, most elaborate, and most significant sites in their regions. And in all three cases, a key dynamic was the ability of the capital to project power over distance.[17]

There are (literally) tons of evidence at Chaco itself for major action—bulk transport—over distance: masses of pottery from the Chuska Valley, about 75 km from Chaco; many tens of thousands of large beams from uplands 80 km and even farther (it's hard to think of anything bulkier than roof beams); and at least the possibility of bulk import of corn (e.g., Benson 2010) and other foodstuffs from comparable distances—distances which did not, apparently, intimidate the ancients.

In chapter 2, I suggested that Chaco's bulk-goods economy routinely operated out to 150 km and its political economy reached 250 km. To repeat: 150 km was Chaco's "inner core," the likely limit for regular transport of bulk goods by porters (Malville 2001; see chapter 2, note 5); and 250 km was Chaco's "outer limit," a distance beyond which it was difficult or maybe impossible to keep power relations in order.

Recent very intriguing "big data" research using pottery and obsidian—rather than architecture and baubles, my favorites—show that the distances I'm suggesting between Chaco and Aztec and between Chaco and its "outliers" aren't too far. Barbara Mills and her colleagues (Mills et al. 2013) looked at huge data sets from post-1200 sites over a wide swath of the Southwest—not at this point including Chaco, but that's coming—and were surprised by what they found. "Following common assumptions that most social interaction took place within a day's round trip walk of home, or ~18 km, we anticipated that sites would have had stronger social connections to proximate sites considering that virtually all travel and movement of goods was pedestrian. . . . Mean [average] distance among sites with strong social connections are surprisingly high, ranging between 70 and 120 km in all but the final period of our analyses" (1450–1500), when the Southwest shattered and things got small (Mills et al. 2014:5788). The average distance between strongly linked sites (omitting the 1450–1500 period) was about 90 km; many strong connections, as measured by pottery and obsidian, sometimes reached as far as 400 km (Matt Peeples, personal communication, August 18, 2013). "One surprising result is the number of strong similarities in ceramic assemblages that exceeded 250 km in a context in which movement was exclusively on foot" (Mills et al. 2014:5789). That's mostly after Chaco and after Aztec—that is, after things fell apart. And we are not talking about bells and feathers; this analysis focuses on sherds and lithics. Distances of 150 km and 250 km were not exceptional; they were the norm. It's a small world, after all.

Jumping over Aztec (to which we will return), let's look at the last of the trio, Paquimé. We know less about its region than we do about Chaco's, but I think we know enough (thanks to Di Peso 1974; Whalen and Minnis 2001, 2009; and others). Whalen and Minnis (2001:194) defined three zones for Casas Grandes, conceptually concentric around Paquimé. First, a "core" with an inner core of 15 km, "which appears to have been directly dominated by the primate center," and an outer core of 15 to 30 km, closely tied but with "somewhat more autonomy." (The core, in this model, was Paquimé's polity.) Beyond the core were "near peripheries" out to about 60 to 75 km ("the outermost limits of a political economy"), and then "intermediate peripheries," and finally "far peripheries," reaching out as far as 150 to 170 km in odd cases like the Animas phase sites of southwestern New Mexico. If I understand correctly, they argue that Paquimé's direct political control was strong out to about 15 km, diminished out to 30 km, and, beyond that, was not much. Whalen and Minnis limited Paquimé effective "political economy" to their middle zone, or 60 to 75 km (Whalen and Minnis 2001:52, 194). They use the term "political economy" differently than I use it here, closer to my bulk-goods economy. Fair enough: 60 to 75 km is about the distance between Chaco and the Chuska Valley, certainly a bulk-goods zone. The basic economic scales were not dissimilar, although tumpline economies could go twice that far (see chapter 2).

A Casas Grandes polity of 15 to 30 km or even 75 km seems small to me (no surprises there, of course).[18] It's worth another look, from another angle. Whalen and Minnis looked outward from the center; what would we see if we looked inward from the peripheries? How far out are the most distant Casas Grandes sites that, according to local authorities working in those areas, are really Casas Grandes? Using data from chapters in a forthcoming edited volume on the Casas Grandes region (Whalen and Minnis 2015), it seems that farthest-out ironclad

FIGURE 3.16
Paquimé's region, approximated from reports of outermost Casas Grandes sites (see text).

Casas Grandes sites form a sort of ring about 150 km from Paquimé (figure 3.16)—gratifyingly close to Chaco's 150 km "inner core." Chaco got out to 250 km; how far did Paquimé go?

Paquimé worked the circuit.[19] Great quantities of seashell at Paquimé came at least 370 km from the nearest ocean—and probably much farther (Bradley 1993). But I'll focus here on ricolite (also called serpentine), a beautiful white-and-green-banded stone not found in the Casas Grandes core or peripheries. There was a lot of ricolite at Paquimé (115 kg). By weight, ricolite was the second-largest nonceramic import to Paquimé (after shell; Di Peso, Rinaldo, and Fenner 1974e:188). Among other things, they made small, low, four-legged stools out of ricolite. "Stool" sounds prosaic, but stools like that were thrones in Mesoamerica, or at least furniture for important people—and Paquimé's stools were made not of wood but of a fancy, expensive stone. The ricolite was geologically sourced to quarries near Redrock, New Mexico (Di Peso, Rinaldo, and Fenner 1974:188), 270 km from Paquimé.[20] Paquimé's prestige-goods economy (my "political economy") reached over 370 km (and beyond) to the shores of the Sea of Cortez, and 270 km to Redrock's ricolite quarries. That was supply; what about demand? Bradley's analysis of Paquimé's shell network reaches the northern Rio Grande, as did small finished ricolite objects—but not stools! I wonder where those went: out to secondary Casas Grandes centers, as badges of office? Or further south?

What about Aztec? Aztec's region appears to be quite a bit smaller than Chaco's (figure 2.5). The most obvious architectural markers for Aztec are bi- and tri-walls (discussed above), and those are clustered in southwestern Colorado—and, of course, at Aztec (Glowacki 2006). Bi- and tri walls appeared throughout the "core" Mesa Verde area—the park and the plains to its west, around Cortez, Colorado—but no further west than Sleeping Ute Mountain (approximately longitude 108°49'). The plains around Cortez were very heavily populated; the area probably played a role in the thirteenth century analogous to the Chuska Valley to Chaco Canyon in the eleventh century: the western breadbasket. The distances were similar: the Chuska Valley is about 75 km west of Chaco; Cortez is 75 km northwest of Aztec Ruins.

In southwestern Colorado, the tri-wall furthest from Aztec Ruins is about 100 km distant. There are at least two more tri-walls outside that core shown on figure 2.5: one in the southernmost Chuska Valley, and the other, the Kin Li Chee bi-wall near Ganada, Arizona—both about 150 km from Aztec Ruins. The "inner core" had become the "outer limit."

Beyond the bi-walls and tri-walls, it's difficult to determine what parts of the old Chaco sphere answered to Aztec. Most (but not all) Chaco-era Great Houses continued to be used for various purposes through the end of the thirteenth century. Many were reoccupied, sort of a "squatter" settlement, or repurposed as crypts or cemeteries. (For whom? Good question! I don't know.) Others almost certainly continued as elite residences, at least some of which presumably answered to Aztec. Some, but not all; the southernmost Chaco Great House "out-liers" around Zuni continued to be community centers (I'd say elite residences or palaces) and a few new, post-Chaco Great Houses were built, but it does not appear they had any engagement with Aztec Ruins, at least directly (Cameron and Duff 2008). It was too far away . . . at least too far for Aztec's diminished power.

But Aztec's world probably extended beyond the geographic limits of bi- and tri-walls. T-doors may be showing us that: the distribution of T-doors was much larger than tri-walls. Absent exotica (which, if you recall, were indeed absent), one type of artifact in Lipe's "central Mesa Verde complex" (my Aztec indicia) that's easy to track is the distinctive Mesa Verde mug (figure 2.3). They are found mostly but not exclusively in the Mesa Verde (i.e., Aztec) region. But examples are known from Kayenta and other non–Mesa Verde areas (made on local potter-ies), with more than a few up to 220 km or 250 km from Aztec (Putsavage 2008: figure 3.1). If mugs were indicia, Aztec's sphere of influence may just possibly have reached the distances of Chaco and Paquimé—but I kind of doubt it.

A MILLENNIUM ON THE MERIDIAN

The Chaco Meridian, as originally proposed, was a four-point problem: North, Chaco, Aztec, and Paquimé. Three of those points are now widely, almost univer-sally, accepted: Chaco moved north to Aztec (e.g., chapters in Reed 2008). I use Chaco-North-Aztec as a litmus test. If today a practitioner denies Chaco-North-Aztec, I dismiss him or her as hopeless. Convivial, perhaps, for a drink and a joke, but useless for practical work.

Paquimé, the fourth point, remains problematic for some (but not for me!), and we will return to that city—"painted in many colors," according to the first Spanish accounts—in chapter 4.

Here I extend my argument (and stretch the truth?) to three more points, two earlier and one later.[21] Introduction to these new players requires, alas, some ar-chaeological jargon: the Pecos System. Not a system for beating the house in Ve-gas, the Pecos System was and is a chronology—a series of historical stages—for the Pueblo Southwest, invented almost a century ago at a meeting at Pecos Pueblo (hence the name). You'd think something that old would have been superseded and replaced, and indeed the Pecos System has given way to myriad local chro-nologies; but for sweeping statements about all of the Southwest, the Pecos Sys-tem remains our best option. It starts off badly with Basketmaker II, an era before the introduction of corn and pottery. Badly because (1) there is no Basketmaker I and (2) Basketmaker II now has corn. Let's just give it a miss and jump right to Basketmaker III, with well-built pithouses, painted pottery, and more corn than Iowa (at least if we believe the optimistic diorama at the Mesa Verde museum). Pueblo I follows with—you guessed it—pueblos replacing pithouses. Pueblo I, II, III, IV, and V (when the Spaniards arrive) unfold the slow and steady progress from the rude and cheerless Basketmakers to the perfection of modern Pueblos. The past wasn't like that. The Southwest had a colorful history of rises and falls, successes and failures, war and peace, and so forth—just like every other region in the inhabited globe (Lekson 2009). But no matter: the Pecos stages reflect real differences in architecture, pottery, and the like. As patterns in the data, they stand up. They got that part right a century ago. The Pecos System tells the wrong story, but its plotline puts the right characters in the right places at the right time.

Here's the kicker: for each of six Pecos stages, from Basketmaker III through Pueblo V, the biggest (by far), most complicated (by far), and most interesting (by far) sites sit on the Chaco Meridian.[22]

Almost as awkward as Pecos System jargon are too-busy graphics. Figure 3.17 shows the Pecos System/meridian argument, but it needs explaining, first across the top and then down the side. Across the top are longitudes, from right to left: 107°50', 107°55' and 108°. The world being what it is—that is, roundish—longitudes converge as they head north, toward St. Nicholas, and diverge as they

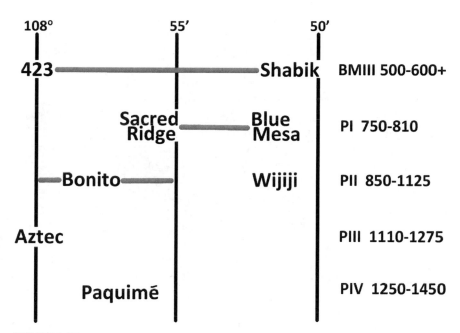

FIGURE 3.17
Longitudes: the longitudes of the biggest, weirdest, most interesting sites of each Pecos System stage (explained in text). Longitude, measured from right to left, as 107°50', 107°55', and 108°. Time and Pecos stages from top to bottom.

head south to the equator. The spread from 107°50' to 108° at Chaco is about 14 km—under 10 miles.

Down the right side are time periods that correspond to the Pecos System stages, starting with Basketmaker III (500–600+) at the top and Pueblo IV (1250–1450) at the bottom. In the body of the diagram are sites: "423" is 29SJ423, and "Shabik" is Shabik'eschee—two huge Basketmaker III sites at either end of Chaco Canyon. Sacred Ridge and Blue Mesa are part of a large Pueblo I complex just south of Durango, Colorado. Bonito, of course, is Pueblo Bonito; the horizontal bar represents downtown Chaco, and the asterisks mark the farthest Great Houses in Chaco Canyon, Peñasco Blanco on the west (left) and Wijiji on the east (right). Downtown Chaco was the center of the Pueblo II world, just as Aztec Ruins was the center of the Pueblo III world. Paquimé—far to the south of all its predecessors—was a whacking big Pueblo IV site. Paquimé, in contrast, was a capital city and a wonderfully cosmopolitan place, the most remarkable site of its time and place—the Pueblo IV world sagged south.

Culiacán is my candidate for the greatest site of the Pueblo V period (the era of colonization). Culiacán was *way* out of the Southwest, and it wasn't even a Pueblo in the sense of Pueblo Indians—but it was the last lonely pueblo in the Spanish sense: the northernmost city on the coast of New Spain. Culiacán was not quite on, but very near, the swampy Sinaloan coast (figure 3.18)—and off my chart. Its longitude must remain approximate (as discussed below, I've never been there, and I'm not planning on going anytime soon). From the safety of Google Earth, from the written reports, I think ancient Culiacán's longitude was *approximately* 107°35', near the modern town of San Pedro (the Spanish moved modern Culiacán a few miles upstream)—that's about 15' east (right) of 107°50'. We'll return to Culiacán and its smeary meridian-ness below.

Figure 3.17, complicated as it is, illustrates that for every Pecos stage, the largest, strangest, and most significant sites were on the meridian. That is, if I've got the right sites—I'll describe the new faces shortly. We've already met Chaco (Pueblo II), Aztec (Pueblo III), and Paquimé (Pueblo IV); and I hope we can agree that for those three Pecos periods, those sites fit the bill. Now let's turn to what came before and what came after. Before: 29SJ423 and Shabik'eschee (423-Shabik on figure 3.17), phenomenal Basketmaker III sites at Chaco Canyon, followed by the amazing Pueblo I complex at Sacred Ridge and Blue Mesa. Then of course came Chaco-Aztec-Paquimé. And after: Culiacán, a Pueblo V period Mesoamerican city, the same distance from Paquimé as Paquimé was from Chaco. And all on or about on the meridian.

I say these sites were, for their respective periods, the biggest, most complex, and most interesting. Relative sizes ("biggest") are fairly solid, and mostly from published compilations for the particular period. Please note that the earlier sites (Basketmaker III and to some extent Pueblo I) are less certain than later sites: it's very true that Basketmaker III sites are not easy to see, and I've been told of other, larger sites—unrecorded, of course. But I am fairly certain about Pueblo I and quite certain about Pueblo II, III, IV, and V. By "complicated" I don't mean "complex" in archaeology's stilted sense of "political." No, I mean complicated: high densities of disparate, odd, weird stuff—both buildings and goodies. "Most complicated" is my opinion but could be quantified. Why bother? It's pretty obvious: each of these sites had much larger varieties of much weirder architecture and artifacts than other sites of their respective times and places—more complicated in both quantity and quality. Indeed, we could substitute the term "weird" for "complicated"—and I do, from time to time. "Most interesting" may sound completely subjective, but that quality too could be demonstrated by the numbers of books, articles, dissertations, and theses published on each site. More ink has been spilled on these sites than almost any others in their times and places. The exception to the large-literature rule is Culiacán, which was investigated only once, very early (Kelly 1945).[23]

Chaco, Aztec, and Paquimé were discussed above; they will reappear in the following section only to bridge from Pueblo I (Sacred Ridge–Blue Mesa) to Pueblo IV (Culiacán). Not by design, but still somehow appropriate, the discussion begins with archaeological minutia of Basketmaker III and ends in conceptual histories of Pueblo V—things seem to get fuzzier as they get closer in time.

Basketmaker III (500–600+)

Basketmaker III, as a Pecos stage, is usually dated from 500 to 700. The dates on figure 3.17 refer to the probable occupation spans of two remarkable Basketmaker III sites in Chaco Canyon, 29SJ423 and Shabik'eschee. "Shabik'eschee" surely gets the nod for names, over the cryptic "29SJ423." Shabik'eschee is Navajo—at least it started off as Navajo before archaeologists wrote it down—and when ungarbled, Shabik'eschee refers to a nearby sun petroglyph (hereafter, mostly "Shabik"). 29SJ423 is simply a code: 29 = New Mexico; SJ = San Juan County; 423 = the 423rd site recorded in that county (hereafter, 423). 423 is at the lower end of Chaco Canyon near the westernmost Great House in the canyon, Peñasco Blanco (Windes in press). Shabik is at the upper end of the built-up area, just above the easternmost Great House in Chaco proper, Wijiji (Roberts 1929; Wills and Windes 1989; Wills et al. 2012). The two Basketmaker III sites are strikingly similar, each with between 80 and 100 pithouses grouped around an early Great Kiva (Windes in press).

We've only recently realized how odd Shabik and 423 are. Almost all other Basketmaker sites have only one or two pithouses, sometimes surrounded by a fence or palisade. If you find a Basketmaker site with ten pithouses, you write your book and retire in rock-star glory. Eighty to one hundred pithouses, it turns out, is phenomenal, colossal, stupendous, unheard-of (cf. Reed 2000). Except at Chaco, where there are two of them.

What to make of that? Shabik'eschee is just too darn big—a complaint heard as soon as other, normal, smaller Basketmaker III sites were excavated. Maybe Shabik is just a grand illusion: the result of reoccupations, time after time, of properly small Basketmaker III groups, possibly attracted by pinyon trees and nuts (Wills and Windes 1989; Wills et al. 2012). In the aggregate, the comings and goings of a handful of people could produce a big archaeological site.[24] But this requires a special pleading for Chaco's Basketmaker III. Elsewhere, Basketmaker III is considered to be relatively sedentary, with permanent occupations and stable relationships—not a sad string of one-night or one-season stands (e.g., chapters in Reed 2000). Moreover, it's pretty clear that Basketmaker III Great Kivas serve large (if sometimes dispersed) groups. If Shabik was a few families picking pinyon nuts, would they need a Great Kiva? No, that takes a village. (And if up-canyon Shabik was a pinyon-nut camp, it's hard to imagine what resource attracted people down-canyon at 423, where pinyon trees are thin on the ground.) Most of us accept that Shabik'eschee and 423 were village-like—if not the rock-solid monumental permanence of Chaco at its height.

And it was probably bigger than just Shabik and 423: Chaco Canyon, it seems, was a teeming, bubbling cauldron of Basketmaker III activity. Indeed, more than a few Basketmaker pithouses were buried deep below Pueblo Bonito (Judd 1964)—I wouldn't be surprised if there was a third big Basketmaker III site lurking beneath the Town Beautiful. "Shabik'eschee and 29SJ423 were not two separate Basketmaker sites or 'villages,' but rather the east and west extremes of a single settlement or community that was stretched out along the entire canyon floor between these two concentrations" (Wills et al. 2012:342), a dispersed site a little over 15 km long, east-west.

I agree: there's a lot more Basketmaker III at Chaco than 423 and Shabik'eschee. To be sure, all those many Basketmaker houses were not occupied simultaneously and permanently through two or more centuries (a pithouse only lasts a decade or so). But however it's sliced, the 15 km aggregate represents a big, big, big Basketmaker III site. If Shabik and 423 stand alone among (known) Basketmaker III sites, the 15 km megasite of Chaco is literally orders of magnitude larger (but recall that we probably don't know Basketmaker III as well as we do later periods).

Something happened in Chaco around 500 that created the biggest, most complicated, most interesting Basketmaker III site in the Pueblo world—however we parse the Chaco megasite.

Sacred Ridge–Blue Mesa (750–810)

During Pueblo I (700–900), Chaco became something of a backwater. There were Pueblo I settlements, of course, but the action shifted emphatically to the north, in a broad band of sites from Blanding, Utah, on the west to Durango, Colorado, on the east (Wilshusen and Van Dyke 2006). Most of that Pueblo I energy was well west of the Chaco Meridian. The remarkable exception was Sacred Ridge–Blue Mesa (figure 3.17), directly north of the 423-Shabik Basketmaker III megasite. Sacred Ridge–Blue Mesa was the biggest, most complicated, most interesting Pueblo I site (Potter and Chuipka 2007a)—and notably offset to the eastern edge of big-time Pueblo I.

Like the Chaco Basketmaker III megasite, Sacred Ridge–Blue Mesa combines multiple units that, for archaeological record keeping, have been called individual sites. They weren't separate settlements; they were all part of one big megasite, from Blue Mesa on the east to Sacred Ridge on the west. Blue Mesa sits high above the Animas River just south of Durango, Colorado (Potter and Chuipka 2007b). Most of it is now under the Animas Airpark, a county airport, but it was big. Blue Mesa by itself was once considered the largest Pueblo I site (Wilshusen and Ortman 1999), but larger by increments not by multiples.

But wait . . . there's more. In 2009, they made a lake by damming up Ridges Basin, a small valley 2.5 km west of Blue Mesa. The dammed creek runs east right through Blue Mesa—the two were connected via a short narrows. CRM (Cultural Resource Management, or "salvage") archaeology preceded the dam. They found wonderful things (Potter 2010): scores of pithouses, and in the middle of the soon-to-be lake, a remarkable complex called "Sacred Ridge"—to which we will shortly return. Dates from the CRM project indicate that the complex began about 750 to 810 (Potter 2010; Potter and Chuipka 2007a). Blue Mesa produced dates from one structure at 831 (Potter and Chuipka 2007b), so the Pueblo I sites lasted at least that long if not longer. Again, these datings (and other Pueblo I datings) will no doubt change with additional work—only a tiny fraction of Blue Mesa has been intensively investigated, and some of it may survive beneath the runway.

CRM archaeology in the Ridges Basin tilted the balance of power from Blue Mesa to Sacred Ridge (Chuipka and Potter 2007b:8). Wilshusen and Ortman (1999) estimated about 200 pit structures at Blue Mesa, absent Sacred Ridge; the Ridges Basin project downgraded Blue Mesa to 74 (Chuipka and Potter 2007b), about the same number as at Ridges Basin itself (for a total of 150 pithouses, still a huge site!). That reduction of Blue Mesa may or may not reflect pride of place— my site's bigger than your site; I suspect Blue Mesa, pre-airport, was in fact larger than Ridges Basin. But Ridges Basin has much more interesting architecture, specifically Sacred Ridge (Chuipka 2009; Duke 1985; Potter and Chuipka 2007a). The excavator, Jason Chuipka, described Sacred Ridge:

> What stands out about Sacred Ridge are all the things that were "not supposed to be there" according to our understanding of the early A.D. 800s in the northern Southwest. The site was too early for towers (there was one at Sacred Ridge); pit structures in the area averaged about 5 m in diameter (most were 50% larger than that at Sacred Ridge); no sites were known to contain more than two or three

contemporary habitations (there were 20 at Sacred Ridge), and in a time of plenty without ecological stress and population pressure there should be peace (instead, there was ample evidence of violence).

The architecture at Sacred Ridge can be summarized as different—structures differed from one another as much as they differed from those in the larger community. The architecture tower was the most distinguishing feature at the site. Visible from nearly every household in the valley it was less of a lookout and more of a building to be looked at—a tall structure standing out from the low mounds of pithouses that dotted the area. The tower was different, highly visible, and had no obvious utilitarian function. There are two types of people that build like that: people with power, and those that wish to look as though they have power. (Jason Chuipka, personal communication, July 22, 2014)

From west to east, from Sacred Ridge to Blue Mesa, a distance of a dozen kilometers, there were more eighth-century houses than at any other Pueblo I site in the northern Southwest. Not urban densities, but taken together a very large, impressive settlement. (The whole greater than the sum, etc.)

Sacred Ridge–Blue Mesa was a big but short-lived bang. The bang: there were very few people (almost none) in the Durango area immediately before, and very few (almost none) immediately after. That is, almost no Basketmaker III and very little Pueblo II, but a *lot* of Pueblo I at Sacred Ridge–Blue Mesa. Battalions of people moved in from somewhere, or more likely several "somewheres": pithouse architecture in Ridges Basin shows details and styles from several other distant regions. An influx created the largest town of its time, on the far eastern edges of hard-core Pueblo I, followed by an exodus to parts unknown. That exodus was marked and perhaps sparked by an act of highest drama.

Sacred Ridge–Blue Mesa was a short big bang, and it ended with a bigger bang—a big bad bang. In the last act at Sacred Ridge, more than thirty people—men, women, and children—were tortured, massacred, cut to pieces, and tossed into two of the oversized pithouses (Chuipka 2009; Osterholtz 2013). The dead were locals—they had grown up in and around Ridges Basin. But that community was far larger than thirty people, so it's quite possible that the locals were killed by other locals—or, also possible, by raiding outsiders.

If the latter, it came out of the blue, so to speak: no part of the large settlement was "defensive." The Sacred Ridge–Blue Mesa people were not anticipating war. So I think it's likely that the killing was an inside job, the brutal climax of social and political tensions that ended Blue Mesa–Sacred Ridge's history—and an event surely remembered for generations.

Chaco, Aztec, Paquimé

We've met Chaco, Aztec, and Paquimé before, so there's no need to describe them again here. Each was the biggest, weirdest, most interesting site of its time.

Chaco was hands down the eight-hundred-pound gorilla of Pueblo II. There can be no demurral on this; if there is, it should be ignored.

Aztec's role in Pueblo III is subject to discussion, because—as everyone knows—Pueblo III was the period of Mesa Verde, America's most famous archaeological park. As well it should be: the experience of walking through the rooms and towers of a perfectly preserved site like Cliff Palace is truly remarkable. But, historically, Mesa Verde was not a big deal. The Mesa Verde region—defined by pottery styles and architectural details—reached from southeastern Utah on the west to Aztec Ruins on the east. Mesa Verde has the best sites to see, but not the biggest sites. Indeed, the largest Mesa Verde towns were not in the national park, but out on the plains to the west, around the modern town of Cortez, Colorado. Yellow Jacket (25 km northwest of Cortez) was the largest of all Mesa Verde sites: 100 acres of rubble, hummocks, and swales are all that's left of 1,200 rooms and 200 kivas. (Cliff Palace—the largest Mesa Verde cliff dwelling—had 150 rooms and 23 kivas, a tenth the size of Yellow Jacket.) Mesa Verde archaeologists have known this for years: the mass of population was not on Mesa Verde but on the plains to its west. This area was in Aztec's region, marked by bi- and tri-walled structures (e.g., the Great Tower at Yellow Jacket), but Colorado archaeologists are loathe to admit that Aztec Ruins in New Mexico played any role in the Mesa Verde sphere. It's Chaco outlier-denier NIMBY nonsense: déjà vu all over again forty years later.

Aztec Ruins was (slightly) larger than Yellow Jacket and hugely larger than Cliff Palace, and it knocks them both off the charts for complications and weirdness. As discussed above, Aztec was laid out to an elaborate cosmological plan (much like Chaco) focused on tri-walled structures. It had roads and massive Great Houses, among the biggest ever built. There's nothing even remotely as weird as Aztec in the rest of the Mesa Verde region. Aztec came to a rough end, more of a whimper than a bang, with decades of out-migration from its region, lots of Sacred Ridge–level violence, and finally the abandonment of the city itself.

Paquimé scores very high—off the charts—for weirdness and interest, but maybe not so much on bigness. It was by far (factor of two or three or more) the largest site in the Casas Grandes region. Recall that Di Peso pegged Paquimé at 0.35 sq km (Di Peso 1974:370); but it might only be half that big (discussed above). If so, Paquimé halved was about the same size as Sapawe, one of the very largest Rio Grande pueblos.

Rio Grande and Hopi Pueblo IV sites were big. The difference: they were farming villages, deliberately simple, typically short-lived. Paquimé was a city—an urban center of remarkable sophistication, central to a very large region. I've argued elsewhere (Lekson 2009) that big pueblos like Sapawe were the reaction to the fall of Chaco-Aztec, people voting with their feet leaving the Chaco-Aztec region and all those annoying noble families, moving into already crowded Pueblo areas. Rejecting class society and nobles, they experimented with ways—mostly ritual—to hold large villages together without all that Chaco-Aztec stuff. For the first century or so—Pueblo IV—it didn't work so well: the big villages lasted only a generation or two, factionalized, and then split into "daughter" villages, or out-migrated to greener pastures. But eventually they sorted it out and became pueblos, as we know them today: large farming villages without kings and nobles. But there were still kings and nobles at Paquimé, until it too fell—for reasons in which we have been curiously uninterested—around 1450. And that's when Culiacán kicked things up a notch.

Culiacán (1450–)

After Paquimé came Culiacán (figure 3.18). The modern Mexican city of Culiacán—the administrative center of both Sinaloa and its eponymous drug cartel—is about 620 km south of Paquimé, a little less than the distance from Chaco to Paquimé. (If you accept Chaco moving to Paquimé—and I hope you do—the next hop from Paquimé to Culiacán shouldn't be dismissed on distance alone.)

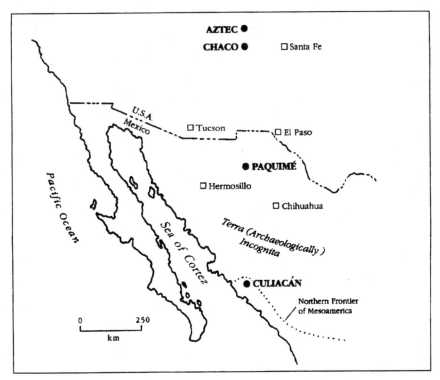

FIGURE 3.18
The US Southwest and northwest Mexico.

Modern Culiacán sits east of Paquimé's longitude and the meridian. Conquistadors relocated the capital; ancient Culiacán was downstream and 40 km off the nominal meridian—the biggest error of any of the six sites, but acceptably and even impressively close, given the rugged terrain between Paquimé and Culiacán—of which, more below.

Culiacán was, geographically, the end of the line: the southern end of a north-south history that reached north up to the mountains of Colorado and ended at Sinaloa's Pacific Coast; and the end of the line, historically, the last act of a story that began around 500 and ended a thousand years later, in 1530, with the arrival of Nuño de Guzman's army of conquest—which we will meet again in chapter 4.

Or . . . maybe Culiacán was all those things. We know very little about its archaeology, so I can't make a case based on architecture or artifacts. The only major excavations happened before World War II (Kelly 1945). I'm told most of Kelly's site, near the modern town of San Pedro, has been leveled for agriculture. I have not seen it for myself. My interest in the site was unfortunately coincident with the rise of the Cártel de Sinaloa. Culiacán is the cartel's headquarters.[25]

So what I know of Culiacán comes from books and the advice of archaeologists of an earlier age, who knew the site. From books and conversations (Kelly 1945; J. Charles Kelley, personal communication), it appears that Culiacán's glory days came around 1450 and after, in the Late Postclassic—the era that ends with conquistadors. It had a history, of course, as the northernmost major center in the earlier Aztatlan Horizon of coastal city-states, which reached—directly? at removes?—the Southwest in the fourteenth and fifteenth centuries (e.g., Kelley 1986, 2000; Mountjoy 2001; Sauer and Brand 1932; Spence 2000). But it is in the sixteenth century, with the arrival of the Spanish, that Culiacán becomes what law enforcement might call a "place of interest." Helmut Publ (1985, 1990) compiled and critiqued colonial accounts, and he describes Culiacán's hegemony:

> Largest and most prosperous of all the provinces in the Aztatlan region, [it] was well known for its fine markets, wealth in precious metals and stones (e.g. gold, silver, turquoise), commerce, as well as a large population. . . . At the time of Spanish contact, Culiacán is said to have had 200 pueblos under its control . . . settlements as far south as Chametla recognized the chief (*cacique*) of Culiacán as ruler. . . . The northern boundary of Culiacán appears to have been the Morocito valley. (Publ 1985:122–123)

. . . or approximately 150 km from the capital, up and down the coast. (There you go again: 150 km of political reach.) The Spanish described a highly stratified society with kings, nobles, and commoners, totaling about 70,000 people in two hundred pueblos or towns, over an area of 12,000 to 13,000 sq km (about 5,000 sq miles; my calculation based on Publ's data)—in short, a polity comparable to

Chaco's 150 outliers and something under 100,000 people, but over a much larger area (see chapter 2).

If I'm right, Culiacán was the end of the line, from north to south. And, apparently, going the other way: from south to north. Culiacán was recognized by its Spanish chroniclers as the northernmost civilized city—shown prominently on an Ortelius map of 1603—on the Pacific coast. Culiacán was a real Mesoamerican (or rather West Mexican) city—nothing at all Southwestern about it. But Culiacán had a northern (i.e., Southwestern) connection, hinted at on antique maps. More than hints, actually—there's a map that walks us right through it in detail.

Alexander von Humboldt (1769–1859) was a Prussian scientist with a jones for geography. His travels took him to Latin America around the turn of his century (1799–1804) and resulted in a monumental, multivolume report of his findings. Among those was a surprisingly accurate map of the Southwest (Humboldt 1803: map of New Spain): "Carte Générale du Royaume de la Nouvelle Espangne dupuis le Parallele 16° jusqu'au Parallel de 38° (Latitude Nord)." This map is highly regarded by historians of cartography as the most accurate map of the West and Southwest to that time and for some time thereafter. The map's accuracy was remarkable because von Humboldt never actually visited the Southwest. He compiled his map in 1803 from maps and other holdings at *Real Seminaria de Meneria* and other archives in Mexico City: collections of new and ancient maps—possibly including Native maps—subsequently lost or dispersed by revolution and war.

Among the many natural and cultural features labeled on the map were three ruins noted as "home of the Aztecs" after they left Aztlan—the mythical homelands of many Nahua groups, including the Aztecs conquered by Cortés. (Von Humboldt identified the Great Salt Lake as Aztlan.) The first of the three was not a specific site, but rather an area south of the San Juan River and north of Hopi's latitude between the confluence of the Animas and San Juan Rivers and the confluence of the San Juan and the Colorado Rivers (I use today's names, not von Humboldt's). South of the San Juan, north of Hopi, east of the Colorado, west of the Animas: a large area, to be sure, but within that large area, the most prominent ruins were Chaco. Here the label says "Premiére demeure des Azteques sortis d'Aztlan en 1160. Tradition incertaine." The second ruin is clearly identified as Casa Grande, the fourteenth-century adobe tower now preserved under a magnificent tin roof, south of the Gila River near Phoenix. "Ruines des Casas Grandes [Casa Grande] Seconde demeure des Azteques d'oú ils passerent de la Tarahumara á Hueicolhuacan"; Hueilcolhuacan is clearly identified as Culiacán on another Humboldt map: "Culiacan l'Ancien Hueilcolhuacan." My translation: "Ruins of Casa Grande, second home of the Aztecs from where they passed through the Tarahumara to Culiacán." The Tarahumara (Ramuri) famously occupy canyons and barrancas of the eastern flanks of the Sierra Madres, traversed by the meridian. The third and final ruin—presumably from where his

Aztecs actually left the Southwest—is unquestionably Paquimé (he warns us not to confuse the two Casa(s) Grande(s), one on the Rio Gila and the other near "Yanos" or Janos; von Humboldt 1811, vol. 2:393–396). The label: "Casas Grandes Troisieme demeure des Azteques"—the third and final Aztec home, before they headed south to Culiacán, over the mountains and through the canyons of the Sierra Madres.

It's worth noting that his map does not show these four sites on the same meridian: latitude was easy, but longitude remained a challenge throughout the eighteenth century.[26] Colonial mapmaking—the basis of von Humboldt's map—was notoriously chancy. The position of Mexico City varied hundreds of miles from one map to the next. Von Humboldt—a gifted geographer—did much to rectify accuracy, but it's the history, not the planimetry, that matters here. Von Humboldt's map showed people moving north-south from what was probably Chaco to Paquimé (via Phoenix?), and from Paquimé to Culiacán.

You might say I'm loading a lot on one map. But this is not just one map: it was a compilation from formidable archives of old and older maps, and a collaboration with Mexico City's leading savants at 1800, when the city was rich and cosmopolitan—a city of palaces, they called it.[27]

Von Humboldt's map almost immediately became political: Zebulon Pike somehow obtained (and appropriated without acknowledgment) a copy for his explorations in 1806. The Mexican government circulated copies widely in the run-up to the Mexican War to demonstrate their claim on territories manifestly destined for their rapacious northern neighbor, those territories later taken by the United States in the Mexican War. A third- or fourth-generation derivative—the Disturnell map used in the negotiations ending that war—showed von Humboldt's Aztec homeland in the Southwest (encouraging modern Latino/a advocates for an American Aztlan). But in von Humboldt's time, the Mexican War was far in the future. In 1804 Mexico was the royal colony of New Spain, and Texas was largely innocent of Texicans. His presentation was scientific and historical, not political.

When the United States took New Mexico from old Mexico in 1846, occupation troops and federal officials were surprised by rumors of Moctezuma and Aztecs. Indeed, Moctezuma loomed then and now as a figure in Pueblo myth (e.g., Parmentier 1979). Through much of the nineteenth century, New Mexico was accepted or at least considered as a possible Aztlan—the mythic homelands of the Aztecs—by many scholars and much of the reading public. Then we nationalized New Mexico's prehistory. American scholars from pioneer archaeologist Adolph Bandelier (1882, 1890–1892) forward dismissed Aztecs and "Azteques" as garbled myths, imposed upon and repeated by gullible Pueblo Indians. Bandelier and others were motivated politically to show that Southwestern ruins were our ruins, not Mexico's.

Today these stories of Moctezuma and Aztlan are dismissed out of hand by modern scholars as imports, brought to Native New Mexicans by Native troops in the service of Spanish conquistadors, and then distorted and mythologized by simple Pueblo peoples. Like chiles: we have been taught that chiles came north with Coronado's Tlaxcalan auxiliaries. Surprise: there were chiles at Paquimé a century before the first Spaniards approached the Southwest (Minnis and Whalen 2010).

And, perhaps, Aztecs—of a sort. Spanish invasions and *entradas* have been framed by historians as playing out European worldviews and fables of the "Seven Cities of Cibola." The Seven Cities were European myth of lost tribes gone west, transferred to the New World. It's a constant leitmotif in histories of Spanish *entradas* into the north. But it seems that many (most?) conquistadors accepted and perhaps even favored Native accounts of Aztlan over Old World fables of Cibola's cities (as we shall see in chapter 4). With "Nueva España" and "Nuevo Leon," Spaniards named conquered regions for Old World places; "Nuevo Mexico"—also of course a Spanish name—presumptively proclaimed validity for Aztec histories.

Confusion comes from the word "Aztec." The name today is synonymous with the Mexica of Tenochtitlan and its empire, which fell to stout Cortés with eagle eyes and all his men in wild surmise. "Aztec," in fact, was an inclusive word, meaning people from Aztlan—and there were many. "Aztec" didn't mean only Mexica, the historical Aztecs; it meant anyone from the north, from Aztlan.

So: who were von Humboldt's Azteques? Perhaps the Aztecs of modern myth, but probably not. Possibly one of many Nahua peoples from the north, groups later conflated with Moctezuma's Mexica.

What should we make of these hints and allegations? The earliest Spanish accounts—to anticipate chapter 4—indicate an important trading route more or less due north out of Culiacán, over the mountains to the last great Southwestern city, Paquimé. Von Humboldt's compilation of old Mexican maps independently reports a movement more or less due south out of Paquimé, over the Tarahumara mountains to Culiacán—and makes it clear that the move south was of historical moment. Was Culiacán the last hurrah, the end of the meridian line? Or is Culiacán another beautiful fact, killed by an ugly theory? Sing the benediction: more research is necessary.

NOTES

1. "Uniquity" is a real word; you'll find it in *really* big dictionaries.

2. Trigger's version of urbanism has been adopted and developed by many currently researching cities, such as George Cowgill (2004), Michael Smith (2005, 2008), and many others.

3. Di Peso made a 13.1 percent adjustment for walls in his calculation; a similar adjustment brings the Chaco total down to about 58,600 sq m.

4. Using the very same data available to Whalen, MacWilliams, and Pitezel (2010), I thought Di Peso had a solid case for Big Paquimé (Lekson 1999). They brought nothing new to the argument but their interpretation. But, as always, I'm open to ideas. Maybe Paquimé was smaller. We'll never know until someone tests the eastern arm/not-an-arm, and that won't happen in our lifetimes.

5. An important caveat: some ethnographic accounts of Axcee on Mexico's northeast sound alarmingly Puebloan, with terraced houses.

6. While Chaco itself was spatially extensive, its major buildings (such as Pueblo Bonito and Chetro Ketl) originated the massed, terraced form later transformed into Pueblo towns; the big Chaco buildings may have been the icons of the Pueblo style (Lekson 1990a; Fowler and Stein 1992). But Chaco buildings were not farming villages; they were elite residences. If Chacoan forms are mirrored in modern pueblos, those forms have been radically repurposed, from palace to pueblo.

Up to 80 percent of the roofed space of buildings like Pueblo Bonito and Pueblo Alto lacked any evidence of domestic functions. They were probably warehouses, offices, monuments, or something else altogether, but the lack of living features indicates that they were not, in any useful sense, "pueblos." It was only after Chaco, in the twelfth and thirteenth centuries, that plateau towns assumed the apartment-like form that we today call "pueblo": tightly aggregated massing, terraced around a central enclosed plaza (Adler 1996; Morgan 1994). That happened first, of course, in Mimbres in the eleventh century (chapter 2), and Mimbres, as we shall see, is implicated in Paquimé's beginnings. What goes around comes around: Möbius logic.

7. Cordell (1984:273) gives it a sentence, and about the same in the 1997 edition; Vivian (1990) doesn't even mention it; Plog (1997:108) limits it to a couple of paragraphs. The north-south alignment of Alto and Tsin Kletsin was simply a curiosity. Today it's taken more seriously (Van Dyke 2003, 2004).

8. Sofaer (2007) calls this "lunar"; I call it "solsticial" (Lekson 2009:293 n. 136). The south-southeastern orientation refers to the way the building faces; it is the perpendicular of lunar standstill and/or solstice alignments—the two are within a few degrees, very close—of rear or stem walls.

9. But the Mound of the Cross did not monument a center axis, as at Chaco and Aztec. Recall that Paquimé may or may not have been U-shaped, like a PIV pueblo: Di Peso (1974) said it was; Whalen, MacWilliams, and Pitezel (2010) say it wasn't. Either way, the Mound of the Cross is "off center": not on the centerline of the U and not on the centerline of the western arm of the U—if Whalen, MacWilliams, and Pitezel are right, the city itself.

10. The cardinals are critical to all Pueblo world making (Dozier 1970:203–207; Ortiz 1972:204–207), except at Hopi, which until recently relied on solar directions (Heib 1979:577–578; Parsons 1996:365 n.). They define Pueblo place, ceremony, and worldview

with particular accuracy. "All peoples try to bring their definitions of group space somehow into line with their cosmologies, but the Pueblos are unusually precise about it" (Ortiz 1972:142). I do not offer this as retroactive, upstreaming "proof" of cardinality at Chaco; there's no particular relevance of modern Pueblo practices for events prior to 1300, when Pueblo society was very different. Rather, I suggest that the meridian continues, sublimated in modern Pueblo worldviews.

11. Adobe had a history in the Aztec area, including the earliest adobe bricks (Cameron 1998). Massive, poured-adobe walls also occurred at a Great House nearer Chaco: Bis sa'ani, a few kilometers northeast of the canyon. Bis sa'ani was a small Great House, dated to 1130–1140—just after construction ended in downtown Chaco and well into Aztec's heyday. Was Bis sa'ani an Aztec "outlier"? Perhaps, but the main point here is that Bis sa'ani was built principally of massive poured-adobe walls, with Chaco-style sandstone masonry on a few exterior walls (Breternitz, Doyel, and Marshall 1982). Massive adobe walls, much like Paquimé's, were used at Bis sa'ani by the early twelfth century.

12. Sandstone seems to have been the stone of choice, but Great Houses were built out of a range of materials: river cobbles, adobe, sandstone, petrified wood. Chaco went to great lengths to achieve particular forms, and they often went to great lengths to acquire materials. But they would sometimes build with what was at hand.

13. Also not making the trip were Great Houses—and those obnoxious elites and nobles.

14. Even the cacao jars of Pueblo Bonito were painted in local designs, or at least widespread designs, used at Great Houses and "unit pueblos." Dorothy Washburn, however, argues that "Chaco design systems may have come, in part, from Mexico into the Hohokam area before it moved northeastward to Chaco Canyon" (Washburn 2008:299).

15. The "buttresses" along the south wall of Kin Kletso and the west wall of Kin Bineola resemble, vaguely, the breeding pens of Paquimé. Neither are structurally convincing as "buttresses." The Kin Kletso example was excavated in 1934 with, unfortunately, no surviving notes about its contents (Vivian and Mathews 1964:44); I think that canyon lore would tell us, however, if the Kin Kletso "buttresses" were found full of macaw bones.

16. Very few copper bells have been found in the northern San Juan: one from Aztec (Morris 1919:100); one bell from Goodman Point near Cortez, Colorado (a large site with a Chaco-era component; Vargas 1995: table 5.1); two bells from the Shield Site (Hayes and Chappell 1962), a Chaco-era ruin very near Goodman Point; and a reported bell from Edge of the Cedars near Blanding, Utah (Vargas 1995:75), another large site with a Chaco-era Great House (Hurst 2000). There are a few others, unattested, floating around the Mesa Verde area. Compared with the numbers of bells from Chaco Canyon (about 25), the Mimbres region (about 25), or the Hohokam region (about 150), the Northern San Juan is cupricly challenged: very few bells from this most intensively investigated area.

There were more birds than bells. Salmon Ruins was planned in the late 1060s and finished by the early 1090s—Chaco's glory days—and excavations produced nine macaws (six as bird burials; Durand and Durand 2008:105–106). Macaws or parrots are frequently depicted on Mesa Verde Black-on-white pottery (Crown 1994:149) and Mesa Verde rock art. No birds have been recovered from the scores of Aztec-era (that is, Mesa Verde–era) sites excavated in the northern San Juan. Salmon and Aztec had what birds there were, and by Aztec's time, there weren't many.

17. One early objection to the Chaco Meridian was the distance involved, even on the short hop: Chaco and Aztec Ruins are about 85 km apart! When the idea of the Chaco Meridian was first presented, some of my colleagues objected that 85 km was a long way, too long for any serious prehistoric interactions—a distance crossing districts, provinces, even separate cultures and ethnicities. I'm not making this up: it happened repeatedly at conferences and in conversations when *Chaco Meridian* first came out. I have neighbors in Boulder, Colorado, who run 100 km in a day for fun (or so they say). Objections about 85 km being "too far" were silly then and largely but not entirely forgotten now.

18. The 15 km inner core—the zone of real political authority, according to Whalen and Minnis—is a half day's walk, there and back again; that is, a zone of potential daily face-to-face interaction. That's a community, not a polity. A polity is composed of many communities.

19. Paquimé had roads (Di Peso 1974) and an extensive line-of-sight signaling system (Swanson 2003), much like Chaco's.

20. Redrock was a place I once knew well—I surveyed the valley in 1974, and later analyzed collections from Paquimé's likely trading partner at Redrock, the Salado-period "Dutch Ruin."

21. Paul Minnis, who gave me the title of chapter 4, also planted a bad seed in a recent offhand comment. He asked, why isn't Cerro Juanaqueña on my meridian? Cerro Juanaqueña is a massively terraced hill on the lower Rio Casas Grandes that dates to about 1250 BCE; the terraces were residential, and the residents were farmers (Hard and Roney 2005). This is the "Early Agricultural period"—one of the most remarkable discoveries of the last two decades in Southwestern archaeology. And I have, elsewhere, claimed that Cerro Juanaqueña is the most remarkable of the known Early Agricultural period sites; indeed, I stated that Cerro Juanaqueña was the first monumental architecture in the Southwest (Lekson 2009:42–43). And it is, indeed, "on" the meridian (107°7'30'—about 15 km west of the Chaco midline). Dr. Minnis meant, I think, to cast doubt on the meridian, and my initial response was, well, Cerro Juanaqueña is far too early, 1750 years before Shabik'eschee. After thinking more about it, I'm not so sure. Cerro Juanaqueña is a spectacular, monumental site, visible for miles. In 1999 I mentioned Culiacán as a sort of odd, unlikely tease; now I think it's for real. Fifteen years from now, Cerro Juanaqueña might make the cut.

22. Make that "on or about on" the Chaco Meridian, which is perhaps 10 km wide. I've used 107°57'25" as the nominal longitude, but the "meridian" is really more smeary, as might be expected when the surveying equipment was a piece of twine and a rock plumb bob, viewed with a naked, uncorrected eye. My eye, at this point in life, is smeary too.

23. Regarding "interest," it's worth pointing out that Chaco, Aztec, and Paquimé are all World Heritage sites. Chaco brings Shabik'eschee and 423 to World Heritage status, on its coattails—and Aztec, too, as a "Chaco Protection Site"—they are all World Heritage (it's a long story). Mesa Verde is the only other prehistoric Southwestern World Heritage site, but it got in more on charm than merit: Mesa Verde is stunningly spectacular, but not particularly significant historically. Sacred Ridge and Blue Mesa are now under the waters of Lake Nighthorse and the tarmac of Animas County Airpark, respectively, and therefore precluded from World Heritage consideration (as far as I know, they weren't even on the National Register of Historic Places). Sacred Ridge had its fifteen-minutes-of-fame interest when word of some grisly discoveries—discussed below—reached the media. Along that line, Culiacán gets enormous amounts of media interest but for all the wrong reasons: the Sinaloa Cartel.

24. "It is absolutely true that Shabik'eschee is enormous compared to most other BMIII sites" (Wills et al. 2012:343), but maintained that it was the result of a hopping, popping, Brownian motion of small-scale, short-term use and reuse—just more of 'em. Small Basketmaker groups "shifted residential locales and agricultural fields easily and frequently within the canyon and its immediate tributaries in response to local inter-annual variation in hydrological conditions and natural resource patterning" (Wills et al. 2012: 328), and—as Wills points out—there were a *lot* of those small groups.

25. The Sinaloa Cartel is one of Mexico's most successful businesses, running a diversified portfolio of criminal activities. The cartel's successes, however, discourage fieldwork. A gray-blond monoglot gringo would not last long snooping through Culiacán cornfields—or so I'm told by those who know. I'm sure Culiacán is a lovely city for those who know its rules; but I don't. So I'm not going—despite a decade of nudging by my (supposed) friend, David Roberts, who knows no fear (Roberts 2015).

26. Britain's Longitude Prize for a functional chronometer, making longitude measurements possible, was awarded in 1765, only a generation before von Humboldt's travels in the New World.

27. Moreover, it's a map by von Humboldt. We don't hear much about von Humboldt in the United States because he barely visited here (stopping briefly to chat up Tom Jefferson), but in Europe and Latin America, von Humboldt is revered like a god, or at least respected as a protean intellect, the like of which they don't make anymore (e.g., Rupke 2008). Native America played foil—the noble savage—to the horrendous European wars that framed the Enlightenment. The humanists needed a model for good—absent the Church—and they invented ahistorical, natural humanity of the New World to fill that role. Von Humboldt—a scientist-humanist—traveled the continents and saw for himself. He questioned the Natives, he "avidly explored vestiges of American cultures in the archives of the viceroyalty" (Kutzinski and Ette 2012:xxvii),

and he decolonized Native American history: "Humboldt was among the very first to bring to Europeans' attention a library in which the former historyless objects of Europe's imperial gaze became subjects whose testimonies and testimonials provided other perspectives on the *conquista* and continue to do so today" (Kutzinski and Ette 2012:xxix). He did as we are adjured to do today: he took Native accounts seriously. *Ad hominem*, I know, but in this case, it's justified. Von Humboldt got some things wrong, but he got a lot more right—quite possibly the *Carte Générale du Royaume de la Nouvelle Espangne.*

4

A Beautiful Fact Killed by an Ugly Theory

Why, sometimes I've believed as many as six impossible things before breakfast.

—*The Red Queen*

The latest round of research at Chaco Canyon is the University of New Mexico's "Chaco Stratigraphy Project" directed by Patricia Crown and Chip Wills, which began in 2004 and continues in new directions today. While the results have not yet been published (Crown forthcoming), the findings are already remarkable (e.g., Crown and Hurst 2009). UNM's is the first major project at Chaco after a hiatus of almost two decades, when the National Park Service sponsored the Chaco Project, from 1971 to 1986.

I was involved in that earlier NPS work. The Chaco Project party line, in the early 1970s, explained Chaco as a Mesoamerican creation (Hayes 1981; Lister 1978). Changes in leadership brought changes in direction, and the new mid-1970s group (of which I was one) did not ratify our predecessors' free-trade agreement. What was all this loose talk about Mesoamerica? Where was it coming from? The obvious candidate for a Mesoamerican (or at least cadastrally Mexican) source was Paquimé, which burst upon the archaeological scene in Charles Di Peso's magnificent 1974 eight-volume report. Paquimé was a real contender.

Di Peso dated Paquimé to 1060–1340 (Di Peso 1974; Di Peso, Rinaldo, and Fenner 1974a:8–35); in the 1970s, the apex Chaco was dated from an undefined something or other in the ninth century to the last construction tree-ring dates at about 1125. Di Peso knew Chaco's dates, and in retrospect we can see he stretched his site's chronology back to its elastic limits, to argue for contemporaneity of

Paquimé and Chaco (Di Peso 1974:653): a six-decade overlap from 1060 to 1125. He didn't make up dates of course, but he accepted noncutting tree dates as real dates, and almost all of those dates were demonstrably too early. To get a uniform diameter for their beams, Casas Grandes carpenters shaved off the outer rim of the logs, and with it of course the outermost rings—which give you the date the tree was cut. Di Peso decided to ignore that problem, and in a way, you couldn't blame him: before his work there were no dates at all for Paquimé, and he had to use what he had at hand. Even today, tree-ring dates are few and far between in Casas Grandes archaeology, which consequently is being built on far less precise radiocarbon (14C) dating (discussed in appendix B).

Di Peso hinted that maybe Paquimé caused Chaco, but he hedged his bets by also suggesting that Chaco and Paquimé could have been the products of the same Mesoamerican *pochteca* explorer-merchants, or even—presaging my arguments in this book—wondering if "remnants of the Late Bonitian peoples, after abandoning Chaco, could have gone to Casas Grandes [Paquimé] about the time that the Paquimians began their urban renewal project" (Di Peso, in Di Peso, Rinaldo, and Fenner 1974a:211). Di Peso covered Chaco-Paquimé to win, place, or show in the chronological race. Mind you, these were all interesting ideas, if infuriating to Chaco archaeologists of that earlier age.

In the end, a local Chaco prevailed over Mexican expansionists. The triumph—if such it was—came not from Chaco data, but from the internal collapse of the Paquimé chronology. Di Peso's early dating of Paquimé (1060–1340) was almost immediately questioned (e.g., Lekson 1984c, among many others), culminating in Jeff Dean and John Ravesloot's dendrochronological restudy (1993:96–98). Dean and Ravesloot demonstrated that Di Peso's Paquimé chronology was simply wrong. By statistically projecting the missing rings, they redated Paquimé from no earlier than 1250 to no later than 1500—and warned that their analysis probably erred on the early side. The chronology of interaction had been turned on its head: Paquimé could never have caused or even affected Chaco, because Paquimé was least 100 years later than Chaco. We will return to Paquimé and its troubled timing later in this chapter (and see appendix B).

"It is no longer necessary to stretch the archaeological record to identify dubious parallels between Paquimé and Chacoan sites," said Dean and Ravesloot (1993:102). While specters of Mesoamerica still fluttered around the dark corners of the Chacoan world, the main contender—Paquimé—was knocked out of the ring. The result was a draconian devaluation of Di Peso. We still honor, in the breach, his monumental report—the book that launched a thousand snipes—with an endless series of critical term papers and devastating dissertations taking Di Peso to task. And, more importantly, after Di Peso died in 1982, a half-dozen follow-up field projects that corrected Di Peso's deficiencies, real or imagined, and added important new data to the corpus.

And so it stood. No one thought of Chaco and Paquimé together, except as anecdotal fodder for the history of the field. But Di Peso's throwaway speculation about Chaco "remnants" moving on south to Paquimé rose, phoenix-like, from the ashes of his old dead chronology. Maybe a group of Chaco people really did walk the long and winding road or, rather, the old straight track from Chaco to Paquimé. That might explain those pesky architectural features and parallels, described in chapter 3. That thought was one of many triggers for the first edition of *Chaco Meridian*.

And where was Aztec in all this brouhaha? Nowhere. Aztec never entered into Chaco-Paquimé discussions, despite its exotic name. "Aztec" appears repeatedly in the index of Di Peso's report, but almost exclusively in reference to the empire of Tenochtitlan. Only once does "Aztec" refer to the National Monument in New Mexico. Southwestern archaeology never took much note of Aztec Ruins. "Aztec Ruins" didn't even make the cut in Stephen Plog's (1997) Southwestern textbook, *Ancient Peoples of the American Southwest*; and in the first and second editions of Linda Cordell's (1984, 1997) *Archaeology of the Southwest*, Aztec appeared only as a historical footnote to the development of dendrochronology. It shows to better advantage in the third edition (Cordell and McBrinn 2012) as a Chaco "outlier"—Chaco's region was defined mainly in the early 1980s, too late for Linda's second edition—and as the "northern center of the post-Chaco era" (a kind nod to the first edition of *Chaco Meridian*).

Until very recently, Aztec can't get no respect—as the poet said. Aztec Ruins was first seen as a refugee colony fleeing Chaco, then as a minor Chacoan agricultural outpost (Lister and Lister 1987:86), or even as a Mesa Verde site with a small barrio of bedraggled Chacoans (Ferguson and Rohn 1987:155). In the mid-1980s, Jim Judge hinted that Aztec Ruins may have been something more: "I submit that there was a shift in the administrative and ritual locus from Chaco to the San Juan area, perhaps to either Aztec or Salmon" (Judge 1989:247).

People started paying attention, and beginning in the late 1980s a lot of good research got done—surveys, mapping, a lot more dendrochronology (e.g., Brown, Windes, and McKenna 2008; Stein and McKenna 1988). That new information changed our view of Aztec. It was not the last twitch of a dying Chaco, but maybe a major player in its own right. As we learned more and more about Mesa Verde, we discovered that there is nothing remotely like Aztec in the northern San Juan (i.e., Mesa Verde) region: its monumental construction is unmatched by any of the scores of large Mesa Verde villages to the west, most of which have now been carefully mapped and documented (e.g., Varien and Wilshusen 2002; Kohler and Varien 2012). Aztec was a big deal.

As noted in chapter 3, Aztec has far fewer exotics and goodies than Chaco: only a few macaws, a couple of bells, and not much turquoise. No one speaks of Aztec Ruins and Mesoamerica except to explain that its name was an early misnomer: no, the Aztecs didn't build Aztec Ruins. But with a new appreciation of size and complexity of Aztec's cityscape (Stein and McKenna 1988) and its dating (now greatly refined: Brown, Windes, and McKenna 2008), Aztec neatly filled the chronological gap between Chaco and Paquimé.

Chaco, Aztec, and Paquimé were north-south of each other, on approximately longitude 107°57'25"—the "centerline" of Chaco Canyon defined by the conspicuous alignment of Pueblo Alto and Tsin Kletsin (figure 2.10), the Chaco Meridian.

I say these three sites are on the Chaco Meridian, but—as discussed at length in chapter 3—they are not precisely on the same longitude. They are more or less on the meridian. The Chaco Meridian was a constructed feature or an event, or a series of events: not a geodetic line.

What does it mean to be "due north" of Chaco? The canyon spans about nine minutes of longitude from Una Vida to Peñasco Blanco (figure 3.18). Aztec Ruins is (really) due north of Penasco Blanco; Paquimé is (really) due south of the highest point on Chaco's South Mesa.

Picking points is an inherent difficulty in this line of work. I was a constant critic of archaeoastronomers at Pueblo Bonito, a semicircular building with radial walls and windows that, in plan, resembles a plastic protractor: look out Bonito's windows and you can span the entire northern sky; look back in and you pick up the southern half. There are lots of radial lines at Bonito, and there are lots of celestial bodies out there to align them with. Is it any surprise that Bonito's windows frame one star or the sun at a particular time? How could they not? With enough points, something will invariably line up with something else. The Fritz line—the line between Pueblo Alto and Tsin Kletzin—was a longitude Chacoans apparently cared about: so I went with that, 107°57'25".[1] But the meridian was less a line than a corridor, not just a length but a bit of width, too.

The fact that Chaco, Aztec, and Paquimé shared a meridian, with allowable errors, should not be at issue: it's on the map. But was that alignment intentional? I argue in this chapter that it was. Chapter 3 reviewed some remarkable similarities and parallels between and among these three ancient cities. Those shared features and details, found (in various combinations) at these three and nowhere else, suggest that *something* was going on. Here, I move beyond arguing for similarities and connections to questions of plausibility and meaning: questions of how and why.

To be clear, I am not testing hypotheses; I'm arguing a case. I present that case legalistically as means, motive, and opportunity. Could they do it, technically—means? Would they do it, ideologically—motive? Did they have the time to do it, chronologically—opportunity? Courtroom clichés, perhaps—standards of proof surely more appropriate for archaeology than "scientific certainty"—but my goal is to demonstrate, if not beyond reasonable doubt then by a preponderance of the evidence, that the Chaco meridian structured or tracked the political history of the Pueblo Southwest.

MEANS: "THEY DO THINGS DIFFERENTLY THERE"

Did Chaco, Aztec, and Paquimé possess the knowledge and technical ability to create a 720 km long alignment on a meridian?

The knowledge? Yes: I suggested in chapter 2 (and detail in appendix C) that Chaco knew the north well before the shift from Chaco to Aztec—thus, it was not a move, blindly, into unfamiliar country. This is fine-tuning an accepted story: we all accept that Chaco moved north of the San Juan, but I'm saying that movement began as early as 1020 (almost a century before Aztec Ruins), while most archaeologists place that expansion at 1075 or later (a few decades before Aztec Ruins) (see appendix C). And in chapter 2, I argued that Chaco knew the south: it was cozy with the Mimbres region, which included the site of future Paquimé. Again, the move southward—from Chaco or Aztec to Paquimé—was into new, but hardly unknown territory. They knew the turf.

The technical ability? Yes: that technology was demonstrated in the Great North Road linking Chaco and Aztec, and the north-south wall at Pueblo Bonito which a skeptical scholar (whose anonymity I honor) declared "the only real archaeoastronomy at Chaco." The wall is worth thinking about. It runs very, very close to true north (less than a quarter degree off north). The direction was clearly significant. The wall, as built, ran over the top of a deep, below-grade Great Kiva. Chaco architects carried the massive wall over the Great Kiva, like a chord across a circle, on several huge beams. Hundreds of tons of sandstone suspended across the kiva roof on telephone poles laid lengthwise. This was not ideal; it was not even wise. But it was, evidently, precisely what they wanted. The problem could have been avoided by deflecting the wall a degree or two off north. It was more important to run the wall due north, even with serious structural challenges; and that's what they did.

The Great North Road was even more remarkable. Chaco's roads were indeed phenomenal (Stein 1989; Lekson et al. 1988; Vivian 1997a, 1997b). Roads, where we can see them, were wide (ca. 9–10 m), remarkably straight, and carefully engineered with cut and fill and elaborate ramps or stairways at slope breaks (Kincaid 1983: chapters 6, 9). Roads fanned out from Chaco Canyon. The South Road runs south-southwest through the Chaco community of Kin Ya'a and to Hosta Butte—a major landmark for the southern San Juan Basin. The West Road (still under study) runs west-northwest toward a densely settled area around modern Newcomb, New Mexico, and perhaps on to a peak in the Chuska Mountains. And the North Road—best studied of all—runs north from Pueblo Alto to Aztec Ruins—to a city, not a mountain. From Aztec, a road shoots off to the northwest, vaguely toward Mesa Verde. Like everything at Chaco, the North Road is a subject of much debate, to which we return below.

In the 1980s, we thought that roads radiated out in all directions from Chaco, linking the center to its outliers. Outside the canyon, only a few roads have been fully studied—it is expensive to research a 60 km long site that, more often than not, is invisible on the ground. The North Road and the South Road received the closest scrutiny, and they were real (Kincaid 1983; Nials, Stein, and Roney 1987). At most outliers, we could see short road segments pointing back to Chaco or to the next outlier, and—given the reality of the North and South Roads—we assumed it was safe to "connect the dots" between those segments (Lekson et al. 1988).

Roads may not have worked that way. Most of the roads radiating out from Pueblo Alto (Windes 1987a) end—or, rather, are no longer visible—after only a few kilometers. John Roney revisited roads projected between prominent outliers and saw nothing (Roney 1992); he concluded therefore that roads—as projected—did not exist. It may have been sufficient to build a short segment pointing in the proper direction; that symbolic alignment did whatever roads were supposed to do. Over the longer hauls, start and end points were enough. But I wonder: are we asking too much for fairly ephemeral features, a thousand years in the wind and rain of northwest New Mexico? Even the most formal roads, such as the North Road, have gaps where we must infer continuity. That may be so for other roads, perhaps for most roads.

The Great North Road was, apparently, a product of later Chacoan times; based on dating of associated structures and ceramic scatters along its route, the North Road was built no earlier than the 1080s and more likely the early 1100s (Kincaid 1983; Sofaer, Marshall, and Sinclair 2008; Stein and McKenna 1988:57). The North Road (figure 4.1) begins at Pueblo Alto in Chaco Canyon and runs at about 15° east of north 3 km to Escavada Wash. At the Escavada, the road corrects course and runs north, deflecting back and forth slightly within an approximately 1.0 km wide corridor for about 50 km over rolling plains. It passes road-related Chacoan buildings at regular intervals—the most spectacular being Pierre's site, a complex of three small Great Houses and a high-point fire-signaling station. About 50 km north of Pueblo Alto, the road reaches the rim of Kutz Canyon, cut 200 m deep. And the fun begins. One school of thought (Marshall 1997) holds that the road ends there, with the depths of Kutz Canyon representing death and the underworld—that is, the road was symbolic, a road to nowhere. Another school of thought (mine, but not mine alone) argues that the road continued and did indeed go somewhere—first to Salmon Ruins, and ultimately to Aztec Ruins.

Up to the rim of Kutz Canyon, the North Road traversed mostly level lands, with only low ridges and a few small valleys breaking the line of sight. Kutz Canyon is very different: genuine badlands, a moonscape of deep clay canyons and precipitous cliffs. Interesting to look at, but I wouldn't want to walk across it. Cliffs and canyons, by and large, were no obstacle to Chacoan engineering; but they were not idiots. At Kutz Canyon, the road descended into the canyon via an

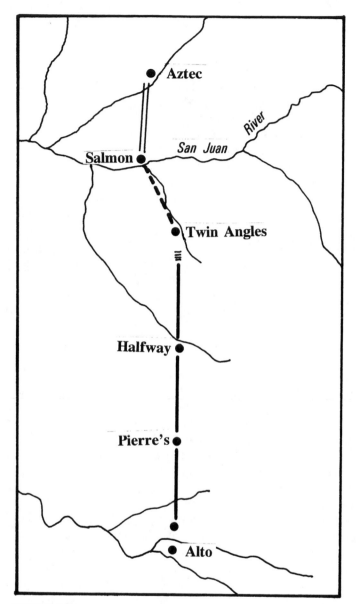

FIGURE 4.1

The Great North Road. The North Road was named "great" in reference to the famous Roman road running north through England. This map combines elements and information from Bureau of Land Management surveys (Copeland 2014; Nials, Stein, and Roney 1987), Solstice Project research (Sofaer, Marshall, and Sinclair 2008), Earl Morris's excavations (Carlson 1966), and my own observations. The North Road was not, of course, perfectly straight as shown here; it zigged and zagged, tacking through a series of slight deflections within a 1 km wide corridor. And it veered off to the northwest down Kutz Canyon; as explained in the text, claims that the road ended at Kutz Canyon are a canard.

elaborate wooden stairway (some of which is still there) and almost certainly deflected 20° west of north, following the relatively straight, relatively level bottom of Kutz Canyon Ruins. The bottom of Kutz Canyon has, of course, been heavily eroded over the last nine centuries.

About 6.5 km down Kutz Canyon, the road passed below a high fin, on which sat Twin Angels Pueblo, an outlier. Twin Angels (named for a two-pointed peak nearby) was almost exactly on the Chaco Meridian—in this case, just a happy coincidence, I think. Twin Angels Pueblo is an odd outlier (Carlson 1966); most outliers were central to communities of small unit pueblos (Lekson 1991), but Twin Angels sits in splendid isolation. There is no associated community, no reason for Twin Angels to be there, looking down into Kutz Canyon, except its positions along the North Road. Very much like Pierre's site, it was a road-related building, and it confirms the road even if we can't see the road on the eroded canyon. At the mouth of Kutz Canyon, the road reached the San Juan River, and immediately opposite, Salmon Ruins—a huge Chaco building, and Aztec's immediate predecessor. Salmon was the road's original destination, and the location of Salmon across from the mouth of Kutz Canyon was not a coincidence. (Möbius logic, I know, but a strong case nevertheless.)

The Kutz Canyon offset to Salmon Ruins puts the road a few kilometers west of its initial longitude at Chaco Canyon. From Salmon, the North Road almost certainly returned to north, running 16 km to Aztec Ruins (Stein and McKenna 1988:57). Today, this final segment is heavily impacted: the land between the two sites is a crazy quilt of well pads, pipelines, and service roads. There have been some sightings, however, and local archaeologists are confident that the North Road connects Salmon and Aztec Ruins (Copeland 2012).

Aztec Ruins, 85 km north of Pueblo Alto at Chaco Canyon, is less than 4 km west of the Chaco Meridian.[2] That's pretty good shooting for people working with naked eyes, a piece of twine, and a rock plumb bob—but not preternaturally good. This isn't amazing or astounding or fantastic: they could have done it. Indeed, they demonstrably did it; that's the beauty of the Great North Road. The road is not an archaeological interpretation or a logical inference; it actually exists on the ground. We can see it and walk on it. The North Road shows us, concretely, Chacoans could survey a long meridian line over broken terrain.[3] We know they did it, and we can speculate to some purpose on how. Only two specific techniques were necessary to survey the North Road: determining north and prolonging a line.

Determining north was easy—but not by reference to the polestar Polaris, which was well off celestial north in the eleventh through thirteenth centuries. A range of simple techniques are known for fixing the parallel (i.e., east-west) from a solar passage or the rotation of stars from horizon to horizon.[4] North was then set by the perpendicular of the east-west parallel. This process required no complex equipment. "For sighting and meridian determination, the [ancient]

Egyptians used a plumb bob, which was observed through a slit cut in the end of a palm leaf" (Multhauf 1985:57), and we can assume that Anasazi technology was at least that sophisticated—or maybe that simple.

Accuracy comes from repeated measurements: make repeated measurements and then average the results, by "eyeball."[5] The periodicity of the measurement is thus of some importance—how often can you repeat the measurement in a reasonable time? Unlike the annual cycles of solstices and eighteen-year-plus lunar standstills, north can be measured daily, indeed multiple times daily. Repeated observations of north were easy, so considerable accuracy could be achieved. Building orientations at Chaco Canyon were very precise for the meridian (less than one degree off at Pueblo Bonito, Hungo Pavi, and Tsin Kletzin) but far less accurate for proposed solsticial and lunar alignments, with their much longer observational cycles (Sofaer 1997).

It should be made very clear that it would not be possible for Chacoans to go to Aztec or to Paquimé and independently determine longitude from the stars or other landmarks. Determination of longitude was far beyond the technical capabilities of the New World (and Old, until relatively recently; Howse 1980; Sobel 1995). It was impossible to locate Aztec or Paquimé on the Chaco Meridian without actually staking out a north-south line, beginning at Chaco, and prolonging a line by visual alignment. That line could be surveyed, on the ground, by backsighting and foresighting on range poles or plumb lines—or something similar, a stick and a rock on a string. Experiments in naked-eye surveying at Chaco demonstrate that lines could be prolonged over broken terrain with remarkable accuracy, for example, about 1 m of error over 2 km (Rolf Sinclair and Anna Sofaer, personal communication, 1988). Surveying from backsight to foresight was simple and straightforward—until terrain blocked the backsight. Every ridge or valley would break the line of sight. Then it would be necessary to reestablish north and begin the process again—a problem that, as it turns out, actually increased accuracy (as described below).[6]

There was nothing complicated about laying out the North Road. A panel of astronomers and archaeologists concluded that only "simple technology—probably not a corps of engineers—was required to perform such tasks as aligning the roads" (Young 1987:231). I've suggested, in public, that a troop of Boy (or Girl) Scouts could lay out the North Road with three bamboo poles, a spool of twine, and a box of truck flares. (I've never actually tried this with Boy or Girl Scouts.) Surveying the North Road required time and patience—the Scouts might have passed from Cub to Eagle by the time they finally reached Aztec—but no technical equipment or esoteric knowledge.[7]

We can actually see this process in the North Road. The road, in some segments, runs very close to the true meridian (Kincaid 1983), but not along its entire length. From ridge to ridge, it tacks ever so slightly, back and forth within a corridor about 1 km wide. There were very slight changes of direction at each ridge line, each break in the line of sight, each place where it would have been necessary to reestablish north. And each time north was reestablished, the total error was reduced, because the error was essentially random—as many errors to the east as to the west. It was "self-correcting."[8]

The North Road where it descends into Kutz Canyon is less than 1' off the longitude where it began its meridian route at Escavada Wash—an error of a little over 1.0 km over a length of more than 50 km. The key to this accuracy was probably the breaks in the line of sight and the consequent need to repeatedly reestablish north and the line's direction. At least three and perhaps four ridge lines broke line of sight along the North Road's route. If the San Juan Basin was flat as a pancake, they might have made do with a single originating measurement, establishing north at Pueblo Alto and then running the line out 50 km. The first measurement, no matter how many times it was repeated and averaged, would almost certainly have had at least a small angle error. A small angle error would be negligible over a short distance, but over 50 km, a small angle becomes a large east-west displacement. So, many short segments are better than one long segment.[9]

What about the longer span from Chaco to Paquimé? Chaco and Paquimé are 630 km apart—thirteen times the distance of the North Road from Pueblo Alto to Kutz Canyon (figure 1.1). We can be pretty sure they didn't do it this way, but what if they backsighted north at Chaco and somehow prolonged that line, straight out; how bad would it be? The error observed on Chaco walls aligned on celestial phenomena—including solstices and lunar cycle—is typically no more than 2° (Rolf Sinclair, personal communication, 1996). An initial 2° angle error would create an east-west error of over 22 km if continued, or prolonged, over 630 km. But, in fact, the Chaco-Paquimé error was only 1 km. This accuracy was achieved because the Chaco-Paquimé line (like the North Road line) was broken up into many short segments. There are about a dozen major breaks in the line-of-sight between Chaco and Paquimé, and each required the reestablishment of north-south, and each introduced small, self-correcting random errors. Ridge lines divided—broke the line of sight and backsight—at approximately 50 to 60 km intervals; at each ridge, a new sighting measurement would have been necessary. Thus, the Chaco-Paquimé line required at least a dozen separate measurements for an equal number of segments of relatively equal length.[10]

Chaco and Paquimé are only about 1 km apart, east-west, in their meridians; that is, the east-west displacement or error is under 1 km over 630 km distance. That's good shooting; but is it unreasonably good? Given the necessity for reestablishing north at least a dozen times, a 1 km error is not astonishing. In fact, it is almost predictable. Formulas have been developed for calculating theoretical errors inherent in repeated measurements, such as segmented meridians. A formula for multiple "independent uncertainties" comes from John R. Taylor's *Introduction to Error Analysis* (Taylor 1982:52–59)—as explained to your mathematically challenged author by Professor Taylor himself, who must be held blameless for any subsequent misuse. All that is needed are the average angle error, the total length, and the number of segments. The likely error for naked-eye sighting at Chaco was typically no greater than 2°. Chaco and Paquimé were 630 km apart, with about a dozen segments of approximately equal length (see note 10). (For those following Taylor's text, I assume that the segments were of exactly equal length, without doing great injustice to topographic reality.)

Error for multiple-segment, "independent uncertainties" is a quadratic sum, rather than a simple sum; that is, the errors accrue as the square root of their summed squares, rather than directly. The theoretical error for a multiple segment model (based on formulas in Taylor 1982) for twelve measurements would be only about 6.7 km, a considerable reduction from the compounded 2° error of 22 km! And, of course, my estimate of the number of segments is minimal; the alignment may have incorporated many more segments, many more measurements, and thus an even smaller theoretical error.[11]

One kilometer offset between Chaco and Paquimé, still, is more accurate than the theoretical value of 6.7 km. Should this concern us? I think not: they got lucky. The theoretical error is, in fact, a statistical bell curve: a 6 km span about a mean, with the chances of 1 km error much higher than an error of 3 km. It is not remarkable that an error of 1 km was achieved on the first (and presumably only) attempt to trace this line on the ground. Had the error been 22 km, for example, we would have to consider nonrandom sources for error. A displacement of 1 km was fortunate, but not fabulous.[12]

We are constantly told that we should be amazed by the astonishing precision of ancient astronomies. And some of the Chacoan measurements were pretty good, by our standards. But why demand this of ancient Pueblo peoples? Why would they hammer themselves for accuracy? Indeed: how would they even know they were in error? They wouldn't; they couldn't. That's our concept, working with GPS and Google Earth, not theirs, measuring the sky with a rock dangling on a string. Remember, longitude was a mystery: they had no way of knowing what longitude they were on. Today, longitudes are measured as degrees west of the telescope in the old Royal Observatory at Greenwich, England; wise as they were, it's unlikely that the lords of Chaco knew about that.[13]

They had no way of knowing that there was any error to correct. Standing at Aztec or Paquimé, there was no way to judge how close or how far they were from the Chaco Meridian. They could only know that a line had been run, a deed had been done. (A ritual accomplished?) One line was probably fine—and, thanks to "independent uncertainties," they (almost) nailed it in one try.

North was the only real direction they had, the only useful direction. Polynesians could go across it and, with some rudimentary sextant work, more or less sail a latitude—as we measure these things. The Chacoans could go with it, north and south, and more or less line a longitude—as we measure these things.

Longitude is our measure; they were simply working toward or working away from north. A meridian, more or less.

MEANS (CONTINUED): "CAN'T GET THERE FROM HERE"

That seems pretty bold: marching off north, marching off south, blindly following a direction. Again: these people weren't idiots. I think the meridian led them into lands they knew, with varying degrees of detail.

Of course, they knew the Chaco-Aztec segment; it fell entirely within the old Chaco region. It's been argued (by my wife) that Chaco did not move north of the San Juan River before about 1075 (Cameron 2009). It's quite true that the boom in Chacoan building up north came after 1075; but at several key Great Houses, there are hints that Chaco arrived earlier, and often in the early eleventh century at places like Chimney Rock, Far View House, and Carhart (the northernmost outlier) (see appendix C). In brief: Beams dating to the 1010s and 1020s were reused in later (1075) buildings. Chacoans did not take wood lightly. They used exactly the wood they wanted. For whatever reason, they wanted those early beams reincorporated into the later Great Houses. I think that reason was an earlier structure, an early presence at those northern locations; that is, Chaco was north of the San Juan (in some form or other) and knew the territory by the early eleventh century. (See appendix C.) Moreover, things—*something*—had been happening back and forth on this approximate longitude from as early as 500 at Shabik-423 and Sacred Ridge–Blue Mesa, for five centuries before Chaco moved north to Aztec. The northern, Chaco-Aztec segment was Chaco's turf, long before the move.

But the long stretch from Chaco south to Paquimé seems like new territory, for archaeology if not for the ancients. It crosses an important line in the sand, the line between Anasazi and Mogollon, two regions you'll find in every textbook. I gave up on that distinction some time ago: Chaco and Mimbres Mogollon make more sense as an ensemble than as two discreet units (chapter 2). (One critic's main complaint was that the Chaco Meridian was impossible because Chaco was Anasazi, while Paquimé was Mogollon, and therefore they could not be related; Vivian 2001.)

The meridian route from Chaco to Aztec spanned 630 km of mountain ranges, hills, plains, and valleys. What knowledge of that long span would Chaco or Aztec have? Recall that the meridian could only be surveyed *from* Chaco *to* Paquimé; the reverse was technically possible. It would be convenient for my argument if Chaco (and, thus, Aztec) knew something about the sunny south before they took off in that direction.

Looking south from Chaco, the first 250 km lies within the Chacoan region; whatever the Chacoan regional system was or was not, we can be reasonably certain that the first 250 km was known to Chaco and presumably to its successor

Aztec. During the Aztec polity's last decades, the southern half of the old Chaco world was booming. Great House societies continued for several decades, and then they were replaced by enormous pueblos, built, abandoned, and rebuilt in an unbroken historical chain that leads to the modern pueblos of Zuni and Acoma. The Chaco Meridian runs right down the traditional "boundary" between Zuni and Acoma territories—archaeological and modern (Ferguson and Hart 1985; Ruppe 1953)—an interesting fact, considering their traditional histories (discussed later in this chapter). So the first third of the meridian would have been familiar territory.

Less than 100 km separates the southern edge of the Chaco region from the northern borders of Mimbres.[14] In chapter 2, I put forth the proposition that Chaco and Mimbres were pretty cozy. The eleventh-century Mimbres region (figure 2.12) encompasses the final, southernmost 300 km of the Chaco-Paquimé meridian, including the site of yet-to-be-built fourteenth-century Paquimé. Mimbres was incorporated to some faint degree into the Chacoan world, or at least knew some things about the Chacoan worldview. Chaco and Mimbres were, at the very least, on the same trade circuits, allied (and aligned) as trade partners. Even if much of the terrain was terra incognita, routes between Chaco and the Mimbres Valley must have been well known (and probably well beaten) in the eleventh century.

To reach the Mimbres Valley, the meridian crossed the west flanks of the rugged Black Range—one of our very earliest "wilderness areas" and it's easy to see why. It's tough country and not a route we'd expect people to take. Likely routes, for us, would follow river valleys (our typical guess for ancient trade routes). But those would be far to the east along the Rio Grande, or far to the west, up the Gila River, over a low divide to the San Francisco River Valley, and then upstream to the Plains of St. Augustine (Kelley 1986; Riley 1976, 1995: map 10). Both routes were later followed by Spanish, Mexican, and territorial roads. That's how we'd do it. But . . . we are thinking of carts and horses and, later, cars and trucks.

I call this "Sauer's error": Native routes necessarily followed rivers. The great historical geographer Carl Sauer, in his seminal study of *The Road to Cibola*, used European logistics to reconstruct Native routes: "Men on horses had the same need of saving distance, of finding easy passes and stream crossings, and of food and drink, that directed the Indian's travel afoot. Footpaths and pack-trails rarely differ" (Sauer 1932:1). But anyone who has seen Jackson Staircase at Chaco Canyon knows that the only way a horse goes up that incline is in pieces. Pueblo trails and Chaco roads were not equine friendly. Why would they be?

Sauer, and all who followed him, assumed that colonial roads ran along the principal precolonial, prehistoric trade routes, and a few did. But Native routes didn't need to follow rivers because Indians didn't have horses and carts; they had feet and knew how to use them. Straight up the side of a cliff, for example, at Jackson's Staircase—and a thousand other stairs and steps hammered into the living rock of Four Corners' cliffs. Sauer didn't recognize that a porter not only can go places a horse or cart cannot, but he also has radically different requirements for "food and drink" than a horse. A porter can pack a lunch, carry a canteen. Consequently, Indian trails went straight over mountains and molehills. Chaco roads favored straightness over ease. When a Chaco road hit a cliff or break in terrain, it didn't go around, or take an easy grade in switchbacks. The road went straight up on stairs, ramps, or whatever. Chaco roads were charged with symbolism, true; but they were designed for pedestrians.

A straight route over the slopes of the Black Range, between Chaco and Mimbres territory, would be impressive—but perhaps not unprecedented. Indeed, when we look at the modern map, a road runs through the west flanks of the Black Range, closely paralleling the Chaco Meridian. It's an old road, probably from the nineteenth century if not earlier. Its current and historic name is the North Star Road—which pleases me very much![15]

Mimbres knew Chaco, Chaco knew Mimbres, and post-Mimbres and post-Chaco (i.e., Aztec) probably remembered it all—perhaps not fondly. The Mimbres Valley was more or less abandoned after 1150 (chapter 2). In the thirteenth and fourteenth centuries, the Mimbres Valley and the deserts into which it flows were occupied by post-Mimbres populations that continued the Mimbres line, if not the Mimbres fashion. Ideologies and material culture changed, but memories—good or bad—of both Mimbres and Chaco would remain.

To summarize: Chacoans demonstrably could survey accurate meridians over long distances with broken terrain. We can see (and measure) their accuracy in the north-south wall at Pueblo Bonito and the Great North Road. Following the meridian from Chaco to Aztec or from Chaco to Paquimé would not require complex technical achievements. Moreover, they were almost certainly long familiar with the routes. The Chaco Meridian traversed well-known country. It did not boldly go where no man had gone before—or no woman, itinerant merchant, or priestly delegation. They had the tools. They had the talent. All they needed was a reason.

MOTIVE (1): "ROADS THROUGH TIME"

Chacoan roads are enigmatic: no wheeled vehicles, no beasts of burden, no bulk transport other than porters. Why a road? Porters walk in line, single file. There was no obvious practical reason to construct 10 m-wide freeways where a foot path would suffice. Chacoan roads climbed up steep slopes when easier, porter-friendly alternate routes were close to hand. There are places—in Chaco and elsewhere—where a road cuts a broad stairway straight up a cliff, and 100 m further along, a line of hand- and toeholds winds its way up the same slope. What are we to make of this? We can probably conclude that Chacoan roads served purposes beyond (but including) pedestrian travel.

The North Road, like other Chacoan roads, was originally interpreted as a transportation corridor, analogous to modern roads (Ebert and Hitchcock 1980). This was not a foolish projection of present into past: bulk goods (construction timbers, pottery, and probably corn) were transported into Chaco Canyon from distant sources. Logistics would have been important. We don't know if bulk goods followed roads or if they moved along trails—easier to walk but harder to find archaeologically.[16]

Perhaps it was not goods, but people. There are situations in which people move in clumps or groups; suggestions range from pilgrim processions going into Chaco (Judge 1989; Malville and Judge 1993; Malville and Malville 2001), to troops marching out (David Wilcox, quoted in Roberts 1996:98), to royal processions visiting the provinces (Lekson 2009). All are possible.

Roads were architecture, not infrastructure. They had symbolic value, perhaps more important than any pedestrian use (e.g., Roney 1992). The North Road, discussed above, has been interpreted as nonfunctional: a purely "cosmographic expression" of spiritual or mythical values (Marshall 1997; Sofaer, Marshall, and Sinclair 2008). That interpretation proceeds from the premise that the North Road had "no clear practical destination" (Sofaer, Marshall, and Sinclair 2008:374)—a road to nowhere, ending at Kutz Canyon (figure 4.1). That's wrong—as hopefully demonstrated above—but still a very interesting idea, recognizing monumentality in roads.

The North Road was not a road to nowhere; it was a road from Chaco to Aztec via Salmon Ruins. But it was indeed a monument. There's something odd about the chronology of its termini: Large-scale construction at Chaco Canyon ended about 1125. Salmon Ruins rose about 1088, and building began at Aztec about 1110—as detailed in a following section. The North Road—far more difficult to date than the buildings it connects—may have been built between the late 1080s and the early 1100s (Kincaid 1983; Sofaer, Marshall, and Sinclair 2008)—that is, during the planning and initial construction at Salmon and Aztec. If so, the road did not connect two existing places; it connected an old place with a new place, an *emerging place*.

At several well-studied locations, Chacoan road segments connect noncontemporary, sequentially built Great Houses and post-Chaco pueblos (Fowler and Stein 1992). In Manuelito Canyon near Gallup, New Mexico, a road links a Chacoan Great House (ca. 1050–1150) to a post-Chaco Great House (ca. 1150–1250) about 3.75 km away; and a second segment spans the 3 km distance between the post-Chaco Great House and a larger, even later pueblo ruin known as "Big House" (ca. 1250–1325). Roads connect noncontemporary things, sequential things. That pattern has been found at a number of widely separated districts, from Mesa Verde to east-central Arizona (Fowler and Stein 1992:116–118).

John Stein and Andrew Fowler call these "roads through time," "time bridges, symbolic umbilicals that linked one age to another" (Fowler and Stein

1992:117). "Roads through time" commemorated the historical linkage between Chaco Great Houses and post-Chaco formations. They showed, on the ground and at some expense, that B did indeed come from A. They legitimized the ritual and social roles of post-Chaco Great Houses and pueblos by a material, landscape reference back to Chaco's mythic or historic power. At the local scale, those linkages spanned distances of 2 to 6 km; but roads through time could cross longer spans. I think the Great North Road was the longest, linking Chaco and Aztec capitals of different eras—an interpretation first offered by Fowler and Stein (1992:119). The North Road was not merely a transportation corridor for beams, troops, or pilgrims—although these may have moved along the road. It was a monument.

MOTIVE (2): DIRECTION AND DISTANCE

In chapter 3, North was presented as the only fixed direction—or at least the most useful fixed direction. Other celestial bodies moved: sun, moon, and planets all swung back and forth or wobbled erratically. The stars themselves revolved around the "heart of the sky." North alone did not move. Other celestial landmarks were long known: the solstices, obviously; lunar standstills; and so forth. But those directions were periodic, seasonal, even generational (the standstills were 18.6 years), and had to be brought down to earth and pinned to peaks or lined by walls. "Celestial landmark" may seem a contradiction in terms, but it exactly describes how the ancients knew the heavens: not with declinations and ascensions, but on horizon calendars—peaks and notches on the horizon where celestial events rose or set. For example, Chimney Rock's twin pillars, between which every 18.6 years the moon rose at standstill. Celestial landmarks only worked for specific vantage points. Unless you were standing at or on the Great House, Chimney Rock's pillars wouldn't work. North wasn't like that: it was available everywhere, every night, for everyone.[17]

North is obvious, with south its obvious reverse. Can't have one without the other. But . . . why head south? Why didn't they just keep moving north? A simple explanation: north of Aztec are the Rocky Mountains. But consider the deeper history presented in chapter 3: they moved north twice. First from 423-Shabik at Chaco to Sacred Ridge–Blue Mesa; that ended in slaughter. So they moved south, back to Chaco. Then they moved north again, from Chaco to Aztec; that ended in violence, collapse, and total abandonment of the region. North wasn't working out so well. I've been told by Pueblo people that in their southward migrations, it wasn't that south was the prescribed direction; it was that north was actively bad, literally the wrong way to go. Perhaps they were remembering their history.

For Chaco's nobles, it wasn't just that north was two times bad. There was more to the south than simple course correction. South was also a move closer to the high civilizations of Mesoamerica.

North (and south) were available and powerful. Powerful for what? What did the meridian mean? I present two possibilities: (1) positional legitimation and (2) moving accurately in a direction. In the first edition of this book, I argued for "positional legitimation": alignment with a prior center legitimized the successor center. I still like this, but I'll also offer a simpler alternative, "moving accurately in a direction": leaving a center and moving either north or south to establish a successor, because north (and its converse, south) were the most useful directions to follow.

First, positional legitimation. Meridian alignment with Chaco somehow legitimized Aztec and Paquimé by reference to the historical and (later) mythical past, using Chaco's own remarkable spatial language. Legitimation by reference to a real or mythic past is a common strategy in emerging political formations. "New developments are more secure when they are invested with the authority of the past" (Bradley 1993:116). The socially ambitious claim association with larger-than-life, never-to-be-equaled pasts. Think of the New World's ultimate social climbers, the Aztecs who helped themselves to mythic/historic Tollan/Tula and the ruins of even earlier Teotihuacan.

In noncartographic, nonliterate societies, place and landscape have an immediacy and importance they lose when reduced to two dimensions on a map (e.g., for the Southwest, Basso 1996). Landscape features, celestial phenomena, and the very directions themselves have a potential for meaning we can probably never recapture on maps or in texts. Chaco, Aztec, and Paquimé may have used directional symbolism for key social and political ends. Other societies do this. Cuzco's *ceques* radiated out to Inca dependencies and borders; a strong case has been made for one *ceque* running about 300 km linking Cuzco to Tiahuanaco, a form of positional legitimation (Zuidema 1982:439). On an even larger scale, Islam's 900 million adherents—from Java to the Horn of Africa—oriented themselves, their places of worship, and their worlds to the Black Rock of the Ka'ba in Mecca. Each mosque has a niche (or other indicator) that points toward Mecca, the alignment called *qibla*. They did this in medieval times without complex surveying technologies, but with remarkable accuracy. Of course, they had sophisticated mathematics and the beginnings of geodesics.[18]

Chaco, as an event, became the stuff of myth and history.[19] It could not easily be forgotten—Chaco transformed the ancient Southwest and set trajectories that carried Pueblo peoples through the thirteenth, fourteenth, and fifteenth centuries. Chaco Canyon, as a place, must have retained enormous ideological and political importance. Any new political formation on Chaco's scale would have to address the historical fact of Chaco—Kubler's prime object (chapter 2)—and either appropriate or reject that first center's memory. "Images of the past commonly legitimate a present social order. It is an implicit rule that participants in any social order must presuppose a shared memory" (Connerton 1989:3). Chaco was everywhere, and everywhere people must have remembered Chaco—it was a shared memory, like a great comet or a volcanic eruption or the Beatles on Ed Sullivan.

First Aztec and then, more distantly, Paquimé appealed to Chaco's memory for validation, through repetition (or appropriation) of Chacoan architectural symbols (colonnades, mounds, massing, cardinality, roads, etc.), but even more through physical alignment via prolongation of the Chacoan regional geometry. The North Road, a road through time that continued the old axis mundi of Chaco, was projected south beyond the Colorado Plateau into the Chihuahuan Desert. The Chaco Meridian was both the mechanism and manifestation of positional legitimation. Alignment between the new (Aztec, Paquimé) and the old (Chaco) demonstrated these connections both actively and passively: by the act of alignment, and by monuments such as the North Road and the Mound of the Cross.

There's my second, less elaborate alternative: the alignment of Chaco, Aztec, and Paquimé (and the earlier and later centers discussed in chapter 3) could have resulted from another mechanism, less *outré* than a *qibla* or a *ceque* or a ley line. The alignment we see on the map could have resulted from the (comparatively) simple act of *moving in a direction accurately*. We know that Chacoan designers could determine cardinals with accuracy comparable to other naked-eye astronomers. If their intent was to go north and then south, and precision was a concern, the result would have been three points on a meridian—the four-point problem, approximately. In this scenario, the direction *back to* the starting point is less important than the direction *away from* the starting point—and the results are exactly the same. Recall Ortiz's comment on the precision of Pueblo directions. This is, I'm told, especially true of ritual and ceremony. Establishing the direction of movement may have been a daily ritual—repeated measurements! They were told to go north or south, and they did so with great care, with unusual precision. Moses had a pillar of fire; Chaco had the Heart of the Sky.

Moving accurately in a direction is an alternative to *positional legitimation*. Both would produce the observed data: three sites more or less on a longitude. Meridian alignment back to Chaco would legitimate successor centers, like a *qibla* to Mecca. But simply leaving Chaco and walking north, leaving Aztec and walking south—accurately—would create the same pattern. Occam's razor is one of the most abused nostrums in the social sciences (second, perhaps, only to Zipf's principle), but if simplicity makes complex histories easier to swallow, then dress the meridian in directional accuracy—and hold the *qibla*.

In either case—positional legitimation or moving in a direction accurately—the act itself was probably as important as monuments. The procedure of alignment, while technically simple, must have been a major, memorable event. It required coordination of labor over large areas and considerable time—perhaps decades. Recall my aging Boy Scouts: the Chaco-Paquimé alignment would have taken a considerable length of time and, with attendant pomp and ceremony, it would have been a remarkable performance for all Southwestern peoples to see. Chaco was nothing if not showbiz. There was little that was modest or subtle about Chacoan architecture. Great Houses were typically built on the high ground, to see and be seen, visually dominating the land around them. Imagine the effect of a procession marching for months south from the ancient city of Chaco, cutting trees for lines of sight, lighting flares and bonfires for backsights, performing ceremonies and rituals, until they arrived at the Casas Grandes Valley. This is the place.

Everybody in the Southwest knew about Chaco in its heyday, directly or by rumor; and everybody would have known about the monumental operations of meridian alignment. There were sound political reasons for public display during the process: the point of legitimation is not simply to comfort the rulers, but to convince and persuade the ruled. The meridian was a giant "road through time," remarkable only for its scale.

OPPORTUNITY: "HOW CAN YOU BE IN TWO PLACES AT ONCE . . . ?"

"How can you be in two places at once, when you're not anywhere at all?" That 1960s acid-vaudeville tag not only dates your author; it describes the chronological conundrum of archaeologists trying to make sense of Chaco and Paquimé. Chaco is pretty well dated—indeed, it is perhaps the best-dated prehistoric archaeological site in the world, with thousands and thousands of tree-ring dates. Paquimé, because it was unexplored until the 1960s, was more of a mystery. Charles Di Peso stretched the Paquimé tree-ring dates to make Chaco and Paquimé contemporary, or very nearly so. He dated Paquimé (and the Medio period, height of Paquimé's prosperity) from 1060 to 1340. The beginning date of 1060, of course, was Chaco boom times. Contemporaneity made sense to Di Peso (and others), given the remarkable parallels between those two major centers (chapter 3). But he stretched it too far, things snapped, and his chronology was shattered by remorseless reanalysis. As discussed above, Dean and Ravesloot's (1993) redating revealed that Chaco (900–1125) was more than a century older than Paquimé (1250–1450). More recently, Michael Whalen and Paul Minnis (2003, 2009:67–70) have argued that, while Paquimé itself postdated 1250 and probably 1300, the Medio period began much earlier, at 1200 or even as early as 1160. Not so much of a stretch as Di Peso, but still a long reach back. Poor Paquimé! Her suitors insist she's older than she is. She's antique, to be sure a *grande dame*, but not so old as they'd have her. It's possible that the Medio period began at 1200 with a century run-up to Paquimé at 1300. Rome wasn't built in a day. But I believe that the run-up was only a few decades at most, with the Medio fun beginning mid-thirteenth century and the full-on Casas Grandes phenomenon— and the city of Paquimé—kicking in around 1300 (see appendix B).

The Chaco-Paquimé dates have changed (several times), but the parallels remained, suggesting connections across that century gap. Di Peso was right: Chaco had *something* to do with Paquimé, or vice versa. How to cross that missing century, from the end of Chaco at 1125 to the beginnings of Casas Grandes (the culture) around 1250? That was a problem when I began to rethink Chaco and Paquimé, many years ago. A series of new dates from Aztec and a new realization of Aztec's scale and importance—work described elsewhere in this book—filled the gap. Aztec, once dismissed as a secondary or refugee site, emerged as the New Chaco—and perhaps the chronological, political, and geographic transition from Chaco to Paquimé.

Construction at Aztec began as the last burst of major construction was ending at Chaco. It's clear now that Aztec was the premier site in the northern San Juan area (including the Mesa Verde region) from 1110 through about 1275. Several other very interesting things coincide, approximately, with that end date at 1275: the beginning of the twenty-five-year-long "Great Drought," the final depopulation of the Four Corners, and the beginning of the Medio phase (ca. 1250?), leading to construction at Paquimé around 1300.

With the addition of Aztec, the meridian chronology works quite well: Chaco, Aztec, Paquimé—bing, bang, boom—in tight sequence. There is one interesting anomaly: Salmon Ruins.

Salmon Ruins is a Bonito-class building (figure 3.3), at a key angle in the Great North Road where it swung north to Aztec Ruins. The vast bulk of Salmon Ruins dates to a fairly tight span from 1085 to 1095, with some major construction through the 1100s (Reed 2006). A cluster of earlier dates around 1070, however, suggest either an earlier small block of rooms later incorporated into the 1085–1095 structure, or reuse of beams from an earlier, probably Chacoan building—a starter-kit Great House. (There may have been similar situations, almost a century earlier, at Chimney Rock, Far View, and even Pueblo Alto: a small Chacoan building preceded larger, later Great Houses, and their wood was very intentionally reused in the later, larger buildings; appendix C.) Be that as it may, Salmon Ruins was built during boom times at Chaco. As, indeed, was Aztec Ruins: construction at Aztec began about 1100, with most of the site completed by 1125—a decade and a half of intensive construction. (It must be emphasized that Aztec Ruins was the single biggest Chacoan construction project ever; not a society on the skids, but Chaco at the height of its organizational and administrative power.) So it's not: Chaco ends, Aztec starts. It's more: Chaco's roaring along and starts Aztec while it can do big things. Making hay while the sun shone—or rather, while the rain fell. The shift from Chaco to Aztec was carefully thought out and planned, not an escape from the canyon one step ahead of angry peasants.

There's probably overlap from Aztec to Paquimé, too; they didn't turn out the lights, lock Aztec's doors, and immediately receive the certificate of occupancy for Paquimé. Paquimé was a very cosmopolitan meeting of West (and probably central) Mexican and Chacoan nobles and elites, with a commoner population of local people joined (swamped?) by in-migrating Mimbres and south Chihuahuan populations. The bright lights of the big city drew wise guys and rubes from miles around.

The city itself was almost certainly built around or more likely after 1300 (Lekson 1984c; Whalen and Minnis 2009), but there may well have been a run-up. The run-up is the rub. As discussed at length in appendix B, recent chronological issues with Paquimé have to do with the Medio period's beginning. In brief: Paquimé was the jewel in the crown of the Medio period (nominally, 1250–1450). The Medio period was preceded by a simpler and sparcer Viejo period (nominally, 700 to 1150). You'll notice a century's gap between the two; that gap, too, is nominal. The terminal dates for the Viejo period come almost entirely from the dating of Mimbres Black-on-white, which is found in Viejo contexts. The conventional wisdom has Mimbres ending about 1130 or maybe as late as 1150. It's possible, of course, that Mimbres pottery was made after 1150 by Mimbres migrants in the Casas Grandes Valley. In fact, I'd kind of like that, since I think most of Mimbres moved to northern Chihuahua (chapter 3), perhaps keeping their ceramic traditions alive a few decades after everyone else gave up.

As recounted in chapter 3, we need to bring in people from somewhere to build Paquimé and its polity. Mimbres, other parts of Chihuahua, wherever; the Viejo period population does not seem to be in place pre-Paquimé to fill the Rio Casas Grandes Valley and northern Chihuahua during the Medio period—which is what happened. It went from a quiet backwater to one of the most densely settled regions in the greater Southwest.

Chihuahua still lacks the detailed demographic data that drives cyber-Anasazi models. But it's clear that at the peak of the Medio period, there must have been several tens of thousands of people living in the central Casas Grandes area (Lekson, Bletzer, and MacWilliams 2004). The basic demographic question is: Were there enough late Viejo period people to create the densely settled Casas Grandes Valley of the Medio phase? Probably not.[20]

I'm sure the Casas Grandes Valley was not an entirely "empty niche"—that's just an expression I've used from time to time, not to be taken literally.[21] There were Viejo period settlements before the Medio period—but maybe not many. Di Peso thought that Viejo period sites were thin on the ground, and I fear that there is little in the recent surveys around Paquimé to contradict that conclusion.

Whatever the size of Viejo period populations—and it's got to be more than we now know—it cannot be stated too strongly (since many people seem to miss this point) that the Chaco Meridian never involved the wholesale migration of tens of thousands of people from the Anasazi area into Chihuahua. No, I suggested in the first edition and repeat here that several hundred elites or nobles—less than a thousand?—made the journey to the Rio Casas Grandes Valley, joining many thousands of *other* in-migrants from nearby areas (specifically the Mimbres and post-Mimbres; see chapter 3), and it's likely that denser Viejo populations in southern Chihuahua (Kelley et al. 1999, 2004; Stewart et al. 2005) added much to the mix—there is an undeniable local cast to Casas Grandes that subsumed most but not all of the outside machinations.

Chihuahua is decades away from the demographic detail that archaeologists now take for granted in the Four Corners states, so arguments for continuity or discontinuity remain just that—arguments. But even absent data, Chihuahua archaeology could be informed by news from the north. With the enormous research investment in the Four Corners states, we have come to realize that movements, migrations, periodic abandonments, "fallow valleys," and reoccupations were *typical* and not extraordinary. Nobody developed *in situ*, jogging in place from simple bands to more complex societies. People marched in and out of the Four Corners for as long as people lived there. A long uninterrupted sequence in place is extraordinary, not the default option. Why would Chihuahua be different?[22]

The Medio phase was supported bottom-up by local people, taking a very broad view of "local," but it was created by elites and nobles, top-down. Shaman-priests or would-be kings, the upper classes almost certainly considered themselves different and distant, engaging ideologies and exchanges and probably even travels from and to faraway places: Chaco or Mesoamerica. Consider the flamboyantly extroverted nature of Paquimé itself: of all the many wonderful places in the ancient Southwest, Casas Grandes seems least likely to be a *truly local development*. However Casas Grandes began, it certainly did not live locally once it was going strong. It thought globally and acted globally.

In summary, opportunities: the chronologies of Chaco, Aztec, and Paquimé allow the proposed movements up and down the Chaco Meridian: bing, bang, boom—Chaco, Aztec, Paquimé.

CLOSING ARGUMENTS: "HIGH CRIMES AND MISDEMEANORS"

Chaco-Aztec-Paquimé planners had means (engineering and terrain knowledge); motive (roads through time, positional legitimation, moving accurately in a direction); and opportunity (sequential chronology) to design and produce the Chaco-Aztec-Paquimé alignment—that is, to commit the Chaco Meridian in the 108th degree. That's the state's case, and the state rests. Now we cross the aisle and mount a defense: it's all just a coincidence. The defense rests.

Coincidence

The alignment of Chaco, Aztec, and Paquimé could be pure chance. Circumstantial evidence alone cannot leap that hurdle: we will always arrive back at the beginning of the Möbius strip. Surely, dots on a map are *testable*. What are the statistical probabilities that the alignment of Chaco, Aztec, and Paquimé was simple coincidence?

There are statistics for testing linearities, lines of sites. Those statistics were originally developed for dealing with "ley lines." (For a useful history, see Williamson and Bellamy 1983.) The term "ley line" was coined by Alfred Watkins (1855–1935), the godfather of ancient alignments. Watkins was the scion of a successful beer-brewing family—not wealthy, but well off—and among many other things a gifted photographer and, to me, a sympathetic character. He dabbled in archaeology and published some important if obscure studies. It was OK, back then, to dabble in archaeology. It was a dilettante's pastime, an antiquarian hobby. Or, rather, it had been. Archaeology was beginning to professionalize in Britain just as Watkins noted the curious alignments of monuments of varying age: a castle, a henge, a cathedral, a dolmen, and so forth. He suggested that later monuments might have been deliberately placed over earlier monuments—think of Spanish churches atop Mexican pyramids—and thus these alignments preserved Stone Age originals, or ley lines. ("Ley" because so many place names the lines crossed ended in "-ly" or "-ley" or "-leigh.") That does not sound unreasonable. Watkins may well have been onto something, but the emerging professionals squashed him like a grape. He was not even allowed to advertise his books in the professional journal, *Antiquity*. Needless to say, Watkins was disgruntled. He died in 1935. Ley lines died sometime before that.

Ley lines were revived in the 1960s and 1970s by hippies and New Agers. Leys became earth energy lines, highly dousable and good for your aura (I guess). The new ley lines projected far beyond England, across oceans and continents. If professional archaeologists needed more fuel for ley's pyre (they didn't), New Age nonsense did it: a seemingly final demolition of ley lines' credibility.

I have reviewed, but not exhausted, the New Age ley line literature—indeed, the reverse: the literature exhausted me. It has a lurid, Roswellian, X-file interest, but let me state plainly: I am not personally interested in earth energies, UFOs, or *feng shui* despite the fact that I now live in Boulder, Colorado, and (in a previous life) resided in Santa Fe, New Mexico—two hotbeds (vortexes?) for this sort of thing.

Ley lines are shunned by all right-thinking professionals, but . . . things do, indeed, line up. Maybe Watkins was right. I suppose partly inspired by *Chaco Meridian*—although one would think it an example of what not to do—a number of archaeologists and scholars have recently lined up Chaco (Doxtater 2002, 2003; Heilen and Leckman 2014:386–389; Van Dyke 2004). Which works, because Chaco lined things up, like the Great North Road.

Given 150 outliers and several scores of peaks and buttes, which lines are real? How do we tell? Watkins recognized the need for statistical tests in his 1920s publications: "What really matters . . . is whether it is a humanly designed fact, an accidental coincidence, or a mare's nest that mounds, moats, beacons, and mark stones fall into straight lines" (quoted in Broadbent 1980:111). There are many monuments on the map (British ordinance maps were perfect for this kind of work); so many that more than a few alignments will appear randomly. Pro and con partisans attempted to statistically test ley alignments (e.g., Pennick and Devereux 1989:232–236). The statistical questions asked of ley lines were two: first, how to discover ley lines and, second, how to evaluate proposed ley lines. In both instances, the crux of the problem was the development of statistical distributions of "colinearities" within a spatial field of uniform, independent, random points— a hypothetical array of candidate sites for alignment.

It should come as no surprise that discovery statistics were developed by ley-line hunters, while evaluation statistics were developed by skeptical archaeologists and statisticians. The latter are of more interest here than the former. A celebrated example concerns fifty-two megaliths scattered over Cornwall—the "Old Stones of Land's End" (e.g., Broadbent 1980; Kendall and Kendall 1980; Michell 1974, 1977). Various ley lines had been proposed for these monuments, and several statisticians evaluated methods for testing their validity. The logic of their tests rested on the numbers of three-point alignments, within fifty-two random points, which might be expected through chance alone. Statistical distributions of those potential random alignments were calculated, and the number of alignments actually observed in the Old Stones of Land's End were compared with that distribution—with mixed results. There were, in fact, more alignments observed than predicted by pure chance. A sizable portion of the alignments could be dismissed as chance occurrences, but which (if any) were "real" and which were random alignments? Are we any closer to a method?

I'm not sure. I'll finesse the whole problem by declaring the Chaco Meridian a statistics-free zone. Bear with me. I've often heard this critique: there are so many sites in the Southwest that something is bound to line up with something else—almost invariably followed by a derisive snort. But there is a difference between Chaco-Aztec-Paquimé and the Old Stones of Land's End, and it is enormously important: the points on the Chaco Meridian alignment were not elements of a larger set of points, but were each of them unique—a case made in chapter 3. There was only one Chaco, one Aztec, and one Paquimé during each of their respective epochs (and that goes for earlier and later co-conspirators, too). Moreover, the alignment itself is not a random, independent line within the 360° of possible alignments. The alignment is north-south, along the meridian, a direction of demonstrable cultural importance at Chaco, Aztec, and Paquimé, and the only fixed feature in the sky, the only real direction. Thus the question does not involve *any* three points along *any* line in an open field of random independent points; the three points are unique, and the line is unique as well. Thus, the question is not—as for ley lines—"What is the statistical probability that X proportion of a field of N points align?" but rather, "What is the chance that three unique, sequential points align, along a unique direction, the meridian?" What sort of test would you use? It's a simple problem, but it's not statistical.[23]

I put this problem, casually, to several statisticians (who will remain anonymous here; no need to drag them through this muck). They found the ley-line machinations engrossing, questioning small points of logic but generally approving the skeptical British approaches. But as various criteria and arguments reduced the set of potential points to smaller and smaller numbers, they became less and less interested. When I made the case that Chaco, Aztec, and Paquimé were each unique in their own times and places—biggest, weirdest, most interesting—and that they were sequential, and that north was culturally charged, they dismissed the case as nonstatistical[24] and went back to useful work.

Statistical probabilities, in this case, are obviated by intention, for there was overriding historical direction in the Chaco Meridian. Our evaluation of Chaco, Aztec, and Paquimé cannot be purely or even mostly statistical. "Chance only matters when it can be shown not to be chance. If it does, but cannot be, it does not" (Hawthorn 1991:9).

Coincidence, Again

Moving away from statistical evaluations of hypothetical points in hypothetical space, we can look at the actual places involved, local ecologies and histories. Were there particular reasons—beyond, before, or besides the meridian—for the locations of Chaco, Aztec, and Paquimé? (The section will be confusing—that is, more confusing than others—because I wind up arguing against myself, doing my due diligence.)

Chaco's location has always been troublesome. As discussed in chapter 2, Chaco was a tough place for farming. Little rain, short growing season, long nasty winter, no water—there's little to recommend Chaco Canyon but sandstone, and sandstone is pretty much everywhere around the San Juan Basin. Chaco was not there because of any overwhelming *local* advantages of its canyon. There is no "there" there—but there once was, a history that overrode the lack of amenities (recounted in chapter 3). Once begun, Chaco flourished in part because it was a strategic, central location (Lekson 2009). I favor out-of-favor explanations that link Chaco's rise to the rich margins of the Chaco Basin, the 150 km inner circle—location! location! location! Chaco took off because it was literally a central place—not perfectly geometrically central, but close enough.

They should have built Chaco on one of the smaller tributaries of the San Juan: reliable water, mountain resources, good schools, low crime, and close to the Super Walmart. And that's what they did next, at Aztec. Aztec was a much nicer place, alongside the Animas River: not too big, not too small, just right for simple canal irrigation. Aztec, unlike Chaco, had lots of water and many trees. But there were many comparably nice places on and around the San Juan River, a point attested by the masses of archaeology that litter the margins of the Animas, La Plata, and Piedra Rivers—all heavily settled tributaries—or the San Juan River itself. There was no particular reason to build Aztec on the Animas instead of the La Plata or the San Juan, and nó particular reason for its precise location on the Animas—no springs, no odd rock formations, no point-specific resource (indeed, the sandstone used for Aztec's construction was brought from quarries several kilometers away). Aztec was a much nicer location than Chaco—but there were many of those. Aztec was precisely where it was because it was north of Chaco, at the end of the Great North Road, on the meridian.

Paquimé was located at a *really nice* spot: just below a narrows where the Rio Casas Grandes enters its productive valley. (Similar settings were favored by the earlier Mimbres towns to the north because they were the best place for canal intakes and headgates; Lekson 2006a). It's a great spot: reliable water, broad floodplains, near perfect for farming, and not too far from the mountains. We all should live in such a nice place! There were, however, a half-dozen other streams that flowed out from the Sierra Madre into northern Chihuahua—Santa Barbara, Conchos, San Pedro, Santa Clara, Santa Maria, Carretas, and others. Those river valleys are full of archaeology (Di Peso, Rinaldo, and Fenner 1974b: figure 284–285; Whalen and Minnis 1996b, 2001, 2009; Stewart et al. 2005). Paquimé could have been built on any of half a dozen rich riverine oases, most of which lie well outside the meridian. The Rio Casas Grandes is the largest of the rivers flowing northeast out of the Sierra Madre, but any of the major streams could have supported Paquimé.[25]

Economically (that is, agriculturally), the progress from Chaco to Aztec to Paquimé was indeed progressive. The sequence from Chaco to Aztec to Paquimé tracked increasing control of local agricultural productivity. Let us descend from the airy realms of meridian alignments and regain the terra firma of subsistence— back to corn-beans-and-squash archaeology.

Chaco's was a rainfall adaptation: Chaco-era populations had long traditions of "dry farming" (that is, relying on rainfall, which in that part of the world means pretty dry). They spread themselves out, hedged their bets with multiple scattered fields, and repositioned themselves to adapt to uncertain precipitation. For the Chaco-era subsistence economy, space was more important than place—except for the heavily subsidized center. At Chaco itself, rainfall was gathered and tweaked and ponded (Vivian 1990, 1991)—most people think for agriculture, but I think more likely as landscape architecture (Lekson 2006c). I'd hate to be a farmer at Chaco; and most of the Navajo families who lived there (before the Park Service tossed them out) had real farms elsewhere, in places with better water. Reliable waters were out and around the edges of the San Juan Basin, Chaco's 150 km "inner core" (e.g., Friedman, Stein, and Blackhorse 2003). That's where Navajos and Chacoans farmed. Chaco imported corn from the Chuska Valley, and grew who knows what in its uncertain gardens. Show corn? Marigolds?

Aztec rose on the Rio Animas, after a false start at Salmon Ruins on the unruly San Juan River. The San Juan was unmanageable, useless for agriculture until Navajo Dam was completed in 1962. (Downriver in Utah, Mormons—hardworking, well organized—had to abandon their pioneer town of Bluff because of the San Juan's bad behavior.) The Rio Animas was a perfect stream for simple, prepump, preconcrete diversion irrigation. Of all the thousands of sites we know in the northern San Juan, only Aztec appears to have had significant canals (Greiser and Moore 1995; Howe 1947). Aztec irrigated fields for itself, but its regional population continued to rely on rainfall (Van West 1996; chapters in Kohler and Varien 2012). Aztec stepped it up a notch over Chaco: Aztec could at least feed itself.

Paquimé was at the best location of the three centers for serious canal irrigation. When the Spanish saw the city in 1565, they remarked Paquimé's "great and wide canals" (Obregón, cited in Di Peso, Rinaldo, and Fenner 1974a:113). In the Chihuahuan Desert, canals were not optional; they were essential. Mimbres and Casas Grandes certainly used the uplands flanking their valleys for water-managed rainfall systems—some quite elaborate (Whalen and Minnis 2001, 2009)—but the bulk of agriculture came almost certainly from canal-fed valley-bottom fields. The long growing season of the Chihuahuan Desert and the moderate flow of the Rio Casas Grandes provided an ideal setting for large-scale irrigation, much better than Aztec's (Doolittle 1993).[26]

The sequence, then, from Chaco to Aztec to Paquimé was an economic progression from Chaco's little gardens fed by gathered rainfall, to ditch diversion at Aztec, to large-scale, regional commitment, to canal irrigation at Paquimé—that is, greater and greater control over the means and modes of local agricultural production. To elevate adaptation over agency (not that I care), the sequential locations of Chaco, Aztec, and Paquimé make sense.[27]

From Chaco to Aztec to Paquimé, the three cities stepped up control of production. Chaco had none, Aztec a little, and Paquimé presided over the breadbasket of northern Chihuahua. Here comes the twister, as the poet said: for my argument, the reverse would have been more useful, rhetorically. It would work better, for me, if Chaco was fixed first in a wonderful spot (the Garden of Eden that Chaco unfortunately was not) and its successors took their chances along a meridian that may or may not have hit happy potential homelands. If, for example, Paquimé was out in Chihuahua's Bolson de Mapimí, a hellhole requiring massive influxes of support, the contingency and historicity of the meridian would be better served. Think Brasilia: not so much *de novo* as *ex nihilo*. If things got worse instead of better, the meridian would trump adaptation. But that's not what happened. Hey, I can live with it—and I expect they said that too.

Historical Connections

What was it, exactly, that was moving north and south along the Chaco Meridian? Not hordes of people: while Chaco, Aztec, and Paquimé played out this grand geographic game, the other 99 percent of Pueblo peoples were just trying to make a living. (But wait for the story of the two brothers, the old hag, and the giant iron rock, below.) The population bases of the Chaco, Aztec, and Paquimé regions were profoundly local—again, I take "local" to mean what most people mean by "regional." Chaco and Paquimé were cosmopolitan places, almost certainly multiethnic and multilingual. Aztec . . . who knows? (And who cares? This story is about the nobles, not the commoners.)

As I've suggested above, my guess is that the movement south, to Paquimé, involved elites and their retainers, handlers, and servants—noble families who were determined to be noble, to continue ruling . . . somewhere. Ben Nelson, in a study of the "spread of the Mesoamerican tradition" (Nelson 2000) links that spread to the movement of displaced nobility. The fall of Teotihuacan sent noble families—whose job it was to rule—out looking for new commoners to rule. As frontier centers waned, their leaders rippled north and northwest to newer areas. They established power through symbols and ceremonies, and claims of ancestry from those now-near-mythical earlier centers. Paquimé, Nelson suggests, was the northernmost of those cities. I like this model; it's the same case I'm making, but I'm making it from north to south. They probably came from both directions at once. Paquimé was the place where Mesoamerica and Pueblo political power finally, physically met: colonnades alongside T-doors, ball courts and Great Kivas, maize gods and *awanyu*.

Historical Connections, Continued

These events were momentous, dramatic, climactic—if they really happened. They should be remembered in Native histories and traditions, and I think that they are. Those Native histories offer a different perspective on historical connections between Chaco, Aztec, and Paquimé.

Oral history is tricky. Professor Henry Jones Jr., perhaps the most influential archaeologist of our time, warned us: "We cannot afford to take mythology at face value"; and Felipe Fernandez-Armesto (1987:154) more academically cautioned against "the aetiological enthusiasm of some historians . . . to detect real places and events in the undergrowth of any myth or legend."

But we should not dismiss Pueblo origin stories and traditional histories as mere myth, as did many early anthropologists, such as Robert Lowie, Elsie Clews Parsons, and others, summarily dismissing Pueblo and Navajo traditions as sources for history.[28] That dismissive view ignores the strong threads of history—warps to myth's woofs?—in rich tapestries of cosmology, eschatology, moralizing, and pure poetry that shapes traditional histories. Origin stories serve many purposes, and chronicle is only one among many duties that shape their rhetoric and content.

Tribal scholars and anthropologists who work closely with tribes declare that "real history is embedded in Native American oral traditions" (Anyon et al.

1997:83), and Indian scholars suggest that traditional history may extend back into the Pleistocene (Echo-Hawk 1993, 1997:91). Indeed, oral traditions have equal status with archaeology and academic history as evidence in laws such as NAGPRA.

How are archaeologists to use traditional history? There are protocols for the critical use of oral histories and traditions (e.g., Vansina 1985; Smith 2011:275–278), but for many reasons, those traditions—still vital and evolving—are not accessible for systematic study. More and more Pueblos are adopting policies prohibiting discussions of history with outsiders—sort of a NAGPRA need-to-know basis. Limited to published accounts or "unofficial" versions, we must take what we can get opportunistically, weaving site data and tree-ring dates with traditional narratives. If we use published information with both ingenuity and respect, we might even show how more open exchanges could lead to even greater insights.

"Scientific methodology may not be appropriate for the research of oral traditions, where more humanistic, holistic, and qualitative approaches are sometimes warranted" (Anyon et al. 1997:83). Mainstream American archaeology is not particularly humanistic or even historical, but there is a narrow penumbra, outside the light of tribal trust but not quite in the utter darkness of old-style ahistorical New Archaeology, in which useful things can, perhaps, be done, teasing out places and events, at considerable risk of error and unintended offense. I tried it in *A History of the Ancient Southwest* (Lekson 2009). It's easy to be wrong—but why stop now?

White House, a place prominent in Pueblo origin stories, is a case in point. White House (not the site of that name at Canyon de Chelly) was a mythic center, shared by several Pueblos' histories, where things happened that shaped subsequent Pueblo life. At White House, the kachinas lived with, fought with, and then left the people—after teaching them the dances and ceremonies that would continue the vital converse between spirit world and this world. White House was a wonder, but the events that transpired there were not ultimately happy or even correct (Lekson 2009:200).

Florence Hawley, then in the employ of the Wetherill Mesa Project at Mesa Verde, determined (perhaps not surprisingly) that Mesa Verde was White House (Ellis 1967). I've suggested that White House was Chaco (Lekson and Cameron 1995; Lekson 2009). Pueblo colleagues have told me that White House, today, refers more to the general Four Corners region than to any one site. That makes sense: a particular problem of White House is its common legacy. Too many tribes claim White House for it to be any one place, like Mesa Verde—there's not enough room for everybody, or rather for everybody's grandparents. The same objection might be made for Chaco, but, as the center of a large region, Chaco was one place that could be shared among many different Pueblos' and clans' histories. Much like Washington, D.C., is common to all US citizens—whether or not we've gone there, or want to go there. Chaco transformed the Pueblo world; people remember things like that. And Chaco/Aztec, in decline, played a role in the rise of kachina ceremony: Chacoan ideology failed and left a void that needed filling. That was Pueblo IV, with its explosion of ideologically charged art, competing cults, and the rise of the kachina symbolism (Lekson 2009).

I suspect that White House refers to both Chaco *and* Aztec, two chapters of the same story where important political and ceremonial decisions were played out, spectacularly and (in the end) unsuccessfully. Chaco and Aztec aren't mythical; they were and are very definite places. White House was both a place and a metaphor for events—some of bad memory—that shaped later Pueblo life when Pueblo people turned away from class societies and reinvented themselves at Hopi, Zuni, Acoma, and along the Rio Grande (Lekson 2009).

Paquimé appears, I believe, as a real place—if unlocated—in the traditional stories of Acoma, Zuni, and Hopi. Evidence comes from key passages in the origin stories of these Pueblos, before the peoples reached their middle places. The narratives were first recorded by Ruth Bunzel (1932), Mathew Stirling (1942), Leslie White (1932), and Frank Hamilton Cushing (1896); my understanding of those texts has benefited from conversations with Petuuche Gilbert at Acoma, Ed Ladd from Zuni, and Michael Kabotie from Hopi.

Acoma accounts were recorded by White (1932) and Stirling (1942); I've heard very similar accounts from Acoma friends and colleagues. In these stories, the people left White House. "They decided to go to the south, where lay a place called Ako. They wished to go there and raise parrots [macaws]" (White 1932:145).[29] They traveled due south, following directions given to them by deities, crossing four mountain ranges and four intervening valleys or plains. The people carried two bird's eggs, one a macaw and the other a crow, given to them by a deity or holy person. They were to choose and open one egg when they reached their destination. One egg was a beautiful blue, and the other was dun colored and plain; no one knew which egg was the macaw egg and which was the crow egg. When they reached Acoma (Ako), they divided into two groups by choosing eggs. The people who chose the blue egg, which they assumed was the macaw's, knew that they would stay at Acoma. But when the blue egg was broken, out flew a crow. The people who had chosen the other egg—the drab macaw egg—continued far to the south. "The rest must journey on to Kuyapukauwak and take the other egg with them. . . . This was a very sad time for both groups. The parrot group left toward the south and it is not known how far they went" (Stirling 1942:83). (Parsons 1996:223 adds, in a dismissive footnote, a statement from an unnamed informant: "No one knows where they are now, perhaps in Central America!")

The Zuni story is very similar (Cushing 1896:386–387; Dutton 1963:112 n. 404; Tedlock 1972:264–266). The people choose between two eggs, and a sizable group follow the parrot or macaw from the plain egg, far south to the Land of Everlasting Sunshine (Ferguson and Hart 1985:22). However, this event is said to have taken place west of Zuni, presumably in the valley of the upper Little Colo-rado (Ferguson and Hart 1985:21). Ed Ladd (personal communication, 1996) adds some important points to the published Zuni accounts. The division of the people occasioned by the choice of eggs happened before either Zuni or Acoma was established. Thus, the people who went south were not "Zuni" (yet); but they looked very much like Zuni people. After the southern people had established their homes in "the land of eternal summer," a few returned as traders, bringing macaw feathers, live macaws and parrots, and seashells.

Macaws were important to Chaco; thirty-four were found at the canyon, and recall the macaw feather sash at the far edge of the Chaco world (chapter 2). Only a few were found at Aztec. Paquimé had hundreds and bred the birds, probably supplying feathers—needed for developing kachina ceremonialism—to all the Pueblos (e.g., Hargrave 1970). "The people wished to go south, and raise parrots," according to the Acoma and Zuni stories; and that's exactly what they did.

There is a specificity to these accounts that belies the generalities of White House. Acoma origin stories even name the southern place: Kuyapukauwak (Stirling 1942:83). This, despite the fact that the people who went south were forever separated from those who stayed behind. The Zuni parrot group—"those who were to go in coral's direction" (Tedlock 1972:265)—passed from the scene and almost from memory, returning only as traders carrying macaws and shells. White House was Pueblo history, and thereby subject to metaphorical displace-ment; Kuyapukauwak was someone else's history and perhaps less useful for Pueblo moralizing. The history of the parrot raisers, leaving Acoma and heading south into memory, was freed from the narrative duties of White House, which was the world before, and Acoma itself, which is the world today. It is geographi-cally telling that Zuni and Acoma (and Zia and, perhaps, Laguna) recount this story; it is, evidently, not part of the common heritage of Hopi to the west or of the Pueblos along the Rio Grande to the east (Parsons 1996:223). Acoma and Zuni lie just east and west of the Chaco Meridian, about 120 km south of Chaco. The meridian line itself coincides loosely with the boundary separating Acoma's and Zuni's territories, both modern and ancient (figure 1.1). The meridian passage occurred during a time of remarkable population growth and cultural formation at both Zuni and Acoma (Kintigh 1985, 1996; Roney 1996)—a pivotal period for these two closely related, yet linguistically distinct cultural traditions.

The Hopi don't have that story (or so I'm told), but they do have histories that might implicate Paquimé—stories of Palatkwapi, the Red City of the South, from which several clans migrated to Hopi. Some identify Palatkwapi with Paquimé (e.g., Di Peso 1974; and I've heard this from Hopis, too); others place Palatkwapi in the Verde Valley (Byrkit 1988) or in southeastern Arizona. Leigh Kuwanwisi-wma, of the Hopi Cultural Preservation Office, noted that Palatkwapi "is not just a place, a village, but an era, a time period in which things occurred; it climaxed with the end of a village and lifeways, but it was a village that was a center of others and a way of life" (quoted in Colwell-Chanthanphonh, Ferguson, and Anyon 2008:70–71)—not unlike my reading of White House as metaphor. Palat-kwapi, in some versions, was destroyed by flood. Paquimé, to the best of anyone's knowledge, was not destroyed by flood—unless it was the now-discredited eastern half of the site that Di Peso mapped on the floodplain (see chapter 3)!

Navajo (Diné) peoples have great funds of knowledge about Chaco and its region. The conventional view is that the Navajo entered the northern Southwest several centuries after Chaco and Aztec; yet the rich details of Navajo traditional histories demand our attention (e.g., Kelley and Francis 1994; McPherson 1992, 2014). I'm certain that Navajos know a lot about Chaco. Navajo people adopted much from the Pueblos: weaving, corn, sheep, and—presumably—a great deal of the knowledge and traditions specific to the country. They were more than neighbors: economic mutualism, intermarriage, co-residence, ritual exchange, warfare and raiding, and even alliance linked Navajo clans and particular Pueblos at various times. Navajo clans living in and around Chaco could well carry stories of its ancient times—Pueblo history of these Navajo places. And, of course, there remains the strong possibility that Navajo were in the area before their consensus archaeological appearance (chapters in Seymour 2012). These may be eyewitness accounts.

One important cycle of stories tells of Noqoilpi, the Great Gambler, a ruler who lived at Chaco Canyon. There are many variants of the Gambler story (e.g., Judd 1954:351–354; McPherson 1992:87–93 and citations therein). Many versions have details that correspond closely to the archaeological reconstruction presented here (for example, in some accounts, the Gambler was shot *due south* from Pueblo Alto into Mexico; John Stein, personal communication, 1998). Other versions name other places and events; for example, in one version, the Gambler was exiled to Tiz-na-zinde, about 30 km west of Pueblo Alto (Judd 1954:354); in another version I've heard, he was killed and buried under a boulder near Chaco.

Rather than picking and choosing details and variants that best fit the Chaco-Aztec-Paquimé sequence, it is more useful to present elements common to most of the Noqoilpi stories that resonate. The Gambler cycle tells of the rise and fall of the Chaco Anasazi. Noqoilpi reduced surrounding peoples (all the tribes, Pueblo and Navajo) to vassalage or slavery by unfailingly winning gambling contests. He "demanded that they build the huge pueblo for his house" (McPherson 1992:87)—Pueblo Alto, the "Chief's House"—and then other big houses for his kin and associates. After a despotic career, the Gambler was overthrown (by the people or by the gods or both) and ejected—in many versions, shot up into the sky like an arrow. "The underlying theme is that they had an extensive knowledge that led to a haughty uncontrolled pride and eventual destruction" (McPherson 1992:91). The Gambler is usually identified as a foreigner: Spanish or Mexican (which may mean a Mexican Indian; David Brugge, personal communication,

1998), or even an Anglo—in any event, someone of different origins and social status. Nobility?

The Gambler story describes a class-structured hierarchy at Chaco. It is specific to that place. Although the rise-and-fall plot is common to many (all?) mythologies, parallels between the Gambler stories and Pueblo accounts of White House are telling: personal aggrandizement, institutionalized political power, and forced departure. These things happened at White House, which I think was Chaco Canyon and Aztec Ruins.

Those are Native stories, from north to south. There also are early Spanish accounts that perhaps shed light on the meridian, historicizing Native traditions. Von Humboldt's cartographic summary of Mexico City thinking circa 1800 was discussed in chapter 3: the first home of the Aztecs in the region of Chaco, the last home of the Aztecs at Paquimé, and then over the Sierras to Culiacán. Humboldt was not projecting Spanish fantasies—the Cities of Cibola were fantasies. Von Humboldt related historicized versions of Native traditions.

There are earlier Spanish sources that are relevant. Two hundred years before Humboldt and a century and a half after the fall of Paquimé, Gaspar Pérez de Villagrá served under Juan de Oñate in the 1598 colonization of New Mexico. Villagrá wrote an epic poem about those events—a poem lauded for its accuracy despite the demands of meter and rhyme (Encinias, Rodríguez, and Sánchez (1992:xx, whose translation I use here). Villagrá recounted a Native tale, heard on the approach to New Mexico, about two heroic brothers, "of high and noble Kings descended, sons of a King, and kin of highest lineage" (canto 1, lines 123–125). The brothers each lead a large column of people, his people—warriors, women, children. They encounter an old hag, with a huge iron boulder:

> They say most certainly she bore
> Upon her head, so great and strong,
> A huge enormous weight, almost in form
> A tortoise shell set upright,
> Exceeding in some eight hundred quintal weight,
> Of iron, massive and well molded. (canto 1, lines 40–44)

There is probably poetic license here: 800 quintal would be about 36.8 metric tons. That's a big rock for a hag to carry, and for a meteorite—which is what it was—about the size of AMNH's famous Ahnighito in New York City. No matter; the hag tells one brother to pass south, to found Tenochtitlan—again, a bit of poetic drama—while the other turns back, founding a city of his own:

> [the story] . . . is proved to us by
> The ruins of that city great
> Which we all see in New Galicia,

Of mighty buildings, all laid waste,
Where they, the natives of the land,
Say it was made and founded there
By those New Mexicans who came
Out of the New Land that we seek. (canto 2, lines 230–236)

. . . which the editors identify as Paquimé (Encinias, Rodríguez, and Sánchez 1992:16 n. 18). The hag's iron rock recalls the famous 1.5 metric ton Casas Grandes meteorite, found in Paquimé by treasure hunters in 1867 (Tassin 1902). The meteorite found its way to the Smithsonian, where you can see it today exhibited with other meteorites. But its iron, "massive and well-molded," may have played a role in the meridian, if only a theme interwoven among other themes.

Three decades before Oñate—closer to a short century after Paquimé's fall—another aborted Spanish *entrada* hints at the meridian, at least its possible last leg, from Paquimé to Culiacán. Culiacán was the northernmost real Native city; it became the jumping-off place for Spanish expeditions and incursions into the interior. The first recorded attempt was by Nuño de Guzman—a particularly thuggish conquistador and Cortés's rival—who conquered Culiacán in 1530 and then set his sights to the north toward, we are told, the Seven Cities of Cibola. The Seven Cities were a European myth transported to the New World, and they pop up a lot in histories of *entradas*. But Danna Levin Rojo (2014) argues that the Spanish were after more than Cibola; they were convinced that New Mexico was Aztlan, the Aztec homelands: "For the Spaniards, Nuevo México *was* Aztlan" (Levin Rojo 2014:187, emphasis original)—and Nuevo México would prove to be as rich as the Aztec's México. Cibola was grafted onto the histories of several Nahua groups who claimed Aztlan as a homeland—not just the Mexica's.

So, the early Spanish *entradas*—like Guzman's—were *looking for Aztlan*, thinking it might also be the European Cibola. "Guzman had this information from a Huastec Indian whose father traded into the back country, exchanging fine feathers for ornaments, by a forty days' journey north, and one which involved the passage of a wilderness" (Sauer 1932:9). Guzman's guide led him not up the coastal plain—the easy, obvious route—but north from Culiacán into the rugged Sierras. Carl Sauer, the great historical geographer, was genuinely distressed that Guzman abandoned Sauer's coastal "Road to Cibola" and foolishly headed into the hills: "It is curious, therefore, that, being in Culiacán, about halfway on the direct [coastal] road to Cibola, Guzman should have altered the direction of his march, away from the supposed objective. At Culiacán he began a series of attempts to scale the mountain barrier" (Sauer 1932:9).

Guzman's men, wagons, and livestock marched north from Culiacán and battered themselves against the mountains. A man on foot could travel straight north from Culiacán through the Tarahumara country in the Sierra and ultimately arrive at Paquimé—but Guzman's *remudas* and *carettas* could not. Guzman eventually gave up, and political troubles brought him back to Mexico City.

Guzman was following his guide, who presumably knew where he was headed. His route was a straight line over the mountains, not to mythical Cibola but to the Southwest's real cities: Chaco, Aztec, and Paquimé—and, perhaps, to Aztlan writ large.[30] Paquimé was only three or four generations gone when Guzman marched out of Culiacán (and back again). Its memory was fresh, certainly to Guzman's guide's father and, we may assume, to the kings of Culiacán, who were quizzed by Guzman and his goons.

Von Humboldt's history (chapter 3) had his "Azteques"—whoever they might have been—traveling south out of Paquimé over the Tarahumara mountains to Culiacán (Hueicolhuacan). Guzman's guide led him north out of Culiacán into those same mountains, toward Paquimé and the fabled cities of the Aztlan/Cibola. These two accounts, as far as we know, were independent of each other—that is, von Humboldt didn't care very much about old Guzman, and Guzman of course knew nothing of the future Prussian and his Azteques. Was Guzman headed for von Humboldt's Aztlan?

A Faulknerian sound and fury, poems and myths telling different versions and visions of the story. But I find a consistency in these mixed messages: first, the details and plots that align with my alignment; and second, the distances and dynamics which suggest that meridian distances were not impossible or even extraordinary for the peoples of those times and places.

Historical Connections, Concluded

The fundamental question facing the Chaco Meridian is, coincidence or intention? It seems likely to me that the four point problem (North-Chaco-Aztec-Paquimé) and the two precursors (423-Shabik and Sacred Ridge–Blue Mesa) and the last lonely post at Culiacán are what we in the trade call "facts." That is, for each major Southwestern epoch, the biggest, weirdest, most interesting sites were on the meridian. Intentional alignment has major implications for Southwestern prehistory, and a cascade of archaeological ramifications. If the alignment was instead coincidental, then that vista of historical possibilities hits what eighteenth-century British landscape architects called a "ha-ha": a boundary offering enticing views but blocking passage into that new country. "Ha-ha," indeed: the joke's on me and on the long-suffering reader, whose patience probably reached its limits many pages past. But I believe that the arguments presented in this chapter reduce the possibility of coincidence to something approaching zero.

I am frustrated by colleagues who follow my argument to this point, nod politely, and then ask, "Well, where's your proof?" I've played all my cards and piled on all my evidence. What more proof could we realistically hope to find? DNA would be nice, but I have no hopes for that in my lifetime. All we have and probably all we will ever have is circumstantial evidence. Absent an ancient map, a *lienzo* showing Chaco and Paquimé and Culiacán connected by a line, or a hoard of surveying tools ornamented in Gallup and Ramos styles; absent a line of identifiably Chaco or Paquimé surveying monuments (copper "brass caps"? core-and-veneer cairns?); absent some other fabulously unlikely discovery, it is difficult to envision proof more effective than the cumulative, independent circumstantial evidence.

There *always* remains a chance that the alignment was purely random, a geographic fluke or freak, a happy or unhappy accident. As Dr. Jones tells us, "There's always another explanation." I think evidence for intentionality is strong, internally consistent, and—perhaps most importantly—independent, from several independent perspectives. The architectural details noted by Di Peso and myself have nothing to do with the meridian. The dating of the sites, by tree rings, was accomplished by archaeologists with no interest vested in the matter: Windes and McKenna for Aztec, Dean and Ravesloot for Paquimé, and a cast of thousands for Chaco. (Indeed, most of the archaeological data were developed by other scholars; I've simply combined their arguments, old and new, in a novel way.) The Native stories and Spanish accounts were recorded without any specific reference to these sites (save Villagrá); those identifications are my or others' interpretations.

The cumulative probability of coincidence seems, to me, infinitesimal. Layers of independent data—historic, chronological, architectural, and contextual—progressively diminish any role for chance. Means, motive, and opportunity: members of the jury, I urge you to convict—or at least to share my conviction.

NOTES

1. One other very obvious line to the south beckoned, about 4 km east of Fritz's centerline: a meridian south from Una Vida (unaccountably translated, sometimes, as "One View") and/or Fajada Butte—the two differ by only 0.1' in longitude. Let's use Fajada Butte, famed for its solstice maker and framed in many a poster. From Fajada Butte, a possible road runs a little west of south through the tower kiva complex at Greenlee and continues 15 km south to the remarkable Rams Pasture *herradura*:

> The visibility from this location [Rams Pasture] is excellent. The structure is located on a line from Greenlee Ruin to Borrego Pass. From this position Huerfano Mesa is clearly visible on the far north horizon and appears to stand directly on top of Fajada Butte! When this feature [Rams Pasture] is viewed from Borrego Pass (20 miles to the south), the notch [setting of Rams Pasture], the cap of Fajada Butte, and Huerfano Mesa all roughly line up, again with Huerfano Mesa standing atop Fajada Butte. Because of the situation of the structure in a notch, visibility is restricted to the east and west. (Nials, Stein, and Roney 1987:182)

From there it goes . . . who knows where. Short north-south road segments were documented at Greenlee and Rams Pasture, but a continuous road (visible in aerial photos) could not be confirmed on the ground (Nials, Stein, and Roney 1987). I recommend this alignment to readers, if any, who are intrigued by my argument and who are looking for something interesting to do in the field.

2. That's an angle error of only 2.5° (Sofaer 1997: table 3), if anyone was shooting angles from Alto—but they weren't.

3. Meridian surveys on this scale were not unprecedented in the preindustrial world. About AD 725, a Chinese court astronomer named I Hsing created a "meridian line of 7973 *li* (just over 3500 km)," stretching from Mongolia to Indochina (Needham 1959:292–293). (This happened at about the same time mosques were first being aligned with Mecca.) The Chinese meridian stations were set for astronomical observations, not for geomantic symbolism; and eighth-century China was rather more complex than the eleventh-century Southwest. More resources could be mobilized than were ever available to Chaco or Aztec or Paquimé. But the tools and technical aspects of the work were similar: finding north is pretty simple, and prolonging a line is fairly basic. Needham notes that not all the points were exactly on a north-south line (1959:293 n. c). Even the emperor of China, with all his power and might, could not command naked-eye surveying to be perfect.

4. With a string for a compass, scribe a large circle on flat ground with open horizons. Hold a straight pole (a gnomon) on the center of the circle. A rock tied on the end of the string will keep everything plumb. The shadow of the head of the gnomon will cross the circumference of the circle twice, once in the morning and once in the afternoon. (Your arm will get tired.) A line connecting those two points defines east-west. Bisect the east-west line using the string as a compass; a perpendicular through the midpoint and the center of the circle (i.e., the gnomon) defines north-south. Nothing more complicated is needed for this operation than a piece of string, a pole, and a rock. This technique has been used to determine north, with considerable accuracy, at Chaco (Kim Malville, personal communication, 1998).

5. For those inclined to ritual, it's easy to imagine this as ceremony, a line of priests fixing and refixing north in an outdoor sand-painting-like event. Humboldt lamented the Spanish repression of Native priests "qui observoient l'ombre meridienne aux gnomons" (Humboldt 1811, vol. 1:400). But I digress.

6. William Calvin, a professor and polymath at the University of Washington, evaluated the Chaco Meridian and independently developed and named the method: "Leapfrogging Gnomons: A Method for Surveying a Very Long North-South Line without Modern Instruments" (Calvin 1997).

Another technique to prolong a line, known in modern surveying as "wiggling in" or "balancing in," could also have been used. (When the Zuni people were seeking their Middle Place, the water spider K'yan'asdebi stretched his legs in the four cardinal directions out to the surrounding ocean; with his belly he literally "wiggled in" on the center of the world, the heart of mother earth; Ferguson and Hart 1985:23.) "Balancing in" involves a trial foresight station that is then aligned and realigned on the original "backsight" station through trial, error, and correction. A station on the line would be established on a high peak or ridge, chosen for its long view to the north. A trial foresight would be set approximately north on the horizon, and from that trial foresight, north would be established astronomically. The alignment of north, "foresight" and "backsight," would establish the error in the trial station. The trial station would then be adjusted, north would be reestablished, the alignment rechecked, and the trial station again adjusted. The process would be repeated until the "foresight" was balanced in due north of the established station. Establishing each station would require several days, since north can be fixed only once a day, but this process could "jump" across big distances. Personally, I think this unlikely, but who knows?

7. Visual alignment of range poles is easy and surprisingly accurate. The Scoutmaster stands on the line the troop is trying to extend (or prolong), somewhere behind the last good point. Several Tenderfeet (Tenderfoots, à la Hobbit usage?) are sent out into the bushes and rocks, each with a tall pole or a truck flare. The Scoutmaster lines them up visually, sighting over the last good point on the line. In fact, the Scoutmaster can simply stick two poles or two flares in the ground, one at the last good point and another at a convenient distance back on the line, and go have a beer. The Tenderfeet backsight on the two poles or flares and line themselves up. They repeat the process until they lose the backsight by crossing a ridge, falling into a hole, or tumbling off a cliff. (This is why you need a whole troop.) When the backsight disappears, it is necessary to reestablish the direction of the line and start all over again. It helps to keep foresights fairly short, and backsights long. Similar techniques are not unlikely in ancient Chaco, which had geometry and, perhaps, standard measures (Hudson 1972).

8. In addition to errors in the determination of north, the North Road's "as-built" alignment reflects an opportunistic use of terrain features (hills, buttes, notches, etc.) that provided convenient visual fore- and backsights along the meridian. Sharply cone-shaped hills or pinnacles, such as the site of "El Faro" at the Pierre's site complex (about 20 km north of Chaco Canyon) are almost on the meridian. Presumably, the North Road was laid out in part by referencing visually prominent features, such as "El Faro," which lay only a few meters off the meridian alignment.

9. Consider the example of Pacific celestial navigation, remarkably accurate over voyages for thousands of km. Self-correction by multiple random errors in this kind of navigation has been proven in experimental voyages. "Navigational accuracy is not a function of the length of the voyage. If anything, longer passages provide a greater opportunity for random sea effects and errors of judgement to cancel each other out" (Lewis 1994:268). "While errors in dead-reckoning occur, these tend to cancel each other out over a long voyage rather than to accumulate, which is opposite to what was thought earlier" (Irwin 1992:46; see also citations under "navigation errors, tending to cancel each other out" in Goetzfridt 1992:291). If meridian alignment were a ritual (see note 5, above), north might have been established and reestablished daily—sun or star ceremonies with practical implications—creating many more short foresights, and higher accuracy.

10. The Chaco-Paquimé meridian spans five major plains of 50 to 60 km in width. From north to south, these are: the southern San Juan Basin, the North Plains, the Plains of St. Augustine, the Deming Plain, and Llano de Carretas. At its southern end, the Rio Mimbres and Rio Paquimé Valleys, which align roughly along this meridian, create a combined 250 km length of relatively flat terrain (incorporating the Deming Plain and the Llano de Carretas).

Between these long plain segments, a series of ridges, hills, and mountains interrupt visibility along the meridian line. From north to south, these are (with their approximate latitudes): the Dutton Plateau (Borrego Pass, 35'30"), the east foothills of the Zuni Mountains (Gallo Peak, 35'), the Sawtooth Mountains (34'15"), the Crosby Mountains (Sugarloaf Peak, 34'8"), Indian Peaks (33'30"), the west slopes of the Black Range (from Alexander Peak 33'30" to Mimbres Peak 32'45"), the Carrizalillo Hills (31'45"), and the southeast foothills of the Sierra Alta (Cerro Grande 31'8").

Most or all of these features would be useful for very long back- and foresights (theoretically, up to 160 km). That is, these high points could have been beneficial in running the meridian line over intervening plains. Only the Black Range, with about 80 km of uninterrupted mountain ridges, poses a major terrain challenge. But the Black Range probably requires no different techniques, merely more time and labor. (Field checks indicate that the Black Range could have been spanned in only one or two jumps, by "wiggling in"; see note 6.) And of course that's the minimum. To extend the ritual fantasy (note 5), what if they reestablished north every day? How many days to walk 630 km over broken country? At least 30.

11. The theoretical error similarly computed for the North Road to Twin Angels Pueblo is 775 m, not far off the observed error of just under 1 km.

12. Complementing the results obtained from Taylor's formula, Joey Donahue of Los Alamos National Laboratory simulated an alignment of 200 miles (320 km) with twenty segments of 10 miles (16 km). At each segment, an independent random error with a standard deviation of 2° was introduced. The model was run 10,000 times and produced a mean predictably very close to zero and, more important, a standard error of only 0.35 miles (0.56 km) (Joey Donahue, personal communication, 1996). Considerable precision was possible over long, segmented distances.

Keith Kintigh of Arizona State University developed a similar program to simulate the alignment process. I quote from his letter, reporting the results (Keith Kintigh, personal communication, 1998):

> If one assumes a 630 km meridian divided into thirteen equal segments (of 48.5 km) and an angular error uniformly distributed between −2° and +2°, simulating the survey 100,000 times provides a mean error near 0, as it should because the error is random, not biased to the east or west (the mean is actually 13 m and the standard deviation is 3.5 km). The more important result is that a survey will produce a displacement less than or equal to the observed 1 km displacement about 22 percent of the time. Thus, we would expect them to do as well or better than they actually did better than one out of five times. The average displacement (ignoring direction) is about 2.8 km. . . . Errors of more than 10 km are quite unlikely. Similar results are obtained if the angular error is normally distributed with a standard deviation of 1°. A survey would result in a displacement of 1 km or less about one out of four times (26%) and the average displacement is 2.4 km.

Accuracy, if that was a goal, could have been achieved by repeated determinations of north at each segment and "averaging" the results; recall that experiments at Chaco obtained north with accuracies of less than a degree by simply repeating measurements and "eyeballing" an average. Accuracy could have been improved even more by running the entire 630 km Chaco-Paquimé meridian many times and "averaging" the location of the final station at Casas Grandes.

13. The Chaco Meridian is approximately 108°. I've had rapturous messages from persons, who will remain nameless, noting in all sincerity that the number 108 means something (I forget what) in Buddhism or Hinduism or the Cabala (I forget which). I'm happy that they're happy, but . . .

14. The northernmost Mimbres site I know is the Montoya site at Canada Alamosa, near Truth or Consequences, New Mexico. Montoya is a medium-sized Mimbres site; the big Mimbres villages are another 70 km further south. Montoya is just over the hill (San Mateo Mountains) and barely 75 km from the southeasternmost Great House I know (described in chapter 2): the wonderfully named "Camelot on the San Augustin."

15. The North Star Road reportedly began as a nineteenth-century military road. As a wagon road, it winds on grades around ridges and through valleys, but its overall trend is notably north-south. The history of the North Star Road remains to be written, but it is not too far-fetched to suggest that the military road followed older routes, perhaps far older routes, deviating from north to accommodate new transportation technologies.

16. The bulkiest of bulk materials was construction timber. A great many beams were brought into Chaco, and perhaps the width of the road reflects the length of the timbers, rolling down to Chaco (Snygg and Windes 1998). But the beams were carried, not rolled; so it seems more likely they were carried end-on, that is, along and not across the line of movement.

17. In *A History of the Ancient Southwest* (Lekson 2009:126–127, 294 n. 136), I suggested a cosmological struggle for the soul of Chaco Canyon—or bragging rights, or percentage of the gross, or whatever—between an older, traditional solsticial (or lunar, Sofaer 1997) orientation and a later, upstart cardinal (solar) orientation: that is, from vaguely south-southeast to rigidly north-south. The earliest Great Houses were solsticial; in the first burst of eleventh-century building, Pueblo Alto was markedly cardinal (solar), while Chetro Ketl retained the earlier orientation. Perhaps the noble families of these two houses battled it out; Alto ultimately won. You can see this play out at Pueblo Bonito, originally facing south-southeast. Pueblo Bonito could not be rotated from its original solsticial orientation, but north found expression in the last construction at that most important building. The very late and very prominent north-south wall (described above) divided the public space, the plaza, into two halves. We don't know what north meant, but—by golly—we know it was important.

18. Orientation eclipsing the Chaco-Aztec-Paquimé meridian in scale and technical achievement is spectacularly evident in the mosques of Islam. Either the mosque itself or the prayer niche (*mihrab*) in its walls is oriented by *qibla*, the direction from the point of prayer to the Kaaba in Mecca. The Quran requires that the *qibla* be an accurate alignment, but in some cases the *qibla* was merely conventional. The frequently realized ideal, however, is an accurate orientation of the mosque to Mecca. *Qibla*, a system of world-scale positional legitimation, structures religious architecture, city planning, and

daily life of 900 million Muslims, from Dakar to Sarawak, and has done so for more than a thousand years.

Positional legitimation developed in the earliest days of Islam. In AD 622, the *hegira* brought Muhammad north from Mecca to Medina; the Quam, written in Medina, prescribed prayer in the direction of the Kaaba. (Coincidence places Medina and Mecca on almost the same meridian. It happens.) The subsequent conquest of Egypt and, particularly, the great intellectual center of Alexandria introduced Arab scholars to Greek astronomy and geometry by about 650. Arab astronomy, in particular, blossomed in large part through the development of Greek ideas to the challenge of accurate determination of *qibla* (King 1979). "Medieval Muslim scientists were able—within the limitations of medieval geography—to determine the direction to Mecca of any locality to within a few minutes of arc" (King 1995:253). Orientation to Mecca was a concrete representation of spiritual and political legitimation of the new regimes in lands conquered by Arab armies. Those lands were vast: by the early twelfth century, *qibla* determined the orientation of mosques from Morocco to the Punjab, and from the Caucasus to the Gulf of Aden.

The determination of *qibla* was one of the principal practical challenges that led to the remarkable florescence of Arab astronomy—completely ideological, nothing adaptive about *qibla*. The critical role of Islamic learning in the history of European science is well known and needs no elaboration here. Positional legitimation, in this case at least, was serious stuff: *qibla* were a major link in the history of modern thought. The Chaco-Aztec-Paquimé meridian is another, much simpler example of a basic domain of human cognition: measuring the world on which we live.

19. Mary Helms explored the relationship of kingly towns or cities to two kinds of "outside centers," creative centers that exist mythically, on a cosmic vertical axis mundi or, more tangibly, on a horizontal axis mundi, "out there" at some distance from the kingly center (Helms 1993:173–175). Chaco could have been both, first to Aztec and later to Paquimé. "Spatially/temporally outside centers are regarded as foci of initial cultural origins and creation, and thus places of cosmological power" (Helms 1993:173). The center of "here and now" appeals to the "center-out-there" through ritual, highly crafted objects; recognizable material styles; and "pilgrimages to the sacred distant place over the horizon" (Helms 1993:175). The Chaco Meridian was both a movement and a monument.

20. As Whalen and Minnis (2003:320) state, "The fact that there are so few recorded Viejo sites in the Casas Grandes area has been used to argue that it had a small population just before the rise of the center" of Paquimé. Well, yes, couldn't have said it better myself; but—as we shall see—I'm taking this quote out of context, for Whalen and Minnis insist the pre-Paquimé population was far larger than the evidence suggests. They tacitly acknowledge the problem of insufficient Viejo populations in their "alternative scenario" for the rise of Paquimé, which "does not require so many local people" to populate the city (Whalen and Minnis 2003:328; see also 2009). That alternative has Paquimé rising from the aggregation of many earlier, smaller Medio period pueblos. Possible—but we still need people to create all those earlier but smaller sites. Where does the buck stop?

Di Peso (1974, vol. 1) traveled over much of Chihuahua and did not see many Viejo period sites (that is, sites that immediately predated Paquimé). Whalen and Minnis (2001, 2004) spent a couple of decades looking for Viejo period sites and did not find many either. They were there, of course, a few Viejo period sites (Di Peso 1974, vol. 1)—but not many, and they were small. Whalen and Minnis's survey "recorded only 15 sites with pure Viejo ceramic assemblages [with a total of 20, adding five sites reported by others]. These sites are small, with a mean area of only 0.7 ha" (2003:319). They suggest, hopefully, that there will be more Viejo hidden under later, larger Medio sites, and that is surely the case. But based on excavations at one large Medio site (Site 204), those buried Viejo components are also pretty small (Whalen and Minnis 2009). At the southern end of Casas Grandes, only one of a dozen investigated Medio period sites had Viejo period underpinnings, and those too were slim (Stewart et al. 2005). But in the south, there were some large stand-alone Viejo period sites (Stewart et al. 2005:171)—apparently the places that appealed to Viejo did not entice Medio. (We'll return to these evidently big Viejo sites in the south later; but note that, so far, big Viejo sites and components are conspicuously absent in the Rio Casas Grandes Valley.

21. But people do. (Some) archaeologists must be among the most literal-minded people on earth, immune to metaphor and allusion. They take my taglines seriously. This has cost me, in absurd reviews that completely miss jokes, glaze over punch lines, and take serious issue with my silly subtitles. I can do boring—I've written reports and deliverables that could put an entire Starbucks to sleep—but if I don't have to, I won't.

22. Well, perhaps because of canal irrigation, which creates long-lived sites à la Hohokam and Mimbres. But that clearly was not the case at Paquimé, with only a few pre-Paquimé structures below Di Peso's excavations.

23. Let us sneak up on the problem from another angle. If we begin with all known sites in the Southwest, we will certainly find many sets of three (and more) that line up. If we restrict our field to sites over one hundred rooms with over a century of occupation, that number drops, and with it the probability of chance alignments. If we further restrict the set to regional centers, rich with exotic artifacts and monumental architecture, the number falls to exactly three: Chaco, Aztec, and Paquimé. When the sample equals the population, statistical bets are off.

24. There are other approaches. A skeptical colleague, reviewing an earlier draft of this chapter, asked, "What is the probability that *any* north-south line drawn through the Southwest would intersect several important sites?" A good question, although the term "important" is problematic. Try it yourself, with a *National Geographic* or a AAA map and a ruler—and Olympian detachment for "important." Consider only the best and brightest, and eschew small scales: look only for meridian alignments over 250 or 300 km in length. As a statistical procedure, it stinks; but as an experiment, it's illuminating.

I find only three other north-south alignments of "important" sites, on this scale, in the Greater Southwest: two come tantalizingly close to defining the eastern and western boundaries of the Chacoan region, and the third marks a remarkable Arizona-Sonora connection. Chacoan Great Houses seem to be confined, along the whole 300 km length of the region, by longitude 107°15' on the east (approximately the longitude of

Chimney Rock and Guadalupe Ruin), and 110° on the west (approximately the longitude of the westernmost Great Houses on Cedar Mesa, upper Polacca Wash, and the Little Colorado River). This Great House geography interests me strangely, of course; but it will probably explode as additional Great Houses are recognized in more distant parts of the Southwest. The third alignment involves sites in Arizona and Sonora: Sunset Crater, Casa Grande, and Las Trincheras. Sunset Crater and Las Trincheras were either entirely or largely natural features; Casa Grande has, perhaps, connections to Paquimé. They all *stick up*, remarkably. Sunset Crater rose first, explosively; Casa Grande and Las Trincheras came a century or two later. Their meridian alignment is problematic, but interesting. Map-and-ruler exercises are "ley hunting" (or "ley lying," to quote Simon Broadbent 1980).

If we must be statistical, we could segment the latitude parallels of Chaco and Paquimé into 1.5 km units and assume that Chaco and Paquimé are each 1.5 km in their east-west dimensions ("width"), and free to fall within any segment of their respective parallels, anywhere around the great big world. Then we could calculate the absolute minimum probability that the two would fall by chance in the same 1.5 km wide longitudinal zone: something less than 0.000000002. Of course, this model could place Chaco in Asia or Paquimé in the mid-Atlantic. If we limit the parallels of Chaco and Paquimé to the Southwest (i.e., between longitudes 104° to 115°), the probability of the Chaco-Paquimé alignment, by chance, increases to a whopping 0.0000026. But there is a temporal dimension to the problem. Chaco comes first, Paquimé second; therefore the location of Chaco is fixed, and only Paquimé is free to move. Recognizing this parameter increases the probability to 0.0016. Better, but not odds on which to wager your life savings.

We could chip away at the problem, tightening this parameter and expanding that dimension, and develop a broad continuum of probabilities. But turn the argument on its pointy little head and go right for its pencil-necked throat: (1) assume that the position of Chaco was fixed as the boundaries of the modern park, that is, between longitudes 107°50' and 108°2'30", or about a 16 km "width"; and (2) assume that Paquimé is 1.5 km wide and free to vary, east-west and north-south, as long as it winds up on the banks of the Rio Casas Grandes above Ascension, a 120 km reach of the north-flowing river with a longitudinal width between 107°53'20" and 108°3'40", or about 15 km. Under these conditions and parameters, there would be about 0.90 chance that Paquimé would fall in the same meridian corridor as some part of Chaco. It could hardly miss.

Stated one way, the chances for alignment are astoundingly small; stated another, the chances of alignment approach certainty. Intentional alignment equals certainty, too. Probabilities, in unique cases, depend entirely on how one formulates the case.

And I've left Aztec out of the mix; a three-part problem would be even more convoluted.

25. Sapawe—one of the very largest northern Rio Grande sites, comparable in size (and age and population) to Paquimé—sits beside a much smaller creek than the Rio Casas Grandes.

26. Indeed, Paquimé was, arguably, at the best spot for canal irrigation due south of Chaco. There's nothing between Chaco and the Mimbres area that's irrigable. About 350 km south of Chaco, the meridian crosses the Rio Mimbres, where canals had fueled

the Mimbres achievement a century earlier. But that nest was fouled (Minnis 1985)—salinated, deforested, dotted with ill-omened ruins of a failed society (chapter 2).

27. Pueblo prehistory shows, in general, a trend from dry farming to small-scale water control to canal irrigation. The Chaco-Aztec-Paquimé sequence was not independent of these larger trends. Much of what we see archaeologically at these three sites reflects much larger regional "background" patterns: pottery design, weapon technology, food-processing methods, architectural fabrics, and so forth developed or evolved largely unrelated to the elite's and noble's political shenanigans. In this case, however, the cities *may* have led the way: the limited, possibly architectural water control at Chaco was in advance (chronologically and technically) of other Pueblo districts of its time; canal irrigation at Aztec was (it seems) all but unique on the plateau; and the scale of Paquimé's putative canal systems was both larger and earlier than Rio Grande systems.

These are points for research. I am not certain that my summary is entirely accurate—we haven't really looked for canals in the Four Corners. Most Four Corners models and simulations of agricultural productivity may share a potentially fatal flaw: most ignore the possibility of irrigation.

28. Elsie Clews Parsons parodied origin stories in her classic *Pueblo Indian Religion*:

> Pueblo history and geography are a series of archaeological or topographical legends, almost as naive and fanciful about near events as about remote or cosmic ones. The general outline is simple: "We came up, we moved southward (or eastward) and built houses, something happened, a quarrel or choosing a fateful egg or being stung by mosquitoes, we moved again, we kept on seeking the middle place until we found it here, where we are to live forever." (Parsons 1996:215)

Joe Sando, a Pueblo historian, champions the accuracy of oral traditions, maintaining that traditional history "was not tilted to adorn the reputation of one or another. . . . Nor was it changed or distorted to supply credibility to the demands of a powerful political structure" (Sando 1992:21). But history may be layered within larger narrative themes. Writers Tessie Naranjo and Leslie Marmon Silko honor the metaphorical nature of traditional stories (Naranjo 1995; Silko 1995). "All stories are considered valid. There is never one version of any story" (Naranjo 1995:248). Meaning transcends historical detail.

Oral traditions—like all good history—are perhaps best understood as *both* historical and metaphorical, varying in degree. Peter Nabokov, in an insightful essay on Native American views of history, concludes:

> The spectrum of American Indian narratives, behaviors, and symbols which carry any information faintly deemed "historical" actually falls on any number of different points between the idealized poles of chronology (history) and cosmology (mythology). (Nabokov 1996:9)

29. Macaws, at most Pueblos, symbolize the direction south (Dozier 1970: table 8). They are today associated with the sun (Tyler 1991:13), and macaws and their feathers are specifically and especially associated with modern kachina *sacra* (Parsons 1996:398). Indeed, macaws, their feathers, and their images were key icons in the early development of kachina ceremonialism. Macaws and parrots appear frequently in eleventh-century

Mimbres art, alongside the earliest kachina-like images (Dutton 1963:166–167 n. 501), and, later, with readily identifiable kachinas on fifteenth-century kiva murals (e.g., Hibben 1975; Smith 1952). Trade in macaws was interrupted by the Spanish conquest (Tyler 1991:22–23) and has never quite recovered, but the association of macaws and kachinas is still strong. Macaws were apparently integral to the early development of kachina ceremonialism and to other "cults" of the post-Chaco world (e.g., the "Southwestern cult" of Crown 1994:149, 167). (Hamilton Tyler states that crows and ravens were more directly associated with kachinas than were macaws; what interesting implications for the Acoma story! Tyler 1991:173ff.)

30. Guzman's guide's father had traveled forty days through wilderness to reach the Southwestern cities. As an exercise, divide 620 km—the distance between Culiacán and Paquimé—by forty days: about 16 km a day. Southwestern archaeology often assumes a standard day's walk of about 35 km (or 22 miles; e.g., Wilcox 1996a) as the preferred pace of prehistory. Lumholtz—who traversed this same territory three centuries later, spoke admiringly of Native porters who walked "twice as far each day as a loaded mule can go . . . thirty or forty miles" (Lumholtz 1902, vol. 2:367–369). At those rates, Culiacán to Paquimé was quite doable in forty days. But the miles (or kilometers) between Paquimé and Culiacán were no cakewalk. They crossed canyons and mountains, and the Barranca del Cobre. Trekking over the Sierra Madre might well take forty days—and keeping on course (due north or due south) would be complicated by deep canyons and high mountains. If Culiacán was the end of the meridian line, its 40 km displacement is not so much a fatal flaw as a remarkable bit of naked-eye navigation.

Conclusions?

I am a bear of very little brain, and long words bother me.

—*Winnie the Pooh*

THE FOUR-POINT PROBLEM, WITHOUT REFERENCES

After five centuries of village life, the Southwest finally got its act together, built a city, and elected a king. There had been cities and kings in Mesoamerica for almost two millennia. Class societies—nobles and commoners—were the rule, not the exception. The question is: what took the Southwest so long?

The first polity at Chaco Canyon began about 850, and really took off around 1000; it soon encompassed a region with a bustling bulk-goods economic core in a radius of about 150 km from Chaco, and a political hegemony out to 250 km. The social organization mirrored a common Mesoamerican model (in Nahua: *altepetl*) with a half-dozen major noble families sharing power and rotating the kingship, scores of secondary noble houses, and tens of thousands of commoners who supported the polity with (moderate) tribute and taxes. In return, the capital maintained peace and distributed exotic trinkets. The capital city was built at Chaco Canyon—an otherwise unlikely place—because of historic/mythic events that happened there centuries before. Palaces of the major noble houses rose at places determined in the cityscape by an esoteric geometry that focused on north and the key north-south axis. Or not so esoteric, perhaps: north was evident to everyone, every night as the "heart of the sky" around which the stars revolved. The north-south (meridian) cosmology competed with an older, traditional cosmology that featured the solstices and annual calendrics. Meridian structures were cardinal; the solsticial structures faced south-southeast.

They lived long and prospered. Chaco's nobles decked themselves in macaw-feather regalia and quaffed cacao (chocolate) from cylinder jars. Turquoise from Chaco's workshops went south; copper bells came north. Slaves did the menial tasks; tribute brought them food, labor, honor, and prestige. All in all, it was good to be king.

Around 1075 to 1080, something happened. Possibly the long-simmering conflict between old and new cosmologies boiled over. Possibly charismatic leaders of competing noble families wanted to keep the kingship in-house. A decision was made to create a new capital on one of the live-water creeks and rivers (which Chaco notoriously lacked) to the north. The position of the new capital was determined by running the Chaco Meridian almost 80 km due north, with a slight deflection where the meridian hit an impassible badland. The first river the meridian (and road) crossed was the San Juan, which proved to be too big and unruly. The meridian was prolonged another 15 km to the site of Aztec Ruins on the manageable Rio Animas. The alignment was commemorated in the Great North Road, a monumental affirmation that Aztec was Chaco's successor. There, the new capital was built from 1110 to 1275. Aztec's location was determined by the meridian, but its cityscape was pointedly solstitial, facing south-southeast. Perhaps the two cosmologies were complementary, not competitive: meridian for some purposes, solstitial for others.

(Aztec Ruins, however, was only about half the size and half the population of Chaco. It's possible that Chaco split at 1080, with half going north and half going south—to Paquimé, our next stop.)

Aztec started strong, with some of the biggest construction projects ever attempted by Chacoan builders. A very nasty drought from about 1120 to 1150 spun things off course. The exotics and foreign symbols of power that made Chaco a wonder fell in short supply—chocolate was soon a distant memory for Aztec's down-at-heels kings. The commoners grumbled. The capital maintained order with a very heavy hand: brute force against commoners who broke the rules (failed to pay taxes? fomented rebellion?). Things fell apart, and by the mid-thirteenth century, whole villages of commoners were leaving for greener valleys—mostly the areas around today's Pueblos. Those who stayed had to defend their villages, possibly against other villages, possibly against the state which had become ruthless and oppressive. More and more commoners fled the region. Another drought from about 1275 to 1300 ended the story: the entire region was abandoned by nobles and commoners alike, many tens of thousands leaving a blighted land.

Most commoners settled well outside Aztec's reach, and reinvented themselves as Pueblos: communal, egalitarian farming villages, held together by a web of ritual and ceremony that prevented the reappearance of would-be nobles or wannabe kings. But scores of noble families, after many generations ruling, wanted none of the new egalitarian ethos. They sought new commoners to rule—

that was their job on earth. There were no takers in the north, so they moved south—along the meridian.

About 1300, the Southwest's last great city rose at Paquimé, on the Rio Casas Grandes in Chihuahua—about 630 km due south of Chaco Canyon. Following the meridian south, Chacoan nobles joined with local and in-migrant populations, drawn from all quarters of the compass, to create a great city with all the trappings of Mesoamerica royalty. Paquimé's region rivaled Chaco's, but the city itself was only half the size and population of Chaco's. (If Chaco split, it's possible that half went south while Aztec oppressed the north; and—amid a class revolt—perhaps few Aztec nobles got out alive.)

Paquimé was smaller than Chaco, but far more cosmopolitan. Where Chaco had thirty colorful tropical macaws (and Aztec had three), Paquimé had three hundred—and actively bred the birds. Paquimé played the Mesoamerican ball game on Mesoamerican-style, I-shaped courts. Its nobles had become Mesoamerican, although their bloodlines were northern. Its commoners, however, remained Southwestern: local Chihuahuans and displaced Mimbres and maybe even Four Corners refugees who still supported the old order.

The mix worked and, for a century and a half, Paquimé was a glittering Paris-on-the-Casas-Grandes. Then it too ended around 1450 or shortly thereafter, possibly falling with violence. When the Spanish arrived a century later, Paquimé was a magnificent ruin. What happened to its people? And its rulers—"of high and noble Kings descended, sons of a King, and kin of highest lineage"—where did they go?

The people of the Hopi mesas, Zuni, Acoma, and the Rio Grande were content in their place. They knew Paquimé only as a distant city far to the south, the source of fabulous goods and ritual necessities. The histories of the northern Pueblos diverged from the political history of Chaco-Aztec-Paquimé, and they developed strong internal controls to prevent the rise of any new elites or nobles. Chaco–Aztec was remembered as a wonderful place (White House), but also a terrible place where things had happened that did not belong in the Pueblo world.

BUT WAIT . . . THERE'S MORE!

Chaco-Aztec-Paquimé was the central narrative of political power in the ancient Pueblo world. It had a backstory and dénouement, before and after. "Before" probably didn't involve political power; "after" escaped the Pueblo world entirely. For each of the Pecos System stages (Basketmaker III, Pueblo I–V), the largest, weirdest, and most interesting sites are on or about the Chaco Meridian. The claims for "largest" and "weirdest" are based mostly on the judgment of expert witnesses not even distantly engaged (or even interested) in my case. "Most interesting" can be judged by World Heritage recognition: all but Sacred Ridge–Blue Mesa (PI) and Culiacán (PIV) have that status.

Basketmaker III: The Shabik'eschee site at Chaco Canyon has long been recognized as anomalously large. Add 29SJ423—a site equal in size—and many other sites-within-a-site at Chaco, and you have by far the largest Basketmaker III known to science.

Pueblo I: Blue Mesa, just south of Durango, Colorado, was long ago singled out as the largest Pueblo I site—and then we learned about Ridges Basin just to the west, which doubles the size of the Pueblo I "site" and adds the astonishing architecture of Sacred Ridge: towers, among other things. Together, the largest, weirdest, most interesting site of its time.

Pueblo II: Chaco Culture National Historical Park, I hope, we can take as given, without the need for corroboration: the biggest, weirdest, most interesting Pueblo II site.

Pueblo III: Aztec Ruins National Monument is (or was) a harder sell: history, mystery, and hype made Mesa Verde National Park the icon for Pueblo III. But the facts are pretty clear: the biggest Mesa Verde villages are not on the national park, but in the canyons and plains to the northwest (sites like Yellow Jacket and Goodman Point). And the biggest Mesa Verde city—largest, weirdest, most interesting—is not even in Colorado, but in New Mexico at Aztec Ruins.

Pueblo IV: Paquimé isn't typically considered as Pueblo IV because it's down in Mexico, in the Mogollon region. Paquimé was more Puebloan than not, and if it was Puebloan in the fourteenth century, then we can reasonably call it Pueblo IV. In Pueblo IV, there can be no doubt it was the biggest, weirdest, and most interesting site: weirdest is *prima facie*; most interesting attested by its World Heritage status—no other Pueblo IV site has that honor now or impact then.

Pueblo V: Here we leave the Pueblo world entirely, with Culiacán on the Sinaloan coast (nearly). "Pueblo V" has no real application; I use it here only as a time period. Culiacán was "Pueblo V" in chronology, and—as the Spanish accounts tell us—it was the largest, most important city in northwesternmost Mesoamerica. Biggest: yes, almost certainly. Weirdest: who knows? Most interesting: yes, to me and to the DEA.

These sequential sites—spanning one thousand years—were all biggest, weirdest, and most interesting sites of their times and places, declared so (most of them) by eminent and impartial authorities. They all line up, more or less; their alignment was a north-south longitude, give or take a few kilometers; and that longitude was the Chaco Meridian.

These are "facts." Big, solid, in your face: not percentages or eigenvalues or Bayesian hocus-pocus. I have yet to meet an archaeologist who, when walked through all this, has major objections to the "fact" of big Pecos System sites lining up on a meridian—save for elusive Basketmaker III, which is hard to see. For the present, Shabik-423 is by far the biggest *known* Basketmaker III site—but that may change.

SO WHAT?

The problem is: what did it mean? Answering that question requires, I fear, deprogramming and retooling, shedding our old mystical view of the Southwest and reuniting our Southwest with their world: Mesoamerica. For my colleagues who see the Southwest through Pueblo-tinted glasses, I advise an alternative therapy: close your eyes, take a few deep breaths, open your eyes, and get in touch with your outer reality. Or, rather, *their* outer reality: the Postclassic Mesoamerican world, Mississippian, and all the lovely complicated political systems that dotted North America from the tenth century onward.

The most important, and perhaps most difficult, new reality to grasp is this: for many centuries, the Southwest supported class-stratified societies—upper and lower classes or, more accurately, nobles and commoners. Around 1300, that social system ended: tens of thousands of common people voted with their feet and left the Four Corners and its political structures. They reinvented themselves as Pueblos: egalitarian, communal, ritual, and all that. The nobles went south, looking for lands to rule.

Nobles? Commoners? Where's the evidence for that? At Chaco, the evidence is 50,000 tons of rock and mud, stacked up thirty feet high over the area of a Major League baseball field. I'm describing Pueblo Bonito—and Chetro Ketl and Pueblo Alto, and the rest. Go to Chaco. Walk through Bonito. Cross the wash, and walk around the "Bc" sites. They were absolutely contemporary, and the contrast is absolute: the architecture of a class society. It's not subtle. It's obvious: nobles lived in Bonito, and commoners lived in "Bc" sites.

I'm bemused when I walk through Bonito and the Bc sites with archaeologists and make my pitch for a class-stratified society, and then I am asked, "Where's your proof?" What is it that makes Pueblo Bonito so hard to see?

We've known about the stark contrast between Bonito and Bc sites for years—since the 1930s. First pottery and then tree-ring dating established that the Bonito and BC sites were contemporary. Early archaeologists explained the differences as different ethnicities. That was partially right: two different kinds of people, classes of people, lived in those very different houses, but they were all part of one polity: nobles and commoners.

The history of Mesoamerica—the kings-and-battles history, anyway—is largely the story of nobles ruling or finding places to rule. That was their job, and commoners apparently accepted it. There was no international border, and variations on the noble-commoner theme played out across the (future) United States, from Chumash elites on the California coast to Calusa nobles in Florida—all contemporary with Chaco, Aztec, and Paquimé. North America from Panama up to the northern limits of corn agriculture was awash in class societies and polities, big and small. The biggest noble-commoner society was Cahokia, the great Mississippian capital near modern St. Louis—and also Chaco's exact contemporary. Judging by the remnants and survivals the French encountered much later among the Natchez, the lords of Cahokia were almost certainly royals and nobles, far removed from the commoners—Natchez nobles called their commoners "stinkards," and bad things might happen if a stinkard looked at a noble.

Chaco was like that—sort of. There were nobles and commoners. The idea of social classes violates our notions of what was right and proper in Southwestern prehistory, but those notions are wrong. All the stuff, all those Great Houses that make Chaco so weird, came from the sweat of commoners living in little houses (like the Bc sites).

Then the capital shifted a short hop north to Aztec, and then a long straight track south to Paquimé—720 km from Aztec to Paquimé, 630 km from Chaco to Paquimé. Why would they do that? Why move south, that far?

South away from north, a direction of bad omen. South toward civilization. With commoners leaving to create new societies—the Pueblos—noble families were left with no one to rule. So, like their Mesoamerican counterparts, the Chaco/Aztec nobles moved again. The nobles' world was Mesoamerica; the commoners were building a regional identity of their own. Mesoamerica was an enormously varied region, but for noble families, all of it was more familiar than the emerging Pueblo world of the Southwest.

Nothing I suggest should trigger notions of great empires or states. Southwestern polities were small, loose, and ultimately unsuccessful. They were indeed states, but secondary states—states inspired by bigger, older polities: knockoffs. There had been states and empires in Mesoamerica for many centuries before Chaco and Cahokia. Any interpretations of Chaco, Cahokia, and other "complex" North American societies must come to grips with the fact of Mesoamerica. No one in North America "invented" villages; no one "evolved" complexity. Everything that happened in North America had already happened, centuries or even millennia before, in Mesoamerica.

With Paquimé's demise around 1450, its noble families—now heirs of centuries of rulership, Kings-R-Us—may have gone south to Culiacán, which reached its greatness just before the conquistadors invaded. Commoners, too, moved south, with or without nobles—Pueblo stories of vanished clans and myths of Aztlan may yet merge. That final chapter remains obscure, yet to be written.

NEW METHODS NEEDED: APPLY WITHIN

When we were very young, my cohort (and adjacent cohorts, ascending and descending) were taught by our teachers that archaeology was science: hypothesis testing, Popperian falsification, quantification, measurement, proof, and all that. I was surprised; I thought archaeology was history, coming to the craft through Pompeii (I spent my formative years in Naples, acquiring bad habits). I should have gone into classics, but I was redirected into anthropology, about which I knew very little. I became an accidental anthropologist, an involuntary scientist.

In the 1970s, American anthropological archaeology tried very hard to be science and all but despised history. The authorities expurgated from my 1978 thesis a chapter which suggested that absent good history, our science might be silly. I thought we should get the story right before we tried to draw broader conclusions ("covering laws," they called them).

Getting the story right: It matters, whether or not there were kings in Chaco. It matters to archaeology throughout the Southwest. It changes the historical and social environments throughout the region. Ecological or demographic case studies of a valley or a study area that ignore history too often (always?) come a cropper over "exterior inputs" or "social factors"—that is, history.

To get the story right, we have to develop methods for writing narrative histories for prehistory. *Chaco Meridian* was my first attempt. *A History of the Ancient Southwest* (Lekson 2009) took it further, with more concern for method. I'm a bit biased, of course, but I think *A History of the Ancient Southwest* is a truer account of what happened, a better narrative history than any others currently available: (1) my methods and assumptions were, I think, sound and explicit, and (2) there are no other narrative histories currently available.

We need methods and methodologies and prehistoriographies. We don't have those yet. When I asked a fairly distinguished archaeological audience if they knew of methodologies for writing history for prehistory, one of the wisest archaeologists I know (an emeritus I greatly honor and admire) considered this issue for a minute and replied: "I thought we were just making it up as we went along." Well, yes, but shouldn't we be just as concerned with prehistoriography as we are with technical methods, social theory, and science? I am not aware of a "Method & Theory" book, course, or journal that's grappled in any sustained way with prehistoriography: how to write narrative history for prehistory.

Science can indeed be done with history and prehistory, but science is not a very good way to know or write history. Consider historians, academic and popular. I doubt we could find more than a handful of historians who consider themselves scientists (and those few mostly poached into history from other disciplines).

The intellectual leadership, back in my callow youth, who urged American anthropological archaeology to shun history and embrace science didn't do us any favors. By "us" I mean both the archaeologists and the ancients who form archaeology's most important constituency. We too often forget that point: our job is to tell, as accurately as we can, the histories of ancient peoples: to do them justice. We skipped the history and turned the ancients into lab rats and petri cultures.

That was when we were very young. I grew up and got over scientism. American anthropological archaeology, largely, has not. Many of my cohort (and cohorts ascending and descending), when confronted with the first edition of this book, or journalistic accounts of it, responded with: interesting hypothesis, how are you going to test it? When I hear stuff like that, I order another drink—for me, not for them—and change the subject. They didn't get the memo; they missed the point: it's not a hypothesis—it's an argument. One reviewer objected to my methods: "circumstantial, anecdotal, juristic" (Vivian 2001). Well, yes: I'm making an argument, building a narrative. Not science, more like a legal case: not scientific certainty, but preponderance of the evidence.[1]

CHACO MERIDIAN

When Chaco Meridian was first proposed, fifteen years ago, all were skeptical—including me. Many rejected it, in whole or part. Brian Fagan—one of our best "popular" archaeological writers—tackled *Chaco Canyon* (Fagan 2005) and devoted a few pages to the matter. He asked around and discovered that "few archaeologists involved with any of the three sites accept Lekson's alignment as historical reality" [what a surprise!] (Fagan 2005:212), and he dismissed the Meridian as "an archaeological myth" (2005:212).

What a difference a decade makes. Today, three of the problem's four points are almost universally accepted: Chaco moved north to Aztec. That's no longer controversial—although it's taking the Park Service a while to catch up. The addition of earlier sites to the mix—Shabik-423 and Sacred Ridge–Blue Mesa—strengthens the case in a circumstantial, anecdotal, juristic way. More evidence to ponder—and more evidence to preponder.

The windup: from 500 to 1280, the center, the capital, the whatever-it-was bounced north and south and north and south along a short 130 km-long corridor. And then the pitch: around 1300 (or maybe 1150?), whatever-it-was launched five times that distance to the south, landing at Paquimé. And two centuries later, it skipped the same distance again, to Culiacán.

People are OK with North-Chaco-Aztec, but balk at Paquimé—and I can imagine the Busby Berkeley eye rolling for Culiacán; extraoculars will be strained. Too far, too far, too far by far! Let's focus on 630 km, the distance from Chaco to Paquimé (and from Paquimé to Culiacán). Is that a long distance, too long by far?

Compared to what? For us, 630 km isn't very far at all: a day's drive at 55. But for them? The world of which the Southwest was a very small part did distances on that scale. The great city of Cahokia was Chaco's exact contemporary. It sported 40,000 or 50,000 people, and the biggest pyramid north of Teotihuacan, and was a legitimate peer to any medium-sized Mesoamerican polity. Aztalan (in southern Wisconsin) was a Cahokia "outlier" comparable, in many ways, to Chimney Rock: amid the Woodland populations of Wisconsin, Aztalan appears as out of place as Chimney Rock among the rustics of the upper Piedra. Aztalan is 495 km north of Cahokia, three and one half times farther than Chimney Rock from Chaco Canyon. I doubt that river systems did much to effectively diminish that distance; indeed, by boat, Cahokia and Aztalan were over 600 km apart, against the current.

On another Mississippian frontier, Spiro Mounds in eastern Oklahoma had very strong ties indeed to Cahokia. Spiro is 555 km from Cahokia! Mississippian archaeologists admit Aztalan and Spiro and Cahokia as a combination worthy of debate and discussion. Five-hundred-plus km is not prohibitive or impossible; indeed, it's interesting.

Postclassic Mesoamerica was the larger world of both Chaco and Cahokia—especially the Early Postclassic, from 950 to 1150. The Postclassic period was marked by the spectacular networks of long-distance trade, broad stylistic horizons, and extensive political alliances (Smith and Berdan 2003). A chestnut (I can't say "classic") question of Early Postclassic is the relationship between two key sites: Tula in central Mexico to Chichen Itza in the northern Yucatán. Monuments at the two sites look as if they were built from the same blueprints. I exaggerate, but the resemblances are so striking that we have books titled *Twin City Tales* (Jones 1995) and *Twin Tollans* (Kowalski and Kristin-Graham 2011) and major exhibits on "The World of Tula and Chichen Itza" (a theme in *Legacy of Quetzalcoatl* at the LA County Museum of Art in 2012). The distance between Tula and Chichen Itza was 1,125 km. Hanky-panky happened on thousand-kilometer scales in Mesoamerica. (In an earlier age, Teotihuacan reached out and touched Tikal, a little over 1,000 km distant—and other places equally far away.)

But Tula and Chichen and Teotihuacan were states, empires! Surely those distances were not possible for simpler societies. Well, many archaeologists believe that Cahokia was just a simple "chiefdom" (they're wrong; Pauketat 2007), and Cahokia distances—chiefdom or whatever—are close to Chaco-Paquimé figures. Those distance impress but do not outrage Mississippian archaeologists. And they clearly don't faze Mesoamerican archaeologists. Why do they alarm Southwesternists?

It's what you expect to see, which myth you follow. Our myth of the Southwest holds that societies were always and forever somehow Pueblo-like: simple, egalitarian, independent farming villages held together by ritual, ritual, ritual. They were firmly fixed as "intermediate" societies: a meaningless category that means something more than hunter-gatherers, but less, much less, than states (Lekson 2010). That may (or may not) be the case for Pueblos of the "ethnographic present," but it surely was not true for the Southwest's ancient past (Lekson 2009). The Southwest (1) had class societies with nobles and commoners, and (2) the nobles, at least, were deeply engaged with Mesoamerica—they were trying to be Mesoamerican. Chaco-Aztec and Paquimé were state-level operations—small, derivative, secondary states, translating Mesoamerican models into local idioms. Political centralization and class societies were roundly rejected by the Pueblos, who distanced themselves from nobles and kings around 1300 and started afresh.

Get the narrative right, and Pueblo and Southwestern history (they are not quite the same thing) makes sense. Get it wrong and we have the endless, hopeless "mystery of Chaco Canyon," a riddle wrapped in a mystery inside an enigma—a phenomenon so unique, no ethnographic model fits. I say bosh. Chaco is not that hard to understand, if you get the history right. It was a small knockoff of a Mesoamerican city-state, an altepetl. And that, as John of the great big waterproof boots said, is that.

NOTE

1. Vine Deloria, Jr., trained in law, once complained to me that archaeologists did not know how to frame an argument. He was right: we don't argue a case; we test hypotheses—a silly way to try to write history, if you think about it.

Appendix A

Chaco as Altepetl

Chaco is a failure of Southwestern archaeology. We know so much about Chaco, yet we agree so little—effectively, not at all—about what Chaco was. Historian Daniel Richter, trying to make sense of Chaco, recently complained that "the surviving physical evidence leads archaeologists to wildly different conclusions," most particularly "about the degree to which Chaco Canyon was politically stratified" (Richter 2011:17). Severin Fowles recently summarized (part of) the range of variation on Chaco:

> There is little agreement on the nature of Chacoan leadership. Some interpretations present the canyon as a pilgrimage center managed in a relatively egalitarian fashion by resident priests. . . . Others claim that at its apex Chaco was a secondary state dominated by an elite who resided in palaces, extracted tribute, kept the masses in place through threat, and occasional practice, of theatrical violence. (Fowles 2010:195)

He concludes, "Chaco polarizes contemporary scholarship" (Fowles 2010:195). And to Fowles's two poles, I'd add a third in Chacoan studies: Chaco as essentially Puebloan, farming villages much like ethnographic Zuni. This was Gwinn Vivian's argument (1990), carried on today in different iterations by Wills (2000) and Ware (2014), among others.

Chaco—we are told—was a canyon of simple farming villages (Chaco as Pueblo), or a ceremonial or pilgrimage center (Chaco as rituality), or a regional capital (Chaco as polity). These interpretations seem quite distinct—and you would think that archaeology could tell them apart. But apparently we can't. Chaco therefore is declared deeply mysterious, because archaeologists can't agree.

And archaeology is declared slightly ridiculous, for the same reason—I've audited too many ranger tours that take precisely this tack.

It's become a commonplace, in Chacoan studies, to declare that "no ethnographic models seem to fit Chaco" (Hays-Gilpin 2011:609). Lynne Sebastian some years ago chided us: "If Chaco fit neatly into some straight-forward organizational box based on common patterns that we see in the modern or historical world, we would have found that box by now. This does not mean that it was some unique specimen never seen before or since in the world; that is theoretically possible, but statistically unlikely. What is more likely is that we haven't looked at enough boxes yet" (Sebastian 2004:99; and see Sebastian 2006:411ff.). I agree: it's hard to believe that Chaco—coming near the end of North American prehistory—was something completely new and unique. Mesoamerica had been rolling along for two millennia blooming and pruning social experiments before Chaco did . . . whatever it did. Chaco almost certainly was derivative, in the best sense, of what went before. (If you want bizarre, look early, not late; for example, Poverty Point or Olmec.)

Sebastian (2006) searched for the right box in sub-Saharan Africa, but I think we'll find the answer much closer to hand. Look south; look to Mesoamerica. Chacoans did; why shouldn't we? So I looked south, to Mexico—but too high, into empires. After much fruitless flailing in codices and accounts of Aztecs and Tarascans, I despaired of finding Mesoamerican models appropriate to the Southwest. I needed to lower my sights, and sites. Those mighty empires were composed of small polities, sort of city-state-ish in size and scale. One term for the form was *altepetl*. (I was introduced to the *altepetl* by my esteemed colleague at CU, Dr. Gerardo Gutiérrez, who knows much about the subject. Dr. Gutiérrez is not responsible for my mistakes and errors in this book.) I am not a Mesoamericanist—although I have come to believe that every archaeologist working anywhere north of Panama should become a North Americanist!—but I've spent a fair amount of time (mine and others) boning up on this subject. My principal references are Bernal García and García Zambrano (2006), Gutiérrez (2003), Hirth (2000, 2003, 2008), Hodge (1997), Lockhart (1992), and Smith (2000, 2008)—Smith is not fond of my use of *altepetl*, but his works are invaluable references.

Chaco was not an empire, certainly not on the scale of the Aztecs or Tarascans. As we shall see, Chaco was almost precisely on the scale of the small sociopolitical unit termed *altepetl* (plural, *altepeme*) in Nahua. (Hereafter, we dispense with italics for "altepetl"; they are hard to read.) The altepetl was the basic local polity over much (most?) of Postclassic Mesoamerica. It's not without controversy: Michael Smith, whose data I use here, much prefers the more general term "city-state," noting that altepetl was specific to Nahua at contact (Smith 2008; see also Charlton and Nichols 1997b). True enough, but other archaeologists argue that the form had legs, both chronologically and spatially, back perhaps as far as the Epiclassic period (discussed below).

I'm interested in altepetl for Chaco because (1) it's real; it's not an anthropological theory like chiefdom or rituality; (2) it comes from Chaco's place and time; Chaco surely would have known about it; (3) it's well attested: we have very specific and useful information about altepeme; and (4) it works: it fits Chaco like a glove—one of those elastic, stretchy gloves. Have we found the right "box" for Chaco? I think so—at least a better-fitting "box" than others on offer. What follows is a description of the altepetl form first in the ideal and then in the real; and that is followed by a short argument for why it works for Chaco.

Our most detailed knowledge comes, of course, from proto- and contact Nahua-related documents, long after Chaco (but as discussed below, the form had antiquity). I will use the Nahua term, but other ethnicities and language groups were structured in much the same local-level sociopolitical units—Smith's city-states.

"Altepetl" means "the water(s), the mountain(s)"—a reference to its territorial land base and a key to the inclusive, coherent nature of the polity: it consisted of both a center *and* a region, nobles *and* commoners. The whole thing was a unit. In brief, "An altepetl consisted of a legitimate king—the *tlatoani*—and a population of nobles and commoners subject to the king. In physical terms, the altepetl was made up of a capital city, a series of smaller settlements (towns, villages, and isolated farmsteads), and the farmlands worked by the polity's population" (Smith 2008:89).

James Lockhart (1992) provides a model of altepeme, based on codices and other textual sources, in *The Nahuas after the Conquest* (especially chapter 2, pp. 14–20). Lockhart describes a theoretical altepetl, with arrangements dictated by Native theology and numerology; real altepeme, of course, varied significantly from this theoretical ideal. According to Lockhart, the "minimum requirements . . . are a territory; a set (usually a fixed canonical number) of named constituent [territorial] parts; and a ruler or *tlatoani* (pl. *tlatoque*)" (Lockhart 1992:16). The "constituent [territorial] parts of the altepetl" were "*culpolli*, a term meaning literally 'big house'" (Lockhart 1992:16); that is, territorial subdivisions were in a sense defined by the palaces (big houses) of noble families who controlled or ruled those subdivisions. The palace or noble house itself was called a *tecpan* or *tecalli* (Hodge 1997:212). The "king" (*tlatoani*) was a central leader elected by a council of the highest nobles, and the office theoretically rotated among those families (i.e., it was not dynastic). "The fixed order of rotation of the *culpolli* was the life thread of the altepetl" (Lockhart 1992:17). The succession of *tlatoani* shifted from noble family to noble family, by vote of the nobles, ensuring that son would not inherit power from father and that no one family would dominate the altepetl—at least in theory. This system successfully "decentralized" authority and prevented the rise of any individual noble family in central rulership. The *tlatoani* himself was the head of his own *calpulli* and ruled directly *only* that unit from his palace (Lockhart 1992:18). In effect, all the highest noble families shared governance.

Altepetl lands were divided in complex ways among the multiple noble families, each of which had one or more palaces in its *calpulli*. Ideally, the numbers of *calpulli* were fixed by canonical numbers (for example, eight) (Lockhart 1992:16), but clearly reality differed from the ideal. Half a dozen seems reasonable. Each *calpulli* had its own leader or lord, often dynastic, and each constituted a distinct (and often discontinuous) territory within the larger altepetl. The *calpulli* "in turn were divided into what may be called wards (no indigenous term emerges) of (roughly) twenty, forty, eighty, or a hundred households, each ward having a leader responsible for land allocation, tax collection, and the like" (Lockhart 1992:17), discussed further below.

There are two ways to look at altepeme: an ideal "type"—what it *should* look like; and the on-the-ground reality—what it *did* look like. Earlier I showed mild disdain for anthropological theories (chiefdoms, ritualities), but isn't a "type" another theory? Not so much in this case, because the "ideal" comes (via ethnohistory) from Native sources: more emic than etic. The reality comes from a combination of archaeology and early colonial sources, compiled by various researchers cited below.

For the ideal model, James Lockhart offers a very influential and intriguing diagram of how an altepetl worked, conceptually (Lockhart 1992: figure 2.1, modified here as figure A.1). Note that this is a diagram, not a map. Figure A.1 unites aspects of territorial organization (division into eight *calpulli*) with the ideal system of rotating rulership among the eight highest noble families. Lockhart indicates clustering of palaces in the center of the diagram; that's quasi-cartographic and will be discussed further, below. Note that each palace—or, rather, the noble families residing in those palaces—was equivalent; the highest noble families were equals, together over a secondary nobility. Of course the palace of the overall ruler, the *tlatoani*, was administratively if not architecturally more important.

Lockhart's diagram (figure A.1) is not a map, but its basic structure can be applied to archaeological situations. Kenneth Hirth (2000:272–273; also Hirth 2003, 2008) convincingly applies Lockhart's altepetl model to a medium-sized (9,000 to 15,000 people) Epiclassic polity—the Epiclassic dates AD 650 to 900, about the time that class structures were beginning to form in the northern Southwest (the proto–Great Houses of Pueblo I).

Territory and boundaries were far less rigid than in modern nation-states. The altepetl was defined by relations of people, not by territory: "Territorial boundaries were important for altepetl definition, but they clearly were subordinate in importance to the social relationships that defined tribute and service obligations between lord and subject" (Hirth 2003:73; see also Gutiérrez 2003 and Smith 2008:91). The altepetl was a tributary system. Commoners owed tribute to their immediate lords (secondary nobility); those lower-tier nobles owed tribute to

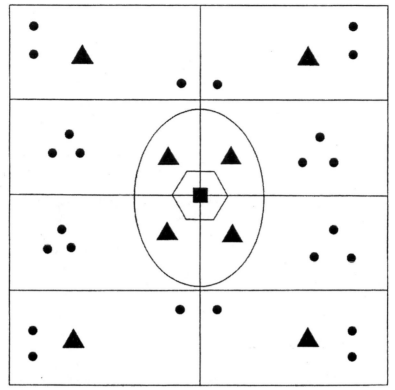

FIGURE A.1
Altepetl, idealized: explained in text (after Lockhart 1992).

higher noble families; the higher noble families owed tribute to the *tlatoani* ruling the altepetl. But tribute from individual commoner families was not oppressive or onerous: a few bushels of corn, a few weeks' labor on nobles' fields or houses, and of course military service in times of war. Again, there was an ideal numerological administrative structure:

> Tribute was provided by mobilizing labor from domestic households on a rotational basis for both private and public (*cuatequitl*) services. Tribute consisted of domestic services and payments of agricultural and craft goods by the individuals who had produced them [organized through the three-tier *cuadrilla*]. The smallest administrative unit was a grouping of 20 households. . . . The second level of *cuadrilla* hierarchy was . . . the group of five *centecpantin* (20 households). . . . At the top of the *cuadrilla* system was the *calpixque* who coordinated the units 100 tribute households. (Hirth 2003:75)

This is important: the altepetl assumes and requires clearly defined classes of nobles and commoners, and a possible middle class. "Elites [nobles] were organized through the 'noble house' (*tecpan* or *tecalli*)"—that is, palaces—while "craft specialists and traders may have formed intermediate social categories" between nobles and true commoners (Hodge 1997:212). "*Calpulli* are often characterized as internally stratified groups of people who lived together, held their land in common, shared a common ethnic or group identity, and engaged in corporate civic and religious activity. Each *calpulli* had a small administrative precinct that could contain a small temple, civic buildings like an elite residence" or palace, a market, and so forth. Importantly, the *telpochcalli* was a house and school for young men (Hirth 2003:75)—a possible function of Chacoan Great Kivas (but that's another story).

Each altepetl had a central cluster of palaces and other civic structures, typically founded at a key place: the site of the initial settlement of the territory, or a notable battlefield, or an otherwise "important" place. Importantly, most (but not all) noble families clustered their palaces around that central spot. This central cluster is a matter of interpretive debate: was it a city? "A key aspect of altepetl organization is that all the major institutions—administrative, religious, and economic—were concentrated in the capital city" (Smith 2008:90)—but not all scholars agree. Lockhart stresses that the altepetl consisted of *both* the central cluster of *tecpans* and the territories around them; together, central cluster and countryside formed the altepetl, with its territorial divisions (*calpulli*). Lockhart (1992:19–20) notes that the term "city" may impose a Western view of capitals and peripheries, and insists that altepetl encompassed both town and country, indivisible. Archaeologically, altepetl landscapes appear to have a central city and multiple secondary centers, but "outlying" major palaces were equivalent, socially and politically, to families in palaces in the central cluster. Smaller secondary palaces were a part of that landscape; they housed lesser noble families that administered subdivisions of larger *calpulli*.

Lockhart, Gutiérrez, and others maintain that this cluster did not constitute a separate city in the Western sense, an urban center to a rural hinterland. Rather the central cluster was constituted of multiple palaces, each corresponding to an individual *calpulli*, and the two were indivisible. There was no urban/rural split: the *calpulli* was the basic unit, and the cluster almost an epiphenomenon. I follow Gutiérrez's summary:

> The concept of "*altepetl*" does not correspond to "city"; rather it refers to the total political-territorial unit of a particular ruling lineage. The *altepetl* may contain locations that present urban characteristics and have "cities." In those cases, a Mesoamerican city is understood to include a concentrated population, political-economic institutions, the ruling lineage, *and* the total territory of the *altepetl*. In pre-Hispanic Mexico, there is no urban-rural dichotomy. If we were to look for

a spatial dichotomy, it would be based on the *pilli-macehualli* relationship—the ruler versus the ruled—and how this relationship determined and dominated the landscape. I believe much of the archaeological data requires reinterpretation based on autochthonous categories. This should not be done mechanically, as it requires the identification of local and chronological variations of the *altepetl*. Despite the variations, given the widespread use of *altepetl* as a political-territorial-ideological structure in Postclassic societies, we need to examine its roots, which undoubtedly lie in the Classic and Formative periods. (Gutiérrez 2003:115)

For the present argument, this disagreement does not greatly matter; it is the scheme or structure that is of interest: things we might see in archaeology. For example, size and scale. How big was an altepetl—center and countryside? I look at two dimensions—population and area—for entire polities and for central settlements.

According to Hodge, the total population of the altepetl or city-state averaged 12,000, and ranged from as small as 2,026 to 40,430; the size of the territory averaged 75 sq km, and ranged from 20 sq km to 228 sq km. "The distance between the urban centers and rural communities in the city-states . . . averages 7.1 km—a walk that could be made in a few hours" (Hodge 1997:218–219). Smith notes that "a typical altepetl in the Basin of Mexico had a population of 10,000 to 15,000 and covered an area of 70 to 100 square km, while in Morelos most altepetl had 5,000 to 10,000 people in an area of 50 to 80 square km" (Smith 2008:90).

And the central clusters? Michael Smith (2008: table 6.1) summarizes the sizes of capitals and second-largest settlements—which he calls cities, and I have no quarrel with that term. From Smith (2008): excluding the huge imperial capitals of Tenochtitlan and Texcoco, twenty Aztec "capital cities" ranged in population size from as few as 600 to 23,000 people. Half were 5,000 or less, and seven were 3,000 or less; that is, one-third of the "capitals" were 3,000 or less in population. The median population size was about 4,750. The median area of the central cluster/capital was 108 ha, with a median population density of 50/ha. Those figures provide a sense of scale for an altepetl central cluster/capital: less than 5,000 people living in an area of about half a square mile. For the second-largest "city" in the polity, Smith found that the median population size was only 465, or about 10 percent of median size of the capital; that is, capitals were an order of magnitude larger than second-largest cities. Comparable data in Hodge (1997:218) for the most part agree with Smith's: "urban center" population ranged from 1,000 to 25,000, "although at least one city-state (Tenanco) in the study area had no urban center (it probably had only elite residential precincts)."

To summarize: the altepetl typically consisted of half a dozen (ideally, eight) noble families occupying palaces, secondary nobles in smaller palaces in a center or city or capital (usually founded at a historically or symbolically important place), and a large population of commoners: between 2,000 and 40,000 people scattered in and beyond the center over the countryside. There was a king, a first among equals, elected from the highest noble families, but the office was not strong, nor did it descend in a kingly line. A hierarchical tributary system moved goods and services up through the secondary and higher nobles and king. Particular commoner families owed tribute only to particular noble families, who then owed tribute to the royal nobility. The tribute or tax was not severe or onerous: a few bushels of corn, a week's work, that sort of thing. Its central "city" had from less than 1,000 to perhaps 5,000 people in about 100 ha; secondary centers were an order of magnitude smaller. "Cities" were defined by civic architecture and monuments, and by geographically clustered noble houses or palaces, each of which controlled groups of commoner families localized in territorial *calpulli*— but sometimes complexly scattered throughout the altepetl. An altepetl on average covered an area of about 75 sq km.

Several key aspects of altepetl "fit" Chaco, and several do not. Let's start with what works. Chaco was a class society, with nobles and commoners—that point is critical. Chaco was the clear regional center/city/capital, with a population in the range of small altepetl cities/centers: 2,500 to 3,000 people. The cluster of seven major Great Houses—elite houses or nobles' palaces—in Chaco Canyon is remarkably similar to the central cluster of noble palaces in altepeme. The seven major Great Houses at Chaco, in this model, represent the altepetl's ideal eight major noble families and their palaces. Other buildings in the altepetl center represent cadet branches, minor nobility, priesthoods, and so forth, much like the minor Great Houses at Chaco, which were residences and warehouses and who knows what.

The demographic scales of altepeme and Chaco are comparable: the largest Aztec altepetl (ignoring the huge imperial capitals) had about 40,000 people, while most had between 10,000 and 15,000. Chapter 2 presented estimates of population in Chaco's core area, the San Juan Basin, of perhaps 55,000 and of the larger Chaco region at perhaps twice that. Chaco's "inner core" population was about the same as the largest altepeme; Chaco's "outer limits" regional population was rather larger.

As in altepeme, the central cluster/city may have been located at Chaco because Chaco Canyon itself was historically important. As noted in chapter 3, centuries before Pueblo Bonito, Chaco Canyon had seen truly remarkable developments in Basketmaker III. We don't know what happened, exactly, but it was something big. Altepetl centers/cities were ideally built at historically or mythically significant places.

Figure A.2 layers Lockhart's ideal (figure A.1) onto Chaco's reality. The pie-slice divisions of Chaco's region, marked by roads radiating out to scores of small, "outlier" Great Houses, parallels the (idealized) subdivisions of the altepetl, with each noble family controlling commoners in its piece of the pie. As with the altepetl, commoner farmsteads were scattered throughout the region and also within

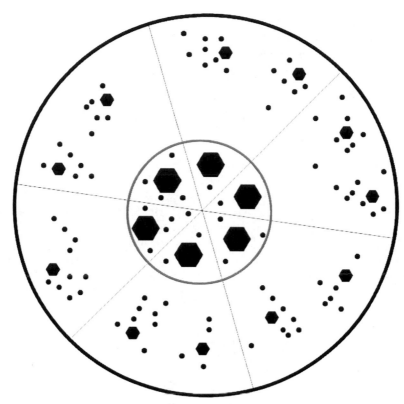

FIGURE A.2
Altepetl, realized: the structure of the Chaco altepetl, combining elements of
Lockhart (1992) and Gutiérrez (2003) with the known form of Chaco's region.

the center/city, with secondary "outlier" Great Houses taking care of business
in the countryside. Like the altepetl, there is no useful separation of center and
countryside: Chaco was not self-sufficient and relied on its region; conversely,
the region focused inward on the center at Chaco Canyon. For both Chaco and
altepetl, the ensemble constitutes the polity.

There were, of course, differences. Chaco translated Mesoamerican forms
into local idioms of architecture, ideology, and cosmology. I'll look at four: first,
ethnic identity; second, absent building types; third, absence of peer polities. A
fourth and more important difference is geographic scale (and related issues of
demographic scale, noted above).

Altepetl is usually understood as an "ethnic state" (Lockhart 1992:14); that
is, the population of the altepetl recognized a common ethnicity or identity.

However, Charlton and Nichols (1997b:169) note that this identity might be fictive, or operational: the "city state" had "a recognized single ethnic identity (although often with a multiethnic composition)." Chaco (taken large) was almost certainly multilingual, perhaps multiethnic; but universal symbols—Great Houses, Dogoszhi-style pottery, and so forth—suggest a shared identity on some level.

Most altepeme centers/cities/capitals had a temple (pyramid) and market (Lockhart 1992:18). Pyramids have been suggested for Chaco (Stein et al. 2007), but it seems likely that this component of Mesoamerican ideologies did not translate into the Southwest and Chaco—if you want to see pyramids, head to the Mississippi Valley. The likely absence of pyramids and the gods they housed suggests that Chaco may have adopted the political form but not necessarily the cosmologies of the south. It has been suggested, from time to time, that the Pueblo world had markets (Kohler, Van Pelt, and Yap 2000; Lekson 2009), but the data are not conclusive. It is noteworthy that markets were far from ubiquitous in Mesoamerican altepetl centers: looking at the Aztec data, "out of 38 city-state centers in the Basin of Mexico, [only] 18 had official marketplaces" (Hodge 1997:212). That is, about one-half of the altepetl capitals actually had markets; and major daily markets were held only in the huge cities of Tenochtitlan and Texcoco.

More telling, perhaps, altepeme existed in the context of other altepeme, or "peer polities"—which some would argue was a necessary condition for city-states. Chaco had no peer on the plateau, at least during its rise and height—Aztec begins in 1110 and Wupatki even later. Was Hohokam a peer polity? Lekson (2009) says yes; Neitzel (2010) says no. Mesoamerica *evolved* the altepetl form; Chaco merely borrowed it and adapted it to Southwestern realities. The absence of peer polities may be more relevant to Chaco's end than its beginning: that is, the altepetl form could be taken out of context, but it could not be sustained out of context.

For me, the major difference between Mesoamerican altepetl form and Chaco is in geographic (and demographic) scale. The average altepetl was 75 sq km with at most 40,000 people; estimates of Chaco's region range from 20,000 to 100,000 sq km with perhaps up to 100,000 people. We might finesse the population issue: if the altepetl is conceived of as an economic-tribute unit, then Chaco's economic "inner core" (see chapter 2) population of 50,000+ is closer to Mesoamerican scales. But differences in geographic scale are, in a word, vast. Geographic scale reflects very different environments. You could feed a lot of people on relatively little land in Mesoamerica, a great place to grow corn. The opposite is true of the northern Southwest and Four Corners: good agricultural land is scattered and patchy, and never reliably productive. The compact altepetl of Mesoamerica reflects the high productivity of its agricultural lands; the same political structure was necessarily "spread out" over the poorer lands of the northern Southwest. Populations were concentrated in Mesoamerica, and spread out in Chaco's region. Chaco developed technologies to make it work: roads and line-of-sight communication networks ensured the coherence of the polity form over the huge Chacoan region. Chaco stretched the altepetl to its extreme limits.

The parallels between Chaco's structure and the idealized altepetl and real Mesoamerican city-states are close, and the differences—while real—are to me more interesting than negatory. Chaco took a form from the rich, bustling south and applied it to a poor, frontier society. It worked for a while but ultimately failed because (1) peer polities were absent to fuel the feedback fission chain that kept city-states going; (2) there was a class revolt by commoners, who voted with their feet, left the Four Corners, and invented Pueblos; and (3) the Southwest is a tough place to start a state, much less an empire. But that's hindsight, our rules: they were making it up as they went along, and it went well for several centuries before the wheels came off.

Appendix B

Dating Casas Grandes

Because the huge pine beams were buried deep in Paquimé ruins, Di Peso had many tree-ring dates. Excavations at smaller sites of that time period don't have that kind of preservation and consequently rely almost entirely on radiocarbon dating, 14C. Most of archaeology uses 14C, but we're spoiled in the Southwest: we expect tree-ring precision and lose patience with 14C's imprecision and ambiguities. Sometimes we try to wring more out of 14C than 14C can deliver.

The issue addressed here is the beginning of the Medio period and the beginning of Paquimé—which probably weren't exactly the same thing. The Medio period was preceded by the long Viejo period of small pithouse sites and—toward its end—pueblo-style villages. Based on the presence of cross-dated ceramics (and particularly Mimbres Black-on-white), Viejo appears to have ended around 1150, when Mimbres Black-on-white ceased to be made. Unless, of course, Mimbres Black-on-white was made longer in Chihuahua than it was in the Mimbres core area of southwestern New Mexico (an interesting possibility, since I argue that Mimbres populations shifted south into Chihuahua).

So the 1150 date for the end of the Viejo period is pretty wobbly; it's simply the date suggested by the pottery, and Viejo could have soldiered on for decades without any new Mimbres pots. But it's the only date we've got.[1] What about the beginning of the Medio period? Paquimé itself is widely accepted to have begun at or shortly before 1300 (Lekson 1984c, 2002; Whalen and Minnis 2009:44), leaving a potential gap from 1150 to 1300. But there was more to the Medio period than Paquimé, maybe an off-site run-up to the big event. So when did the Medio period begin away from Paquimé? The discussion hereafter turns technical and presupposes the reader is familiar with Whalen and Minnis's excellent reports and articles—most importantly the chronological analysis in "Dating the Medio

Period" in their *Neighbors of Casas Grandes* (Whalen and Minnis 2009: chapter 2).

Di Peso suggested a Medio period sequence, with a beginning, a broad middle, and an ugly end—the Buena Fé, Paquimé, and Diablo phases. Whalen and Minnis rejected his chronology (correctly, in my opinion): "Di Peso's three phases of the Medio period have been criticized extensively and no longer should be used" (Whalen and Minnis 2009:44). So there's just a big solid Medio period, *e pluribus unum*.

Absent new excavations at Paquimé itself—unlikely in our lifetimes—we must look elsewhere for chronological clarity. Whalen and Minnis (2003, 2009) excavated four Medio period sites in the Casas Grandes region, looked carefully at chronometry and chronology, and concluded that "the Medio period clearly is underway by A.D. 1200, although there are hints in the Casas Grandes area and elsewhere that it may have begun a little before this date" (Whalen and Minnis 2009:68), suggesting graphically that the Medio period began as early as 1160 (Whalen and Minnis 2009:69). That mid-eleventh-century Medio—if real—met the Mimbres-dated Viejo at 1150: presto, gap closed! 1160 pushes Medio back to Di Peso days, and must in turn expect some pushback. And here it comes.

Tree-ring dating was unsuccessful at their sites, so Whalen and Minnis (2009) rely on 14C dating (and two archaeomagnetic dates, not discussed here). From their work at several sites, they obtained eighty-four 14C dates, "nearly all of which are from Medio period contexts" (Whalen and Minnis 2009:45; the dates are presented in commendable detail in chapter 2 of that report; see also Whalen and Minnis 2003). Fifty-five of the dates were processed with extended count techniques, which should "reduce the standard deviation of each date" (Whalen and Minnis 2009:45).

All but six of those eighty-four dates were obtained from wood, from both fuel and construction contexts (the other six were obtained from maize—none, alas, relevant to the detail that follows). Wood often produces dates that are too old: that is, wood dates may substantially predate targeted events. Only the outermost rings on trees actively fix atmospheric carbon; inner tree rings in effect store older, "fossil" carbon, set in place during the years when inner rings were outer, active rings. Thus a 14C date on wood will almost invariably produce a date older than the actual felling of the tree—the infamous "old wood problem." Radiocarbon dates from wood are problematic for tight problems like the Medio phase—arguments about decades, not centuries.

Within particular contexts, Whalen and Minnis employed a series of statistical procedures to eliminate statistical "outlier" dates and then combined or pooled 14C dates using Keith Kintigh's (2002) programs (Whalen and Minnis 2009:45–47), producing a single probability distribution for each feature or context or site. "The dates used in this analysis must be expressed as radiocarbon years before present (BP) since calibrated dates are not normally distributed" (Whalen and

Minnis 2009:50); the resulting distributions are then calibrated—although it's not clear to me exactly how that works. No matter.

The two key contexts for this argument are an adobe room block at the Tinaja Site (Area 1, Mound A, Site 204) and the earliest levels of a midden at the same site ("lower midden"). These are the best candidates for "early Medio"—that is, pre-1250 Medio period contexts.

Ten dates from Area 1, Mound A, Site 204 (the sole early Medio architectural context) combined to produce a tightly peaked distribution with a mode at 760 BP with a standard deviation of 60; Whalen and Minnis 2009:50–51, figure 2.2). The one standard deviation range, "68 percent of the combined date distribution—820–700 BP, for which the calendar date is cal A.D. 1150–1330 (2σ)"— should "2σ" be "1σ"?—was then assumed to represent *the occupation span* of an early component at the site (Whalen and Minnis 2009:50, figure 2.4). This is a critical point: the standard deviation of the probability distribution was interpreted as the occupation span of the site/context.[2]

A Gaussian statistical range is not an occupation span. The statistical combination of multiple 14C determinations should (or could) increase precision of dating *an event*: that is, of increasing the precision of 14C year determinations around a central tendency, presumably a single date or event. Eliminating "outlier" dates, of course, should also increase precision of dating an event. Pooled means and eliminated outliers do not (of themselves) define *spans*; they increase precision for *events*. (Note I'm discussing precision, not accuracy.)

The standard-deviation calibrated range from the early Medio architectural context (Area 1, Mound A, Site 204) of 1150 to 1330 is offered directly as the actual occupation span of the context: that is, Area 1, Mound A, Site 204 was occupied from 1150 to 1330 (Whalen and Minnis 2009:50). This is not entirely clear in the text but becomes very clear in their figures 2.2 through 2.12—which present the probability distribution of grouped dates from each context and site—to figure 2.14, "Estimated occupation spans of five Medio period sites" (Whalen and Minnis 2009:47–70). A one-standard deviation range (with normal distributions) represents approximately a 67 percent probability that the actual date—the target event—falls within that range, far more likely near its center (mode) than toward either of its two truncated tails. Indeed, the probability of the event falling at either end of a one-sigma range is actually small (17 percent or less). Consider the one-sigma span of 1150 to 1330: the chances of the actual date (*event*) being either 1149 or 1331 is less than 8.5 percent (as an *event*, the probability becomes one-tailed; the event can't be both 1149 *and* 1331). The actual date of the pooled 14C determinations would much more likely be near the center of the distribution, the mode if the distribution was normal or near normal, or within the probability space between "peaks" if the distribution was multimodal—anywhere but out on the edges! Based on the CALIB calculations (see figure B.1), I'd say that Area 1, Mound A, Site 204 most likely dated around 1285 and very likely between 1255

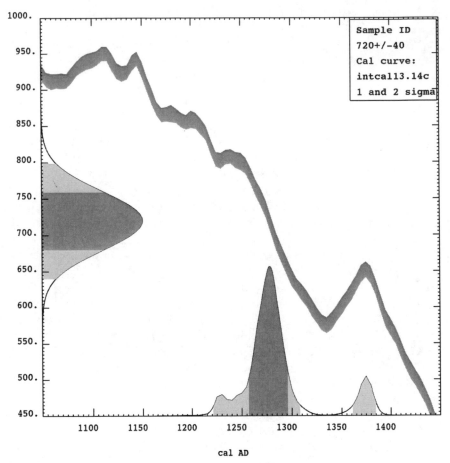

FIGURE B.1
"Early Medio" 14C dates, calibrated (OxCal).

and 1295—and remember, all determinations were on wood, so the calibrated date is probably at least a bit too old.

The other early Medio context—and it's a good one!—which suggests a pre-1250 date is the lower midden of Mound A, Site 204 (Whalen and Minnis 2009:58–61). Significantly, the sizable ceramic assemblage of this context lacked both Ramos and Gila Polychromes, both of which date to approximately 1300 and after (Whalen and Minnis would say 1280 for Ramos Polychrome; Whalen and Minnis 2009:117). Their "early Medio period" ceramic assemblage is a very significant and important discovery (see also Rakita and Raymond 2003); and chronometrically they may have a winner: calibrating the same six dates used in their analysis of the "lower midden" (Whalen and Minnis 2009: table 2.11, figure 2.8) with CALIB produces a one-sigma span of 1155 to 1215, and a two-sigma span of 1045 to 1250, with no clear mode (figure B.2). The lower-midden samples almost certainly predate 1250, and most likely predate 1215. Remember, however: all these dates are on wood. So the jury is still out, but "early Medio" in the lower midden looks pretty solid.

With the advent of Bayesian models for 14C, it is possible to model somewhat tighter dates using the groupings and selections exactly as presented by Whalen and Minnis (2009); that is, with no reevaluation of the architecture, stratigraphy, and contexts of these dates, which I have no reason whatsoever to question.

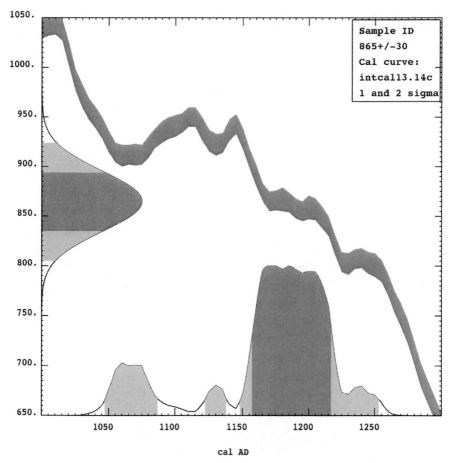

FIGURE B.2
"Lower Midden" 14C dates, calibrated (OxCal).

Exactly the same groupings, selections, and so forth used by Whalen and Minnis are used here in a Bayesian analysis based on the OxCal program.[3] Only one major stratigraphic sequence ("phase" in Bayesian terms) was used: Whalen and Minnis's distinction between "lower" and "upper" Mound A at Site 204 (Whalen and Minnis 2009: figure 2.11). It would be possible, of course, to build tighter stratigraphic relationships through a Harris matrix, but that would necessarily be a job for the primary excavators and analyses, not for a secondary analysis. The analysis was run from oldest to latest, which of course favors the prior probability of earlier rather than later dates. I was tempted to run it in reverse, to favor later datings, but resisted the impulse.

Bayesian analyses produce probability curves, or "posterior density functions," based on data from prior (in this case, earlier) date determinations. When those functions are unimodal with relatively low variance (that is, sharply "peaked), modal values obviously represent the most likely dates. In this case, the Bayesian analysis had the desired result of producing tightly peaked distributions. For key "events" in the sequence, the following estimates were obtained, with modal values to the nearest half decade followed by the two–standard deviation range:

End of late Medio = 1420 (1415–1450)

Beginning of late Medio = 1230 (1215–1250)

End of early Medio = 1220 (1190–1250)

Beginning of early Medio = 1210 (1155–1235)

Remember, almost all dates were on wood and therefore are biased toward determinations older than the target event. Even so, there is little chronological support for early Medio before 1200, or for late Medio before 1230. In the absence of tree-ring dates, I think the best we can hope for are decadal precisions—and precision is not accuracy. To be accurate: early Medio began in the early to mid-thirteenth century, late Medio began in the mid- to late thirteenth century and ended in the mid- to late fifteenth century. That's probably as close as we will get, absent an intense redating program of many more AMS datings on maize or other annuals, followed by a rigorous Harris-matrix-structured Bayesian fandango. Another good project for someone's dissertation.

NOTES

1. There's not a lot of information on the Viejo period (see Pitezel and Searcy 2013). That is an indication of the relative "youth" of Chihuahua archaeology—and/or a real paucity of Viejo period sites in the Casas Grandes area.

2. There is something else odd here: calibrating the same ten 14C determinations from Area 1, Mound A, Site 204 (Whalen and Minnis's 2009: table 2.3, excluding the same three dates excluded by them), with CALIB produces a strongly modal distribution with a clear mode at cal 1285, a one–standard deviation range of 1255–1295, and two–standard deviation spread of 1220–1385 (figure B.1). (Try it yourself: 800±60, 800±40, 800±40, 780±40, 770±40, 760±40, 760±40, 750±40, 750±50, 720±40; http://calib.qub. ac.uk/calib; and remember, all these dates are on wood.) Two different programs, two different distributions?

3. Of course, there's a reason statisticians banned Bayes for a couple of centuries—and why Bayes's heresies have been revived almost exclusively by the looser, weaker sciences (i.e., the social sciences). Bayes cheats: picking and choosing dates, modes, and so forth that fit one's preconceptions (or the statistical preconceptions built into OxCal). May the odds be ever in your favor.

Appendix C
Alto, Far View, and Chimney Rock

I'll make some large arguments from a very small number of tree-ring dates, because some of the key events in the early eleventh-century Chacoan region are represented (I think) by only a few interesting, anomalous dates. I anticipate uneasiness from archaeologists accustomed to great numbers of lockstep tree-ring dates. At Chaco and Mesa Verde, we do dendro by battalions, ranks and files of 1057r marching, with two or three 1056v and 1054v a step behind, and we spurn the odd or anomalous date, 987r straggling far to the rear. "Reused" or "old" wood is tossed on the bonfire of conformities; but those odd unwanted dates meant something to someone, somewhere, sometime. Give 'em a break.

Here are two interesting facts about Chaco:

- Fact #1: Although three of Chaco Canyon Great Houses began in the late ninth or very early tenth century, Chaco's glory days are understood to be 1020 to 1120. What happened from 920 to 1020?
- Fact #2: Major Chacoan expansion to the north of the San Juan River (that is, into the Mesa Verde area) is widely and solidly dated after 1075 (Lipe 2006; Cameron 2009).

I will consider several unusually or "anomalously" early tree-ring dates at some interesting Chacoan sites—Chimney Rock near Durango, Colorado; Far View House at Mesa Verde; and Pueblo Alto at Chaco—which have been lost amid far more numerous later dates. These dates fall into Chaco's missing century and may push Chaco north of the San Juan long before it's wanted.

Anomalous early dates are often dismissed as reused wood or old wood, particularly amid arrays of later dates. Surely expediency was the rule, in many times and places. But perhaps not for Chacoan architecture: monumentally overbuilt, symbolically charged, and conspicuously nonexpedient. Chacoan architectural canons were profligate but purposeful in wood use. I suspect that Chaco construction used precisely the type of wood wanted for the purpose—including old wood. For example, consider "radial-beam pilasters," typical of Chaco "kivas," which usually have six or eight such pilasters spaced around the "bench." The "pilaster" consists of a short section of log lying flat on the bench. They typically go only a few centimeters into the kiva wall and were cut a few cm in from the edge of the bench. The wooden beam in the pilaster was usually encased in a masonry "box," a carefully constructed veneer of small stone elements (that is, nice looking but lacking compressive strength), leaving the uppermost and inward-most aspects of the beam exposed and visible. In the exposed top of the wood, very often a small, round repository was carefully carved into the beam, sometimes fitted with a lid. Several such repositories contained turquoise fragments and other deposits consistent with offerings. The radial-beam pilaster looks, to me, much like a wood shrine.

The wood in radial-beam pilasters was often scabrous and nasty and anomalously old—a motley of species and dates in a single kiva. Varied species, anomalous datings, and the sometimes rough condition of these elements might be dismissed as the use of old, expedient wood—using whatever was lying around. Not, I think, at Chaco. Chaco builders used precisely the wood they wanted, and went to great lengths to get it. They mustered labor to harvest, prepare, transport, and install hundreds of thousands of specific wood elements. The sizes and species used in the roofing of even deep, dark interior storage rooms were often highly standardized. At Aztec, they lavished aspen on storerooms! If Chacoans used "old wood" in radial-beam pilasters, it was probably for an explicit architectural, symbolic, or cosmological decision: they wanted those particular pieces of wood in those key architectural contexts. Old wood was not simply expedient, but highly meaningful. I strongly suspect the pilasters commemorated old buildings, distant forests, events, directions, whatever. In Chacoan buildings, old wood *meant something.*

Of course, the mixture of older and younger wood elements in particular contexts might also indicate less symbolically charged interpretations. For example: reroofing. When floors and roofs were replaced, solid older elements might be retained; not everything at Chaco was woo-woo. But much of it was: the very act of building (and rebuilding) probably had ideological (and political) significance (e.g., Crown and Wills 2003; Van Dyke 2004), like cyclic rebuilding in Mesoamerica. How would we see this? Lintels and other wood elements firmly embedded in the masonry fabric sometimes date significantly earlier than far more abundant secondary roof beams, suggesting actual construction at an earlier date, and roofing or reroofing at a later date—or deliberate incorporation of earlier, reused beams. It could go either way. The point is that Chacoan building wasn't like other Ancestral Pueblo building, before or after: Chaco architecture was rule-bound and highly particular. Wood—old or new—at Chacoan buildings probably meant as much as fancy masonry and stylized doorways and all the rest of the Chacoan canon. Other building traditions, maybe not so much: sometimes—perhaps most of the time—old wood is just old wood.

With that deliberately disorienting introduction, let's look at three Chacoan structures: Pueblo Alto, Chimney Rock, and Far View House. I will argue that anomalous early dates link these three sites in a network with implications for Chaco's missing century (920 to 1020) and for Chaco's expansion north across the San Juan River.

CHIMNEY ROCK

Chimney Rock near Pagosa Springs, Colorado, is "the ultimate outlier" (Malville 2004); a broad consensus among normally aconsensual archaeologists is that Chimney Rock was built to Chacoan plans by Chacoan masons—the same guys who built Pueblo Bonito and Chetro Ketl, or fellow members of the Chaco Local of the Union of Bricklayers and Allied Craftworkers.

The first and most extensive excavations at Chimney Rock were those of J. A. Jeançon of the Colorado Historical Society, in the 1920s (Lister 1997). Frank Eddy's excavations in 1970 produced scores of tree-ring dates (Eddy 1977; figure C.1). Our work in 2009 produced numbers proportionate to the much smaller scale of our excavations (Todd and Lekson 2010)—a small collection with a couple of interesting early anomalies (figure C.1). Our samples repeat and confirm Eddy's dates, particularly the clear evidence of roofing (or reroofing?) in 1093. But two of the recent dates are, indeed, anomalous: cutting dates at 1011 and 1018. Both of these dates were almost certainly architectural elements. They had "a characteristic surface patina and smoothness, which develops on the exterior surface of beams" stripped of bark, which was originally defined as characteristic of Chaco beams but which now extends to a few beams from other building traditions, but still occurs "disproportionately on Chaco specimens" (Jeffrey Dean, personal communication, 2010). That is, the beams that produced 1011 and 1018 dates were not pieces of wood that were just lying around; they were produced to be architectural elements. Beyond these two dates, there is little or no evidence of occupation of Chimney Rock Mesa or the surrounding area in the early eleventh century (Jason Chuipka, personal communication, 2010). I believe that these dates indicate either (1) construction of the Chimney Rock Great House in the early eleventh century, followed by reroofing in 1093, or (2) more likely, an earlier Chacoan structure on or near the location of present Chimney Rock pueblo, with purposeful reuse of its timbers in the later Great House.

```
87     5
-----
100
101    1 8
102    4
103
104
105    3 5 5
106    6
107    0 3 6 9
108    0 1 2 3 4 4 5 6 7 7 9
109    0 0 1 2 2 2 2 3 3 3 3 3 3 3 3 3 3 3 3 3 3 3 3 3 3 3 3 3 3 3 3 3 3 3 3 3
```

CUTTING DATES:

1011	Minor lunar standstill
1018	Major lunar standstill
1070	
1076	Major lunar standstill
1093	Major lunar standstill

(Major standstills in 1037, 1056 not represented in tree ring sample)

FIGURE C.1
Chimney Rock tree-ring dates (N = vv; <u>N</u> = single v; **<u>N</u>** = cutting).

Chimney Rock's masonry, as seen in our excavations and in prestabiliza-tion photography from the 1920s, is Style II, much like the initial construction at Pueblo Alto. Style II dates from 1020 (and perhaps earlier) to about 1050. (Chimney Rock's masonry was greatly altered in 1970s stabilization; it looks a lot nicer now than it used to—we have photos from the 1920s.) Style II was no longer used by Chacoan builders by 1093, either in Chaco Canyon or in major Great Houses like Salmon Ruins. By 1093, Styles III and IV (and the misnamed "McElmo" style) were in fashion. Maybe Chimney Rock masons were slow, or just didn't get it. However, the East Kiva is a perfect example of a Chaco kiva; and that, for me, is highly significant: I think kivas closely reflect the identities of their occupants. Early masonry and early dates—rare as they might be—suggest that Chimney Rock may well have been constructed, at least in part, in the early eleventh century, and reroofed a final time in 1093. Or, if masonry lagged in the provinces, in the late eleventh century the Great House may have replaced and in part incorporated an early eleventh-century structure.

FAR VIEW HOUSE

Far View House at Mesa Verde is a classic "outlier" Great House presumably constructed during the latter decades of Chaco's peak, perhaps 1075 to 1125—although contrary interpretations persist. Some people are oblivious or perhaps impervious to Far View's Chacoan charms. An undated (but fairly recent) trail guide published by the Mesa Verde Museum Association includes the following quote: "Far View House was built and occupied between A.D. 1100 and 1300—during the Classic Pueblo Period of Mesa Verde Ancestral Puebloan occupation." (Ain't no Chaco here, no siree.)

Far View House tree-ring dates come from a variety of field operations, all long after Jesse Walter Fewkes cleaned the place out in 1916. Most are provenienced only to rooms, at best. We do not know the original functions of almost all the beams (only one or two are described as lintels, for example), but I will assume that most were from collapsed roofs. In any event, of seventy-six tree-ring dates, twenty-one predate 1000, forty-one fall between 1020 and 1120, fourteen postdate 1120, and no dates are later than 1243 (figure C.2). Of course, those totals include many "vv" dates; limiting the dates only to cutting or near-cutting (single "v") dates, there are only fourteen:

- 890 (Kiva C*)
- 932v (miscellaneous)
- 1018, 1018 (Room 33)
- 1049 (Room 33)
- 1059, 1059, 1059, 1059, 1059 (Room 33)
- 1069v (Room 32)
- 1243, 1243, 1243 (Kiva C*)

The earliest date of 890 comes from Kiva C, which also produced the latest dates of 1243. Kiva C appears to be a Mesa Verde phase unit intruded into the earlier Chacoan structure—a very common phenomenon in the northern San Juan. Those Mesa Verde guys lost all decency and routinely used lots of old wood, whatever was lying around. Another early date, 932v from an unknown provenience, suggests that either an early Great House or wood from an important PI building was incorporated in the later Great House. Almost all the remaining cutting and near-cutting dates come from a single unit, Room 33, with multiple cutting dates at 1018 and 1059. "However, these could represent reused timbers from one of the many sites in the vicinity" (Robinson and Harrill 1974:63), an interpretation consistent with the Mesa Verde Museum Association trail guide

67	1

77	2

80	9

87	3
88	6 7
89	**0** 7
90	5
91	
92	
93	<u>2</u> 3
94	3 8
95	8
960	
97	4 8
98	4 8 8
99	6 9
100	4 4 7 8
101	0 3 5 7 **8 8**
102	1 1 1 2 3
103	0 8 8
104	0 <u>0</u> 3 2 4 8 <u>**9**</u>
105	4 6 <u>**9 9 9 9 9**</u>
106	4 5 <u>9</u>
107	8
108	4
109	
110	7
111	7
112	0 0
113	
114	
115	
116	3 5
117	
118	0
119	
120	6
121	
122	1 6
123	9 9 9
124	2 3 <u>**3 3 3**</u>

FIGURE C.2
Far View tree-ring dates (N = vv; <u>N</u> = single v; <u>**N**</u> = cutting) (Robinson and Harrill 1974:59–60).

quoted above. (There are, indeed, many sites in the Far View community; dates from those sites include a number of cutting dates from the span 898–899, and many later "vv" dates—but no cutting dates at or around 1018 and 1056, for potential reuse in Far View; Robinson and Harrill 1974:60–62).

A conventional interpretation might have Room 33 built in 1059, expediently reusing much earlier wood cut in 1018. That may indeed be the case, but, alternatively, the anomalous early dates at 1018 might (1) represent deliberate incorporation of wood from earlier significant construction, or (2) indicate that Room 33 was actually built in 1018 and reroofed in 1059. The final near-cutting date of 1069v from Room 32 supports the interpretations that most of Far View House (minus obvious later modifications, such as Kiva C) was built during the Chacoan era, and that—far less certainly—the roofing and reroofing spanned decades.

PUEBLO ALTO

Pueblo Alto, high atop the North Mesa at Chaco Canyon, produced 136 tree-ring dates, including a very conspicuous cluster at 1044–1045, with over thirty cutting or near-cutting dates (Windes 1987a: table 8.2) (figure C.3). This cluster suggests "major, perhaps the initial, period of construction. . . . The earliest date of A.D. 1021 [discussed below] does not rule out earlier construction . . . the two dates are closely related in time and present the strongest case for the A.D. 1045 period of initial construction unless a major hiatus occurred between construction of walls and roofs" (Windes 1987a:213).[1]

Dozens of 1045 specimens were recovered from the Trash Mound; the single 1021 specimen came from the walls of the building itself. The Trash Mound dates have become the accepted dating for Alto, but let's look further at tree-ring dates actually from the building. "Only seven tree-ring dates, three from wall-clearing, were obtained from room excavations at Pueblo Alto" (Windes 1987:210). Of these seven, five are noncutting dates, ranging from 911vv to 1016vv. A near-cutting date of 1004v was obtained from roof fall of Room 142; and a 1021r cutting date came from an intramural beam built into the north wall of Room 110 (Windes 1987a: table 8.2). Thus, there are two cutting or near-cutting dates of 1004v and 1021r, and five noncutting dates, none of which are later than 1016.

The 1004v date came from the "floor fill" (Layer 6) directly above the floor of Room 142. (Full disclosure: I excavated Room 142—but that was a long time ago, and I don't recall the details.) Thanks to Tom Windes's careful and complete report on Pueblo Alto, we learn that Layer 6 included "large chunks of adobe roofing. . . . The density of artifacts was greater in this than in any other above Floor 1, and probably represent debris left scattered over the roof at abandonment" (Windes 1987b:72). Windes discounts this date: "Its association with room construction is dubious, however, because of its context and because it was superseded by a more recently dated specimen (A.D. 1016vv) used as a roof sup-

```
90
91    1
92
93    5
94    9
95
96    6
97
98
99
100   4
101   6
102   1
103
104   3, 4! 5!*
```

*over 35 @ 1053, 1044 and 1045 cutting dates, represent one or more burned roofs in trash mound

CUTTING AND SINGLE V DATES:
1004v
1021
1044, 1045

FIGURE C.3
Pueblo Alto tree-ring dates (N = vv; N = single v; N = cutting).

port in the same room" (Windes 1987a:210). But I think the 1004v date is worth consideration: probably a roof element, possibly a lintel from a collapsed door in the south wall of the room, but—as for most Chaco dates—probably meaningful. Room 142 was part of the first major construction phase at Pueblo Alto, a line of very large rooms backed by paired storage rooms, which Windes dates to 1020–1040, favoring the later, upper limit of that span in light of the Trash Mound 1045 date cluster (Windes 1987a:151–152). The ceramic assemblage associated with construction of these rooms was represented in good, sealed contexts: a pure Red Mesa Black-on-white assemblage (Windes 1987b: figures 2.11, 2.16), which agrees better, in my opinion, with the 1004v date than with the 1040s dating—by the 1040s, later types were appearing.

The other date from actual construction contexts, 1021r, came from an intramural beam in Room 110 in the west wing of the site which Windes dates to 1020–1050—again, I think, reflecting the 1045 cluster in the Trash Mound. The 1021r date comes from a (literally) rock-solid context: not a beam floating in fill but a beam built into the masonry, never to be seen again. The 1021r date is also consistent with the Red Mesa ceramic assemblage associated with initial room construction (Windes 1987b:261). However, Windes states: "We did not recover other supportive tree-ring evidence for construction this early, whereas ceramic cross-dating and other absolute dates suggest construction may have taken place a decade or two later," again leaning toward construction in the 1040s. The Red Mesa assemblage is consistent with a 1021 date for initial construction; the "other absolute dates" from the first floor of the unit consisted of a 14C date that Windes interpreted as 1024± and an archaeomagnetic date of 1170±22 (Windes 1987a: table 8.8). Needless to say, both of these dates are problematic—although Windes's interpretation of the 14C fills me with (muted) joy. But I think we can trust the strong association of a solid Red Mesa ceramic assemblage, which supports initial construction at 1021 or shortly thereafter.

Datings in the 1040s are consistent with the array of all tree-ring dates from Pueblo Alto, especially if we weigh the importance of dates by frequency: over thirty dates at 1044–1045 versus single cutting or near-cutting dates at 1004v and 1021. In this case, we have only two dates from architectural contexts; of course, they could be reused from an earlier structure—as I argued above for radial-beam pilasters—but we don't have a suite of later architectural dates against which 1004 and 1021 would appear anomalous; they're the only dates we've got *from the building*. (I know, I know: I've flipped my logic. Bear with me: a foolish consistency is the hobgoblin of little minds, and I am a bear of very little brain.) I think the earliest construction at Pueblo Alto could well be represented by the 1004v date from Room 142, and/or the 1021 date of the intramural beam of Room 110. If they were *not* reused wood, those early eleventh-century dates may better represent initial construction than does the demolished 1045 roof found in the Trash Mound.

Alto, in its remarkable location high above the valley floor, may well have seen initial construction in a span represented by only 2 out of 136 tree-ring dates: 1004v and 1021r. Alto sits on Chaco's north; in the early eleventh century, what was going on to the north?

PUEBLO ALTO, FAR VIEW HOUSE, AND CHIMNEY ROCK

Pueblo Alto, Far View House, and Chimney Rock form an interesting triangle, or an open V. Far View and Chimney Rock were both about 150 km across relatively open country from the vertex at Pueblo Alto. Far View and Chimney Rock were about 100 km from each other, but the HD Mountains rise between them. Whether they could or could not see Pueblo Alto is a matter of real interest.

All three are conspicuously up high, with sweeping views: Pueblo Alto on North Mesa at Chaco, Far View on a narrow ridge running up to the northern scarp of Mesa Verde, and Chimney Rock atop its spectacular ridge.

Why was Pueblo Alto built where it was? In part, almost certainly, because the spot marked the north end of a highly significant north-south alignment defining

Chaco's basic urban structure—the Chaco Meridian. The spot had been marked, a short time before construction of the Great House, by a small but substantial structure, Rooms 50 and 51 under the very center of the later building. It is possible that the 1004v date, which came from a room subsequently built atop the older Room 50–51 building, was purposefully reused from that earlier structure; but the 1004v date is also consistent with the Red Mesa ceramic assemblage associated with early Pueblo Alto. In addition to defining the north end of the central meridian of Chaco Canyon, Alto's position atop North Mesa gave it a stunning field of view, especially to the north, where Huerfano Butte dominates the northern skyline. The south was largely blocked by the south rim of South Mesa. It is reasonable to conclude that Alto's location was selected in part for its viewshed to the east, north, and west—but not to the south.

Why were Far View and Chimney Rock built where they were? Far View House was the largest (but not the only) Chacoan Great House at Mesa Verde National Park. Its location is puzzling, on the narrow neck of a mesa, with very limited watershed and arable lands. Most settlements of 975–1075 (Mancos phase—the early Chaco era) were down in valleys, near reliable water and good farmlands (specifically in Morefield and Prater Canyons), not high atop mesas—although mesa-top settlements were by no means unknown. I'd guess it was the view: Far View was aptly named (but I don't know who named it!). I am aware of no analysis of its viewshed, but it certainly covered most of the San Juan Basin, from the Chuska Mountains on the west, and to the east, to the toe of the La Plata Mountains and, beyond, the HD Mountains.

Neither Far View nor Chimney Rock could see Pueblo Alto—I think. Alto was not visible from Chimney Rock, and viewshed GIS programs indicate that Alto was not visible from Far View. (These somewhat uncertain "facts" could be easily checked with a few truck flares at night—a good project for someone's master's thesis.) The common point visible from and to all three sites was Huerfano Butte, a very prominent landmark in the northern San Juan Basin and an important place for Natives, ancient and modern.

Chimney Rock was in the most striking setting of the three sites—indeed, in one of the most spectacular settings of any site in the Four Corners. High atop a knife-edge ridge, Chimney Rock's field of view was in fact rather circumscribed: surrounded by taller mountains (the HD Mountains to the west blocked line of sight to Far View), its most notable long-distance vista was a straight shot down the Piedra River Valley, which allowed a limited but precise view of Huerfano Butte. If the Great House were shifted 20 m down its ridge, that line of sight would vanish. (It's not possible to shift it, even hypothetically, further up the ridge because the ridge ends in a scary cliff.) An oversized firebox (still extant, contrary to popular belief) was found at the end of the ridge. It had been burned repeatedly, bright red; and they weren't toasting marshmallows. A fire from Chimney Rock could signal a repeater station at Huerfano, where other similar fireboxes have been found, and thence a signal into Pueblo Alto. This was a dandy science fair project for Katie Freeman (Freeman, Bliss, and Thompson 1996).

I am reasonably confident that Chimney Rock Great House was built at its specific location in large part to see Huerfano (as well as two sandstone pillars, Chimney and Companion Rocks, with astronomical implications). And it seems clear that Pueblo Alto was built atop North Mesa at least in part to see Huerfano, the key "repeater" station in the line-of-site communication system. I believe—but can't yet prove—that Far View House was built high up on Mesa Verde to see Huerfano Butte, for the same reasons as Chimney Rock: line-of-sight communication with Chaco. And I believe that these three Great Houses, or earlier versions of them, were in place by the early 1020s—a half century before Chaco's 1075 expansion north of the San Juan. Most of the considerable Great House construction north of the San Juan River dated to 1075 or later. But the few anomalous dates suggest that construction at Far View, Chimney Rock, and Pueblo Alto began as early as 1004v, 1011, or 1018. Or, conversely, that structures worth commemorating were built at those locations at those times, to be replaced by the later, larger buildings we see today.

To these I add a cutting date from a radial-beam pilaster at Carhart Pueblo (Baxter 2010), the northernmost Chaco outlier (chapter 2): 1017c.

Chaco's regional expansion at 1075 may have been preceded by an earlier presence, in the early eleventh century, at key sites—into an area that was then largely depopulated. Why is a good question. Chimney Rock appropriated or confiscated the remarkable lunar monuments of its twin pillars; the Great House effectively blocked viewing of the 18.6-year lunar events to any but the Chacoan residents. Far View, as far as I know, had no such properties. It had a far, far view, but no other obvious attractions. Perhaps it was not looking at the skies but at the lands below: the rich agricultural lands atop and around Mesa Verde. Time will tell.

NOTE

1. Some years earlier, Windes dated initial construction "in the early 1000s, perhaps as late as 1030 or 1040" (Windes 1984:205, in Lekson 1986).

References

Adams, E. Charles
  1991   *The Origin and Development of the Pueblo Katsina Cult.* Tucson: University of
          Arizona Press.

Adler, Michael A., ed.
  1996   *The Prehistoric Pueblo World, A.D. 1150–1350.* Tucson: University of Arizona
          Press.

Akins, Nancy J.
  1985   Prehistoric Faunal Utilization in Chaco Canyon Basketmaker III through
          Pueblo III. In *Environment and Subsistence of Chaco Canyon, New Mexico,*
          edited by Frances Joan Mathien, pp. 305–445. Publications in Archaeology
          18E. Albuquerque, NM: National Park Service.
  1986   *A Biocultural Approach to Human Burials from Chaco Canyon, New Mexico.*
          Reports of the Chaco Center 9. Santa Fe, NM: National Park Service.

Akins, Nancy J., and John D. Schelberg
  1984   Evidence for Organizational Complexity as Seen from the Mortuary Practices
          at Chaco Canyon. In *Recent Research on Chaco Prehistory,* edited by W. James
          Judge and John D. Schelberg, pp. 89–102. Reports of the Chaco Center 8.
          Albuquerque, NM: National Park Service.

Anyon, Roger, and Steven A. LeBlanc
  1980   The Architectural Evolution of Mogollon-Mimbres Communal Structures.
          Kiva 45(3):253–277.
  1984   *The Galaz Ruin, a Prehistoric Mimbres Village in Southwestern New Mexico.*
          Albuquerque: University of New Mexico Press.

Anyon, Roger, T. J. Ferguson, Loretta Jackson, Lillie Lane, and Philip Vicenti
  1997   Native American Oral Tradition and Archaeology: Issues of Structure,
          Relevance, and Respect. In *Native Americans and Archaeologists: Stepping*

Stone to Common Ground, edited by Nina Swidler, Kurt E. Dongoske, Roger Anyon, and Alan S. Downer, pp. 77–87. Walnut Creek, CA: AltaMira Press.

Ashmore, Wendy
1991   Site-Planning Principles and Concepts of Directionality among the Ancient Maya. *Latin American Antiquity* 2(3):199–226.

Aveni, Anthony F.
1977   Concepts of Positional Astronomy Employed in Ancient Mesoamerican Architecture. In *Native American Astronomy*, edited by Anthony F. Aveni, pp. 3–19. Austin: University of Texas Press.

Aveni, Anthony F., E. E. Calnek, and H. Hartung
1988   Myth, Environment, and the Orientation of the Templo Mayor of Tenochtitlan. *American Antiquity* 53(2):287–309.

Bandelier, Adolph F.
1882   The "Montezuma" of the Pueblo Indians. *American Anthropologist* 5(4):319–326.
1890–1892   *Final Report of Investigations among the Indians of the Southwestern United States, Carried on Mainly in the Years from 1880 to 1885.* American Series 3–4. Cambridge, MA: Archaeological Institute of America.

Basso, Keith
1996   *Wisdom Sits in Places: Landscape and Language among the Western Apache.* Albuquerque: University of New Mexico Press.

Baxter, L. Erin
2010   Explorations at Carhart Pueblo: A Great House Community in the Northern San Juan Region. MA thesis, University of Colorado, Boulder.

Benson, Larry V.
2010a   Factors Controlling Pre-Columbian and Early Historic Maize Productivity in the American Southwest, Part 2: The Chaco Halo, Mesa Verde, Pajarito Plateau/Bandelier, and Zuni Archaeological Regions. *Journal of Archaeological Method and Theory* 18:61–109.
2010b   Who Provided Maize to Chaco Canyon after the Mid-12th-Century Drought? *Journal of Archaeological Science* 37:621–629.

Bernal García, María Elena, and Angel Julián García Zambrano
2006   El Altepetl Colonial y sus Antecendentes Prehispanicos: Contexto Teórico-Historiográfico. In *Territorialidad y Paisaje en el Atlepetl del Siglo XVI*, edited by Federico Fernández Christlieb and Angel Julián García Zambrano, pp. 31–113. México, D.F.: Fondo de Cultura Económica and Instituto de Geografía de la Universidad Nacional Autónoma de México.

Bernardini, Wesley
1999   Reassessing the Scale of Social Action at Pueblo Bonito, Chaco Canyon, New Mexico. *Kiva* 64:447–470.

Blake, Michael, Steven A. LeBlanc, and Paul E. Minnis
   1986   Changing Settlement and Population in the Mimbres Valley, SW New Mexico. *Journal of Field Archaeology* 13:449–464.

Blanton, Richard E.
   1994   *Houses and Households: A Comparative Study.* New York: Plenum Press.

Borson, Nancy, Frances Berdan, Edward Stark, Jack States, and Peter J. Wettstein
   1998   Origins of an Anasazi Macaw Feather Artifact. *American Antiquity* 63(1):131–142.

Bradley, Bruce A.
   1996   Pitchers to Mugs: Chacoan Revival at Sand Canyon Pueblo. *Kiva* 61(3):241–255.

Bradley, Richard
   1993   *Altering the Earth.* Monograph Series 8. Edinburgh: Society of Antiquaries of Scotland.

Bradley, Ronna J.
   1993   Marine Shell Exchange in Northwest Mexico and the Southwest. In *The American Southwest and Mesoamerica: Systems of Prehistoric Exchange*, edited by Jonathan E. Ericson and Timothy G. Baugh, pp. 121–152. New York: Plenum Press.
   2000   Networks of Shell Ornament Exchange: A Critical Assessment of Prestige Economies in the North American Southwest. In *Archaeology of Regional Interaction: Religion, Warfare, and Exchange Across the American Southwest and Beyond*, edited by Michelle Hegmon, pp. 167–187. Boulder, CO: University Press of Colorado.

Brand, Donald D.
   1935   The Distribution of Pottery Types in Northwest New Mexico. *American Anthropologist* 37(2):287–305.

Brandt, Elizabeth A.
   1994   Egalitarianism, Hierarchy, and Centralization in the Pueblos. In *The Ancient Southwestern Community*, edited by W. H. Wills and Robert D. Leonard, pp. 9–23. Albuquerque: University of New Mexico Press.

Breternitz, Cory D., David E. Doyel, and Michael Marshall, eds.
   1982   *Bis sa'ani: A Late Bonito Phase Community on Escavada Wash, Northwest New Mexico.* Navajo Nation Papers in Anthropology 14. Window Rock, AZ: Navajo Nation Cultural Resources Management Program.

Broadbent, Simon
   1980   Simulating the Ley Hunter. *Journal of the Royal Statistical Society Series A* 143(2):109–140.

Brody, J. J.
   1977   *Mimbres Painted Pottery.* Albuquerque: University of New Mexico Press.

Brown, Gary, Thomas C. Windes, and Peter J. McKenna
  2008   Aztec Anamnesis: Aztec Ruins or Anasazi Capital? In *Chaco's Northern Prodigies*, edited by Paul Reed, pp. 231–250. Salt Lake City: University of Utah Press.

Brumfiel, Elizabeth M., and Timothy K. Earle, eds.
  1987   *Specialization, Exchange, and Complex Societies*. Cambridge: Cambridge University Press.

Bunzel, Ruth L.
  1932   Zuni Origin Myths. In *Forty-Seventh Annual Report of the Bureau of American Ethnology, 1929–1930*, pp. 545–609. Washington, DC: Government Printing Office.

Byrkit, James W.
  1988   The Palatkwapi Trail. *Plateau* 59(4).

Cabana, Graciela S. and Jeffrey J. Clark
  2011   Migration in Anthropology: Where We Stand. In *Rethinking Anthropological Perspectives on Migration*, edited by Graciela Cabana and Jeffrey Clark, pp. 3–15. Gainesville: University Press of Florida.

Calvin, William H.
  1997   Leapfrogging Gnomons: A Method for Surveying a Very Long North–South without Modern Instruments. *The Calvin Bookshelf* (January 3, 1997), http://wever.u.washington.edu/~wcalvin/gnomon.htm.

Cameron, Catherine, and Andrew I. Duff
  2008   History and Process in Village Formation: Context and Contrasts from the Northern Southwest. *American Antiquity* 73(1):29–57.

Cameron, Catherine M.
  1998   Coursed Adobe Architecture, Style, and Social Boundaries in the American Southwest. In *The Archaeology of Social Boundaries*, edited by Miriam T. Stark, pp. 183–207. Washington, DC: Smithsonian Institution Press.
  2009   *Chaco and After in the Northern San Juan: Excavations at the Bluff Great House*. Tucson: University of Arizona Press.
  2013   How People Moved among Ancient Societies: Broadening the View. *American Anthropologist* 115(2):218–231.

Carlson, Roy
  1966   Twin Angels Pueblo. *American Antiquity* 31:676–682.

Carpenter, John P.
  1996   Rethinking Mesoamerican Meddling: External Influences and Indigenous Developments at Guasave, Sinaloa. Paper presented at the 61st Annual Meeting of the Society for American Archaeology, New Orleans.
  1997   Passing through the Netherworld: New Insights from the American Museum of Natural History's Sonora-Sinaloa Archaeological Project (1937–1940). In *Prehistory of the Borderlands*, edited by John Carpenter and Guadalupe Sanchez, pp. 113–127. Anthropological Series 186. Tucson: Arizona State Museum.

Chaco Research Archive
2010   Chaco Research Archive. http://www.chacoarchive.org/cra.

Charlton, Thomas H., and Deborah L. Nichols
1997a   The City-State Concept: Development and Applications. In *The Archaeology of City-States*, edited by Deborah L. Nichols and Thomas H. Charlton, pp. 1–14. Washington, DC: Smithsonian Institution Press.
1997b   Diachronic Studies of City-State: Permutations on a Theme, Central Mexico from 1700 B.C. to A.D. 1600. In *The Archaeology of City-States*, edited by Deborah L. Nichols and Thomas H. Charlton, pp. 169–207. Washington, DC: Smithsonian Institution Press.

Chuipka, Jason P.
2009   *Ridges Basin Excavations: The Sacred Ridge Site*. Animas–La Plata Project 12. SWCA, Inc.

Clark, Jeffrey J.
2001   Tracking Prehistoric Migrations: Pueblo Settlers among the Tonto Basin Hohokam. Anthropological Papers of the University of Arizona 65. Tucson: University of Arizona Press.

Clarke, Grahame
1986   *Symbols of Excellence: Precious Materials as Expressions of Status*. Cambridge: Cambridge University Press.

Cobb, Charles R.
1993   Archaeological Approaches to the Political Economies of Nonstratified Societies. In *Archaeological Method and Theory*, vol. 5, edited by Michael B. Schiffer, pp. 43–100. Tucson: University of Arizona Press.

Colwell-Chanthaphon, Chip, T. J. Ferguson, and Roger Anyon
2008   *Always Multivocal and Multivalent: Conceptualizing Archaeological Landscapes in Arizona's San Pedro Valley*. In *Archaeologies of Placemaking: Monuments, Memories, and Engagement in Native North America*, edited by Patricia E. Rubertone, pp. 59–80. Walnut Creek, CA: Left Coast Press.

Connerton, Paul
1989   *How Societies Remember*. Cambridge: Cambridge University Press.

Copeland, James M.
2014   Heaven on Earth: The Chaco North Road. In *Astronomy and Ceremony in the Prehistoric Southwest, Revisited*, edited by Gregory E. Munson, Todd W. Bostwick, and Tony Hull. Albuquerque: University of New Mexico Press.

Cordell, Linda S.
1984   *Prehistory of the Southwest*. Orlando, FL: Academic Press.
1994   *Ancient Pueblo Peoples*. Montreal: St. Remy Press.
1997   *Archaeology of the Southwest*. 2nd edition, retitled. San Diego: Academic Press.

Cordell, Linda, and Maxine McBrinn
2012   *Archaeology of the Southwest*. Walnut Creek, CA: Left Coast Press.

Cosgrove, H. S., and C. B. Cosgrove
   1932   *The Swarts Ruin: A Typical Mimbres Site in Southwestern New Mexico.* Papers
           of the Peabody Museum of American Archaeology and Ethnology 15(1).
           Cambridge, MA: Peabody Museum.

Creel, Darrell
   1989   A Primary Cremation at the NAN Ranch Ruin, with Comparative Data on
           the Other Cremations in the Mimbres Area, New Mexico. *Journal of Field
           Archaeology* 16:309–329.
   1997   Interpreting the End of the Mimbres Classic. In *Prehistory of the Borderlands:
           Recent Research in the Archaeology of Northern Mexico and the Southern
           Southwest*, edited by John Carpenter and Guadalupe Sanchez, pp. 25–31.
           Arizona State Museum Archaeological Series 186. Tucson: University of
           Arizona Press.
   2006   *Excavations at the Old Town Ruin, Luna County, New Mexico, 1989–2003*, vol.
           1. Cultural Resources Series 16. Santa Fe, NM: Bureau of Land Management.

Creel, Darrell, and Charmion McKusick
   1994   Prehistoric Macaws and Parrots in the Mimbres Area, New Mexico. *American
           Antiquity* 59(3):510–524.

Crown, Patricia
   1994   *Ceramics and Ideology: Salado Polychrome Pottery.* Albuquerque: University of
           New Mexico Press.

Crown, Patricia, ed.
   Forthcoming   *The Material Culture of the Pueblo Bonito Mounds.*

Crown, Patricia L., and W. Jeffrey Hurst
   2009   Evidence of Cacao Use in the Prehispanic American Southwest. *PNAS*
           106(7):2110–2113.

Crown, Patricia L., and W. H. Wills
   2003   Modifying Pottery and Kivas at Chaco. *American Antiquity* 68(3):511–532.

Cushing, Frank Hamilton
   1896   Outlines of Zuni Creation Myths. In *Thirteenth Annual Report of the Bureau
           of American Ethnology, 1891–92*, pp. 321–447. Washington, DC: Government
           Printing Office.

Dean, Jeffrey S.
   1996   Demography, Environment, and Subsistence Stress. In *Evolving Complexity
           and Environmental Risk in the Prehistoric Southwest*, edited by Joseph A.
           Tainter and Bonnie Bagley Tainter, pp. 25–56. Santa Fe Institute Studies in the
           Sciences of Complexity Proceedings 24. Reading, MA: Addison-Wesley.

Dean, Jeffrey S., William H. Doelle, and Janet D. Orcutt
   1994   Adaptive Stress: Environment and Demography. In *Themes in Southwest
           Prehistory*, edited by George J. Gumerman, pp. 53–86. Santa Fe, NM: School
           of American Research Press.

Dean, Jeffrey S., and G. Funkhouser
  2002   Dendroclimatology and Fluvial Chronology in Chaco Canyon, Appendix A.
          In *Relation of "Bonito" Paleo-Channels and Base-Level Variations to Anasazi
          Occupation, Chaco Canyon, New Mexico*, edited by E. R. Force, R. G. Vivian,
          T. C. Windes, and J. S. Dean, pp. 39–41. Arizona State Museum Archeological
          Series 194. Tucson: Arizona State Museum.

Dean, Jeffrey S., and John C. Ravesloot
  1993   The Chronology of Cultural Interaction in the Gran Chichimeca. In *Culture
          and Contact: Charles C. Di Peso's Gran Chichimeca*, edited by Anne I. Woosley
          and John C. Ravesloot, pp. 83–103. Amerind Foundation New World Studies
          Series 2. Albuquerque: University of New Mexico Press.

Di Peso, Charles C.
  1974   *Casas Grandes: A Fallen Trading Center of the Grand Chichimeca*, vols. 1–3.
          Dragoon, AZ: Amerind Foundation.

Di Peso, Charles C., John B. Rinaldo, and Gloria Fenner
  1974a   *Casas Grandes: A Fallen Trading Center of the Grand Chichimeca*, vol. 4:
          Dating and Architecture. Dragoon, AZ: Amerind Foundation.
  1974b   *Casas Grandes: A Fallen Trading Center of the Grand Chichimeca*, vol. 5:
          Architecture. Dragoon, AZ: Amerind Foundation.
  1974c   *Casas Grandes: A Fallen Trading Center of the Grand Chichimeca*, vol. 6:
          Ceramics and Shell. Dragoon: Amerind Foundation.
  1974d   *Casas Grandes: A Fallen Trading Center of the Grand Chichimeca*, vol. 7: *Stone
          and Metal*. Dragoon, AZ: Amerind Foundation.
  1974e   *Casas Grandes: A Fallen Trading Center of the Grand Chichimeca*, vol. 8: *Bone-
          Economy-Burials*. Dragoon, AZ: Amerind Foundation.

Diamond, Jared
  2005   *Collapse: How Societies Choose to Fail or Succeed*. New York: Penguin.

Doolittle, William E.
  1990   *Canal Irrigation in Prehistoric Mexico*. Austin: University of Texas Press.
  1993   Canal Irrigation at Casas Grandes: A Technological and Developmental
          Assessment of Its Origins. In *Culture and Contact: Charles C. Di Peso's Gran
          Chichimeca*, edited by Anne I. Woosley and John C. Ravesloot, pp. 133–151.
          Amerind Foundation New World Studies Series 2. Albuquerque: University of
          New Mexico Press.

Douglas, Amy
  1990   *Prehistoric Exchange and Sociopolitical Development in the Plateau Southwest*.
          New York: Garland Press.

Downum, Christian E.
  2004   Wupatki Construction Sequence. Excerpted from: An Architectural Study
          of Wupatki Pueblo (NA 405) by Christian E. Downum, Ellen Brennan, and
          James P. Holmlund. Northern Arizona University Archaeological Report
          1175, 1999. http://jan.ucc.nau.edu/d-antlab/Wupatki/construction.htm.

Doxtater, Dennis
1984   Spatial Opposition in Non-Discursive Expression: Architecture as Ritual
        Process. *Canadian Journal of Anthropology* 4(1):1–17.
1991   Reflections of the Anasazi Cosmos. In *Social Space: Human Spatial Behavior
        in Dwellings and Settlements*, edited by Ole Gran, Ericka Engelstad, and Inge
        Lindblom, pp. 155–184. Odense, Denmark: Odense University Press.
2002   A Hypothetical Layout of Chaco Canyon via Large-Scale Alignments between
        Significant Natural Features. *Kiva* 67(5).
2003   Parallel Universes on the Colorado Plateau: Indications of Chacoan
        Integration of an Earlier Anasazi Focus at Canyon de Chelly. *Journal of the
        Southwest* 45(1–2).

Doyel, David E.
1991   Hohokam Exchange and Interaction. In *Chaco and Hohokam*, edited by
        Patricia L. Crown and W. James Judge, pp. 225–252. Santa Fe: School of
        American Research Press.

Doyel, David E., Cory D. Breternitz, and Michael P. Marshall
1984   Chacoan Community Structure: Bis sa'ani Pueblo and the Chaco Halo. In
        Recent Research on Chaco Prehistory, edited by W. James Judge and John D.
        Schelberg, pp. 37–54. Reports of the Chaco Center 8. Albuquerque: National
        Park Service.

Doyel, David E., and Stephen H. Lekson
1992   Regional Organization in the American Southwest. In *Anasazi Regional
        Organization and the Chaco System*, edited by David E. Doyel, pp. 15–21.
        Papers of the Maxwell Museum of Anthropology 5. Albuquerque: Maxwell
        Museum of Anthropology, University of New Mexico.

Dozier, Edward P.
1970   *The Pueblo Indians of North America*. New York: Holt, Rinehart and Winston.

Drennan, Robert D.
1984   Long-Distance Transport Costs in Prehispanic Mesoamerica. *American
        Anthropologist* 86:105–112.

Duke, Phillip G.
1985   *Fort Lewis College Archaeological Investigations in Ridges Basin, Southwest
        Colorado: 1965–1982*. Occasional Papers of the Center of Southwest Studies 4.
        Durango, CO: Fort Lewis College.

Durand, Kathy Roler, and Stephen R. Durand
2008   Animal Bone from Salmon Ruins and Other Great Houses. In *Chaco's
        Northern Prodigies*, edited by Paul F. Reed, pp. 96–112. Salt Lake City:
        University of Utah Press.

Durand, Kathy R., Meradeth Snow, David Glenn Smith, and Stephen R. Durand
2010   Discrete Dental Trait Evidence of Migration Patterns in the Northern
        Southwest. In *Human Variation in the Americas*, edited by Benjamin M.
        Auerbach, pp. 113–134. Occasional Paper 38. Carbondale: Center for
        Archaeological Investigations, Southern Illinois University.

Dutton, Bertha P.
   1963   *Sun Father's Way: the Kiva Murals of Kuaua*. Albuquerque: University of New
           Mexico Press.

Earle, Timothy
   1997   *How Chiefs Come to Power: The Political Economy in Prehistory*. Stanford, CA:
           Stanford University Press.

Ebert, James I., and Robert K. Hitchcock
   1980   Locational Modelling in the Analysis of the Prehistoric Roadway System
           at and around Chaco Canyon, New Mexico. In *Cultural Resources Remote
           Sensing*, edited by T. R. Lyons and F. J. Mathien, pp. 157–172. Reports of the
           Chaco Center 1. Albuquerque: National Park Service.

Echo-Hawk, Roger C.
   1993   Exploring Ancient Worlds. *SAA Bulletin* 11(4):5–6.
   1997   Forging a New Ancient History for Native America. In *Native Americans and
           Archaeologists: Stepping Stones to Common Ground*, edited by Nina Swidler,
           Kurt E. Dongoske, Roger Anyon, and Alan S. Downer, pp. 88–102. Walnut
           Creek, CA: AltaMira Press, Walnut Creek.

Eddy, Frank W.
   1977   *Archaeological Investigations at Chimney Rock Mesa: 1970–1972*. Memoirs
           of the Colorado Archaeological Society 1. Boulder: Colorado Archaeological
           Society.

Eggan, Fred
   1983   Comparative Social Organization. In *Handbook of North American Indians*,
           vol. 10: *Southwest*, edited by Alphonso Ortiz, pp. 723–742. Washington, DC:
           Smithsonian Institution Press.

Ellis, Florence H.
   1967   Where Did the Pueblo People Come From? *El Palacio* 74(3):35–43.

Encinias, Miguel, Alfred Rodríguez, and Joseph P. Sánchez
   1992   Historical Overview, in *Historia de la Nueva Mexico, 1610: A Critical and
           Annotated Spanish/English Edition*, by Gaspar Pérez de Villagrá, translated
           and edited by Miguel Encinias, Alfred Rodríguez, and Joseph P. Sánchez, pp.
           xxv–xliii. Albuquerque: University of New Mexico Press.

Evans, Roy H., R. Evelyn Ross, and Lyle Ross
   1985   *Mimbres Indian Treasure*. Kansas City, MO: Lowell Press.

Fagan, Brian
   2005   *Chaco Canyon: Archaeologists Explore the Lives of an Ancient Society*. Oxford:
           Oxford University Press.

Ferdon, Edwin N., Jr.
   1955   *A Trial Survey of Mexican-Southwestern Architectural Parallels*. School of
           American Research Monograph 21. Santa Fe, NM: School of American
           Research Press.

Ferguson, T. J., and E. Richard Hart
  1985   *A Zuni Atlas.* Norman: University of Oklahoma Press.

Ferguson, William M., and Arthur H. Rohn
  1987   *Anasazi Ruins of the Southwest in Color.* Albuquerque: University of New Mexico Press.

Fernandez-Armesto, Felipe
  1987   *Before Columbus: Exploration and Colonization from the Mediterranean to the Atlantic, 1229–1492.* Philadelphia: University of Pennsylvania Press.

Fields, Virginia M. and Victor Zamudio-Taylor eds.
  2001   *The Road to Aztlan: Art from a Mythic Homeland.* Los Angeles: Los Angeles County Museum of Art.

Fowler, Andrew P., and John R. Stein
  1992   The Anasazi Great House in Space, Time, and Paradigm. In *Anasazi Regional Organization and the Chaco System,* edited by David E. Doyepp, 101–122. Papers of the Maxwell Museum of Anthropology 5. Albuquerque: Maxwell Museum of Anthropology, University of New Mexico.

Fowler, Andrew P., John R. Stein, and Roger Anyon
  1987   *An Archaeological Reconnaissance of West-Central New Mexico: The Anasazi Monuments Project.* Santa Fe, NM: Office of Cultural Affairs.

Fowles, Severin
  2010   A People's History of the American Southwest. In *Ancient Complexities,* edited by Susan M. Alt, pp. 183–204. Salt Lake City: University of Utah Press.

Frazier, Kendrick
  2005   *People of Chaco.* New York: Norton.

Freeman, Katherine, Robert Bliss, and Jennifer Thompson
  1996   Visual Communication between Chimney Rock and Chaco Canyon. Paper presented at the Oxford V Conference on Archaeoastronomy, Santa Fe, New Mexico.

Friedman, Richard A., John R. Stein, and Taft Blackhorse Jr.
  2003   A Study of a Pre-Columbian Irrigation System at Newcomb, New Mexico. *Journal of GIS in Archaeology* 1:4–10.

Frisbie, Theodore R.
  1978   High Status Burials in the Greater Southwest: An Interpretive Synthesis. In *Across the Chichimec Sea,* edited by Carroll L. Riley and Basil C. Hedrick, pp. 202–227. Carbondale: Southern Illinois University Press.

Fritz, John M.
  1978   Paleopsychology Today: Ideational Systems and Human Adaptation in Prehistory. In *Social Archaeology: Beyond Subsistence and Dating,* edited by Charles L. Redman et al., pp. 37–59. New York: Academic Press.
  1987   Chaco Canyon and Vijayanagra: Proposing Spatial Meaning in Two Societies. In *Mirror and Metaphor: Material and Social Constructions of Reality,* edited by D. W. Ingersoll and G. Bronitsky, pp. 313–348. Lanham, MD: University Press of America.

Fuller, Steven L.
1988   *Cultural Resource Inventories for the Animas–La Plata Project: The Wheeler and Koshak Borrow Sources.* Four Corners Archaeological Project Report 12. Cortez, CO: CASA.

Gabriel, Kathryn
1991   *Roads to Center Place: A Cultural Atlas of Chaco Canyon and the Anasazi.* Boulder, CO: Johnson Books.

Garcia-Mason, Velma
1979   Acoma Pueblo. In *Handbook of North American Indians*, vol. 9: *Southwest*, edited by Alfonso Ortiz, pp. 450–466. Washington, DC: Smithsonian Institution Press.

Glowacki, Donna M.
2006   The Social Landscape of Depopulation: The Northern San Juan, A.D. 1150–1300. PhD dissertation, Department of Anthropology, Arizona State University, Tempe.

Goetzfridt, Nicholas J., compiler
1992   *Indigenous Navigation and Voyaging in the Pacific: A Reference Guide.* New York: Greenwood Press.

Greiser, Sally T., and James L. Moore
1995   The Case for Prehistoric Irrigation in the Northern Southwest. In *Soil, Water, Biology, and Belief in Prehistoric and Traditional Southwestern Agriculture*, edited by H. Wolcott Toll, pp. 189–195. New Mexico Archaeological Council Special Publication 2. Albuquerque: New Mexico Archaeological Council.

Gumerman, George J., and Alan P. Olson
1968   Prehistory in the Puerco Valley, Eastern Arizona. *Plateau* 40(4):113–127.

Gutiérrez Mendoza, Gerardo
2003   Territorial Structure and Urbanism in Mesoamérica: The Huaxtec and Mixtec-Tlpanec-Nahua Cases. In *Urbanism in Mesoamerica*, vol. 1, edited by William T. Sanders, Alba Guadelupe Mastache, and Robert H. Cobean, pp. 85–115. Instituto Nacional de Antropología e Historia and Pennsylvania State University.

Hammond, G. P., and Agapito Rey, eds.
1929   *Journal, Expedition into New Mexico made by Antonio de Espejo, 1582–1583.* Los Angeles: Quivira Society.

Harbottle, Garman, and Phil C. Weigand
1992   Turquoise in Pre-Columbian America. *Scientific American* 266(2):78–85.

Hard, Robert J., and John R. Roney
2005   The Transition to Farming on the Rio Casas Grandes and in the Southern Jornada Mogollon Region. In *The Late Archaic across the Borderlands*, edited by Bradley J. Vierra, pp. 141–186. Austin: University of Texas Press.

Hargrave, Lyndon L.
  1970   *Mexican Macaws: Comparative Osteology and Survey of Remains from the Southwest.* Anthropological Papers of the University of Arizona 20. Tucson: University of Arizona Press.
  1979   A Macaw Feather Artifact from Southeastern Utah. *Southwestern Lore* 45(4):1–6.

Harrod, Ryan P.
  2012   Centers of Control: Revealing Elites among the Ancestral Pueblos during the "Chaco Phenomenon." *International Journal of Paleopathology* 2(2–3):123–135.

Haury, Emil W.
  1936   *The Mogollon Culture of Southwestern New Mexico.* Medallion Paper 20. Arizona: Globe.
  1950   A Sequence of Great Kivas in the Forestdale Valley, Arizona. In *For the Dean*, edited by Erik K. Reed and Dale S. King, pp. 29–39. Santa Fe, NM: Southwestern Monuments Association.
  1958   Evidence at Point of Pines for a Prehistoric Migration from Northern Arizona. In *Migrations in New World Culture History*, edited by Raymond H. Thompson. Tucson: University of Arizona Press.
  1986   Thoughts after Sixty Years as a Southwestern Archaeologist. In *Emil W. Haury's Prehistory of the American Southwest*, edited by J. Jefferson Reid and David E. Doyel, pp. 435–464. Tucson: University of Arizona Press.
  1988   Recent Thoughts on the Mogollon. *Kiva* 53(2):195–196.

Hawthorn, Geoffrey
  1991   *Plausible Worlds: Possibility and Understanding in History and the Social Sciences.* Cambridge: Cambridge University Press.

Hayes, Alden C.
  1981   A Survey of Chaco Canyon Archaeology. In *Archaeological Surveys of Chaco Canyon, New Mexico*, edited by Alden C. Hayes, David M. Brugge, and W. James Judge, pp. 1–68. Publications in Archaeology 18A. Washington, DC: National Park Service.

Hayes, Alden C., and Clifford C. Chappell
  1962   A Copper Bell from Southwest Colorado. *Plateau* 35(2):53–56.

Hayes, Alden C., Jan Nathan Young, and A. H. Warren
  1981   *Excavation of Mound 7, Gran Quivira National Monument, New Mexico.* Publications in Archaeology 16. Washington, DC: National Park Service.

Hays-Gilpin, Kelley
  2011   North America: Pueblos. Chapter 38 in *The Oxford Handbook of Archaeology of Ritual and Religion*, edited by Timothy Insoll, pp. 601–622. Oxford: Oxford University Press.

Hegmon, Michelle, and Margaret C. Nelson
  2006   In Sync, but Barely in Touch: Relations between the Mimbres Region and the Hohokam Regional System. In *Hinterlands and Regional Dynamics in the*

Ancient Southwest, edited by Alan P. Sullivan III and James M. Bayman, pp. 70–96. Tucson: University of Arizona Press.

Hegmon, Michelle, Margaret C. Nelson, Roger Anyon, Darrell Creel, Steven A. LeBlanc, and Harry J. Shafer
1999   Scale and Time-Space Systematics in the Post-A.D. 1100 Mimbres Region of the North American Southwest. *Kiva* 65:143–166.

Hegmon, Michelle, Margaret C. Nelson, and Susan M. Ruth
1998   Abandonment and Reorganization in the Mimbres Region of the American Southwest. *American Anthropologist* 100(1):148–162.

Heib, Louis A.
1979   Hopi World View. In *Handbook of North American Indians*, vol. 9: *Southwest*, edited by Alfonso Ortiz, pp. 577–580. Washington, DC: Smithsonian Institution Press.

Heilen, Michael, and Phillip Leckman
2014   Place, Community, and Cultural Landscape: Anasazi Occupation of the Chuska Valley. In *Bridging the Basin: Land Use and Social History of the Southern Chuska Valley*, vol. 4: *Synthesis*, edited by Monica L. Murrell and Bradley J. Vierra, pp. 319–398. Albuquerque, NM: Statistical Research.

Helms, Mary W.
1988   *Ulysses' Sail: An Ethnographic Odyssey of Power, Knowledge, and Geographical Distance*. Princeton, NJ: Princeton University Press.
1992   Long-Distance Contacts, Elite Aspirations, and the Age of Discovery in Cosmological Context. In *Resources, Power, and Interregional Interaction*, edited by Edward M. Schortman and Patricia A. Urban, pp. 157–174. New York: Plenum Press.
1993   *Craft and the Kingly Ideal: Art, Trade, and Power*. Austin: University of Texas Press.

Herr, Sarah A.
2001   *Beyond Chaco: Great Kiva Communities on the Mogollon Rim Frontier*. Anthropological Papers of the University of Arizona 66. Tucson: University of Arizona Press.

Herrington, Selma Laverne
1982   Water Control Systems of the Mimbres Classic Phase. In *Mogollon Archaeology: Proceedings of the 1980 Mogollon Conference*, edited by Patrick H. Beckett, pp. 75–90. Ramona, CA: Acoma Books, Ramona.

Hibben, Frank C.
1975   *Kiva Art of the Anasazi at Pottery Mound*. Las Vegas: KC Publications.

Hirth, Kenneth G.
1996   Political Economy and Archaeology: Perspectives on Exchange and Production. *Journal of Archaeological Research* 4(3):203–239.
2003   The Altepetl and Urban Structure in Prehispanic Mesoamerica. In *Urbanism in Mesoamerica*, vol. 1, edited by William T. Sanders, Alba Guadelupe Mastache, and Robert H. Cobean, pp. 57–84. Instituto Nacional de Antropología e Historia and The Pennsylvania State University.

2008 Incidental Urbanism: The Structure of the Prehispanic City in Central Mexico. In *The Ancient City*, edited by Joyce Marcus and Jeremy A. Sabloff, pp. 273–297. Santa Fe, NM: SAR Press.

Hirth, Kenneth G.
2000 Ancient Urbanism at Xochicalco: The Evolution and Organization of a Pre-Hispanic Society. In *Archaeological Research at Xochicalco*, edited by Kenneth G. Hirth, vol. 1. Salt Lake City: University of Utah Press.

Hodge, Mary G.
1997 When Is a City-State? Archaeological Measure of Aztec City-States and Aztec City-State Systems. In *The Archaeology of City-States*, edited by Deborah L. Nichols and Thomas H. Charlton, pp. 209–227. Washington, DC: Smithsonian Institution Press.

Hosler, Dorothy
1994 *The Sounds and Color of Power: The Sacred Metallurgical Technology of Ancient West Mexico*. Cambridge, MA: MIT Press.

Hough, Walter
1907 *Antiquities of the Upper Gila and Salt River Valleys in Arizona and New Mexico*. Bulletin 35. Washington, DC: Bureau of American Ethnology.

Howe, Sherman S.
1947 *My Story of the Aztec Ruins*. Farmington: Times Hustler Press.

Howse, Derek
1980 *Greenwich Time and the Discovery of Longitude*. Oxford: Oxford University Press.

Hudson, Dee T.
1972 Anasazi Measurement Systems at Chaco Canyon, New Mexico. *Kiva* 38(1):27–42.

Hudson, L. B.
1978 A Quantitative Analysis of Prehistoric Exchange in the Southwestern United States. PhD dissertation, Department of Anthropology, University of California, Los Angeles.

Humboldt, Alexander von
1803 Map of New Spain. http://www.utulsa.edu/mcfarlin/speccoll/collections/maps/humboldt.
1811 *Essai politique sur le royaume de la Nouvelle-Espagne et Atlas Géographique et physique du royaume de la Nouvelle Espangne*. 4 vols. Paris: Chez F. Schoell.

Hurst, Winston B.
2000 Chaco Outlier or Backwoods Pretender? A Provincial Great House at Edge of the Cedars Ruin, Utah. In *Great House Communities across the Chacoan Landscape*, edited by John Kantner and Nancy M. Mahoney, pp. 63–78. Anthropological Papers of the University of Arizona 64. Tucson: University of Arizona Press.

Irwin, Geoffrey
  1992   *The Prehistoric Exploration and Colonisation of the Pacific*. Cambridge:
           Cambridge University Press.

Irwin-Williams, Cynthia, ed.
  1972   *The Structure of Chacoan Society in the Northern Southwest, Investigations at
           the Salmon Site—1972*. Contributions in Anthropology 4(3). Portales: Eastern
           New Mexico University.

Jett, Stephen C., and Peter B. Moyle
  1986   The Exotic Origins of Fishes Depicted on Prehistoric Mimbres Pottery from
           New Mexico. *American Antiquity* 51(4):688–720.

Jones, Lindsay
  1995   *Twin City Tales: A Hermeneutical Reassessment of Tula and Chichen Itza*.
           Niwot: University Press of Colorado.

Judd, Neil M.
  1954   *The Material Culture of Pueblo Bonito*. Smithsonian Miscellaneous Collections
           124 (whole volume). Washington, DC: Smithsonian Institution.
  1959   *Pueblo Del Arroyo, Chaco Canyon, New Mexico*. Smithsonian Miscellaneous
           Collections 138(1). Washington, DC: Smithsonian Institution.
  1964   *The Architecture of Pueblo Bonito*. Smithsonian Miscellaneous Collections
           147(1). Washington, DC: Smithsonian Institution.

Judge, W. James
  1979   The Development of a Complex Cultural Ecosystem in the Chaco Basin, New
           Mexico. In *Proceedings of the First Conference on Scientific Research in the
           National Parks, Part 3*, edited by R. M. Linn, pp. 901–906. Washington, DC:
           National Park Service.
  1984   New Light on Chaco Canyon. In *New Light on Chaco Canyon*, edited by David
           Grant Noble, pp. 1–12. Santa Fe, NM: School of American Research Press.
  1989   Chaco Canyon-San Juan Basin. In *Dynamics of Southwest Prehistory*, edited
           by Linda S. Cordell and George J. Gumerman, pp. 209–261. Washington, DC:
           Smithsonian Institution Press.
  1991   Chaco: Current Views of Prehistory and the Regional System. In *Chaco and
           Hohokam*, edited by Patricia L. Crown and W. James Judge, pp. 11–30. Santa
           Fe, NM: School of American Research Press.
  1993   Resource Distribution and the Chaco Phenomenon. In *The Chimney Rock
           Archaeological Symposium*, edited by J. McKim Malville and Gary Matlock,
           pp. 35–36. General Technical Report RM-227. Fort Collins, CO: USDA Forest
           Service, Rocky Mountain Forest and Range Experiment Station.

Judge, W. James, William B. Gillespie, Stephen H. Lekson, and H. Wollcott Toll
  1981   Tenth-Century Developments in Chaco Canyon. In *Collected Papers in Honor
           of Erik Kellerman Reed*, edited by Albert H. Schroeder, pp. 65–98. Papers of
           the Archaeological Society of New Mexico 6. Albuquerque: Archaeological
           Society of New Mexico.

Kantner, John
  2004   *The Ancient Puebloan Southwest*. Cambridge: Cambridge University Press.
Kantner, John W., ed.
  2003   The Chaco World. Special issue, *Kiva* 69(2).
Kelley, J. Charles
  1986   The Mobile Merchants of Molino. In *Ripples in the Chichimec Sea: New
          Considerations of Southwestern-Mesoamerican Interactions*, edited by Frances
          Joan Mathien and Randall H. McGuire, pp. 81–104. Carbondale: Southern
          Illinois University Press.
  1993   Zenith Passage: The View from Chalchihuites. In *Culture and Contact:
          Charles C. Di Peso's Gran Chichimeca*, edited by Anne I. Woosley and John
          C. Ravesloot, pp. 227–250. Amerind Foundation New World Studies Series 2.
          Albuquerque: University of New Mexico Press.
  1995   Trade Goods, Traders, and Status in Northwestern Greater Mesoamerica. In
          *The Gran Chichimeca: Essays on the Archaeology and Ethnohistory of Northern
          Mesoamerica*, edited by Jonathan E. Reyman, pp. 102–145. Aldershot:
          Avebury.
  2000   The Aztatlan Mercantile System: Mobile Traders and the Northwestward
          Expansion of Mesoamerican Civilization. In *Greater Mesoamerica: The
          Archaeology of West and Northwest Mexico*, edited by Michael S. Foster and
          Shirley Gorenstein, pp. 137–154. Salt Lake City: University of Utah Press.
Kelley, Jane H., Joe D. Stewart, A. C. MacWilliams, and Loy C. Neff
  1999   A West Central Chihuahuan Perspective on Chihuahuan Culture. In *The
          Casas Grandes World*, edited by Curtis F. Schaafsma and Carroll L. Riley, pp.
          63–83. Salt Lake City: University of Utah Press.
Kelley, Jane H., and Maria Elisa Villalpando C.
  1996   An Overview of the Mexican Northwest. In *Interpreting Southwestern
          Diversity: Underlying Principles and Overarching Patterns*, edited by Paul R.
          Fish and J. Jefferson Reid, pp. 69–77. Anthropological Research Papers 48.
          Tempe: Arizona State University.
Kelley, Jane H., Joe D. Stewart, A. C. MacWilliams, and Karen R. Adams
  2004   Recent Research in West-Central Chihuahua. In *Identity, Feasting, and the
          Archaeology of the Greater Southwest*, edited by Barbara J. Mills, pp. 295–310.
          Boulder: University Press of Colorado.
Kelley, Klara Bonsack, and Harris Francis
  1994   *Navajo Sacred Places*. Bloomington: Indiana University Press.
Kelly, Isabel
  1945   *Excavations at Culiacán, Sinaloa*. Ibero-Americana 25. Berkeley: University of
          California Press.
Kendall, David G., and Wilfrid S. Kendall
  1980   Alignments in Two-Dimensional Random Sets of Points. *Advances in Applied
          Probability* 12(2):380–424.

Kincaid, Chris, ed.
1983   *Chaco Roads Project Phase 1: A Reappraisal of Prehistoric Roads in the San Juan Basin.* Albuquerque, NM: Bureau of Land Management.

King, David A.
1979   Kibla. *Encyclopedia of Islam* 5:82–88.
1995   The Orientation of Medieval Islamic Religious Architecture and Cities. *Journal for the History of Astronomy* 26:253–274.

Kintigh, Keith W.
1985   *Settlement, Subsistence and Society in Late Zuni Prehistory.* Anthropological Papers of the University of Arizona 44. Tucson: University of Arizona Press.
1996   The Cibola Region in the Post-Chacoan Era. In *The Prehistoric Pueblo World, A.D. 1150–1350,* edited by Michael A. Adler, pp. 131–144. Tucson: University of Arizona Press.
2002   *Tools for Quantitative Archaeology: Programs for Quantitative Analysis in Archaeology.* Tempe: K. W. Kintigh.

Kintigh, Keith W., Todd L. Howell, and Andrew I. Duff
1996   Post-Chacoan Social Integration at the Hinkson Site, New Mexico. *Kiva* 61(3):257–274.

Kohler, Timothy A., Scott G. Ortman, Katie E. Grundtisch, Carly M. Fitzpatrick, and Sarah M. Cole.
2014   The Better Angels of Their Nature: Declining Violence through Time among Prehispanic Farmers of the Pueblo Southwest. *American Antiquity* 79(3):444–464.

Kohler, Timothy A., and Kathryn K. Turner
2006   Raiding for Women in the Pre-Hispanic Northern Pueblo Southwest? *Current Anthropology* 47(6):1035–1045.

Kohler, Timothy A., Matthew W. Van Pelt, and Lorene Y. L. Yap
2000   Reciprocity and Its Limits: Considerations for a Study of the Prehispanic Pueblo World. In *Alternative Leadership Strategies in the Prehispanic Southwest,* edited by Barbara J. Mills, pp. 180–206. Tucson: University of Arizona Press.

Kohler, Timothy A., and Mark D. Varien, eds.
2012   *Emergence and Collapse of Early Villages: Models of Central Mesa Verde Archaeology.* Berkeley: University of California Press.

Kohler, Timothy A., Mark D. Varien, and Aaron M. Wright, eds.
2010   *Leaving Mesa Verde: Peril and Change in the Thirteenth-Century Southwest.* Tucson: University of Arizona Press.

Kowalski, Jeff Karl, and Cynthia Kristan-Graham, eds.
2011   *Twin Tollans: Chichen Itza, Tula and the Epiclassic to Early Postclassic Mesoamerican World.* Washington, DC: Dumbarton Oaks.

Krupp, E. C.
1997   *Skywatchers, Shamans, and Kings: Astronomy and the Archaeology of Power.* New York: Wiley.

Kubler, George
  1962   *The Shape of Time: Remarks on the History of Things.* New Haven, CT: Yale
          University Press.

Kuckelman, Kristin A., ed.
  2003   *The Archaeology of Yellow Jacket Pueblo (Site 5MT5): Excavations at a Large
          Community Center in Southwestern Colorado.* http://www.crowcanyon.org/
          yellowjacket.

Kutzinski, Vera M., and Ottmar Ette
  2012   The Art of Science: Alexander von Humboldt's Views of the Cultures of the
          World, an Introduction. In *Views of the Cordilleras and Monuments of the
          Indigenous Peoples of the Americas by Alexander von Humboldt*, pp. xv–xxxv.
          Chicago: University of Chicago Press.

Larkin, Karen Burd
  2006   Community Reorganization in the Southern Zone of the Casas Grandes
          Culture Area of Chihuahua, Mexico. PhD dissertation, University of
          Colorado, Boulder.

Lazcano Sahagún, Carlos
  1998   *Explorando un Mundo Olvidado: Sitios Perdidos de la Cultura Paquimé.*
          Mexico City: Editorial México Desconocido.

LeBlanc, Steven A.
  1983   *The Mimbres People, Ancient Pueblo Painters of the American Southwest.*
          London: Thames and Hudson.
  1986a   Development of Archaeological Thought on the Mimbres Mogollon. In *Emil
          W. Haury's Prehistory of the American Southwest*, edited by J. Jefferson Reid
          and David E. Doyel, pp. 297–304. Tucson: University of Arizona Press.
  1986b   Aspects of Southwestern Prehistory: A.D. 900–1400. In *Ripples in the
          Chichimec Sea: New Considerations of Southwestern-Mesoamerican
          Interactions*, edited by Frances Joan Mathien and Randall H. McGuire, pp.
          105–134. Carbondale: Southern Illinois University Press.
  1989   Cultural Dynamics in the Southern Mogollon Area. In *Dynamics of Southwest
          Prehistory*, edited by Linda S. Cordell and George J. Gumerman, pp. 179–207.
          Washington, DC: Smithsonian Institution Press.
  1999   *Prehistoric Warfare in the American Southwest.* Salt Lake City: University of
          Utah Press.

Lekson, Stephen H.
  1983a   Dating the Hubbard Tri-Wall and Other Tri-Wall Structures. *Southwestern
          Lore* 49(4):15–23.
  1983b   Chacoan Architecture in Continental Context. In *Proceedings of the Anasazi
          Symposium 1981*, edited by Jack E. Smith, pp. 183–194. Mesa Verde, CO:
          Mesa Verde Museum Association.
  1984a   Standing Architecture at Chaco Canyon and the Interpretation of Local and
          Regional Organization. In *Recent Research on Chaco Prehistory*, edited by W.
          James Judge and John D. Schelberg, pp. 55–73. Reports of the Chaco Center 8.
          Albuquerque, NM: National Park Service.

1984b   Mimbres Settlement Size in Southwestern New Mexico. In *Recent Research in Mogollon Archaeology*, edited by Steadman Upham, Fred Plog, David G. Batcho, and Barbara E. Kauffman, pp. 68–74. Occasional Papers 10. Las Cruces, NM: University Museum, New Mexico State University.

1984c   Dating Casas Grandes. *Kiva* 50(1):55–60.

1986a   *Great Pueblo Architecture of Chaco Canyon, New Mexico*. Albuquerque: University of New Mexico Press.

1986b   The Mimbres Region. In *Mogollon Variability*, edited by Charlotte Benson and Steadman Upham, pp. 147–155. Occasional Papers 15. Las Cruces, NM: University Museum, New Mexico State University.

1986c   Mimbres Riverine Adaptations. In *Mogollon Variability*, edited by Charlotte Benson and Steadman Upham, pp. 147–155. Occasional Papers 15. Las Cruces, NM: University Museum, New Mexico State University.

1988a   The Mangas Phase in Mimbres Archaeology. *Kiva* 53(2):129–145.

1988b   The Idea of Kivas in Anasazi Archaeology. *Kiva* 53:213–234.

1988c   Socio-political Complexity at Chaco Canyon, New Mexico. Unpublished PhD dissertation, University of New Mexico, Albuquerque.

1989a   Kivas? In *The Architecture of Social Integration in Prehistoric Pueblos,* edited by William D. Lipe and Michelle Hegmon. Occasional Papers of the Crow Canyon Archaeological Center 1. Cortez, CO: Crow Canyon Archaeological Center.

1989b   Sedentism and Aggregation in Anasazi Archaeology. In *The Sociopolitical Structure of Prehistoric Southwestern Societies*, edited by Steadman Upham, Kent G. Lightfoot, and Roberta A. Jewett, pp. 333–340. Boulder, CO: Westview Press.

1989c   The Community in Anasazi Archaeology. In *Households and Communities*, edited by Scott MacEachern, David J. W. Archer, and Richard D. Garvin, pp. 181–183. Calgary: Archaeological Association of the University of Calgary.

1989d   Regional Systematics in the Later Prehistory of Southern New Mexico. In *Fourth Jornada Conference: Collected Papers*, edited by Meliha Duran and Karl W. Laumbach, pp. 1–37. Las Cruces, NM: Human Systems Research.

1990a   The Great Pueblo Period in Southwestern Archaeology. In *Pueblo Style and Regional Architecture*, edited by Nicolas C. Markovich, Wolfgang F. E. Preiser, and Fred G. Sturm, pp. 64–77. New York: Van Nostrand Reinhold.

1990b   *Mimbres Archaeology of the Upper Gila, New Mexico*. Anthropological Papers of the University of Arizona 33. Tucson: University of Arizona Press.

1991   Settlement Pattern and the Chaco Region. In *Chaco and Hohokam*, edited by Patricia L. Crown and W. James Judge, pp. 31–55. Santa Fe, NM: School of American Research Press.

1992   Mimbres Art and Archaeology. *In Archaeology, Art, and Anthropology: Papers in Honor of J. J. Brody*, edited by Meliha Duran and David T. Kirkpatrick, pp. 111–122. Albuquerque: Archaeological Society of New Mexico.

1993   Chaco, Mimbres, and Hohokam: The 11th and 12th Centuries in the American Southwest. *Expedition* 35(1):44–52.

1996a   Scale and Process in the American Southwest. In *Interpreting Southwestern Diversity: Underlying Principles and Overarching Patterns*, edited by Paul R. Fish and J. Jefferson Reid, pp. 81–86. Anthropological Research Papers 48. Tempe: Arizona State University.

1996b   Southwestern New Mexico and Southeastern Arizona. In *The Prehistoric Pueblo World, A.D. 1150–1350*, edited by Michael A. Adler, pp. 170–176. Tucson: University of Arizona Press.

1999a   Was Casas a Pueblo? In *The Casas Grandes World*, edited by Curtis F. Schaafsma and Carroll L. Riley, pp. 84–92. Salt Lake City: University of Utah Press.

1999b   Unit Pueblos and the Mimbres Problem. In *La Frontera: Papers in Honor of Patrick Beckett*, edited by David Kirkpatrick and Meliha Duran, pp. 105–125. Albuquerque: Archaeological Society of New Mexico.

1999c   Great Towns in the American Southwest. In *Great Towns and Polities in the American Southwest*, edited by Jill Neitzel, pp. 3–21. Albuquerque: University of New Mexico Press.

2000   Salado in Chihuahua. In *The Salado Culture of Southern Arizona*, edited by Jeffrey S. Dean, pp. 275–294. Albuquerque: University of New Mexico Press.

2002   *Salado Archaeology of the Upper Gila, New Mexico*. Anthropological Papers of the University of Arizona 67. Tucson: University of Arizona Press.

2004   Geophysical Research in the Aztec North Mesa District, Aztec Ruins National Monument, New Mexico. Report submitted to Aztec Ruins National Monument, Aztec.

2006a   *The Archaeology of the Mimbres Region, Southwestern New Mexico, U.S.A.* British Archaeological Reports International Series 1466. Oxford: Archaeopress.

2006b   Lords of the Great House: Pueblo Bonito as a Palace. In *Palaces and Power in the Americas, from Peru to the Northwest Coast*, edited by Jessica Joyce Christie and Patricia Joan Sarro, pp. 99–114. Austin: University of Texas Press.

2006c   Chaco Matters. In *The Archaeology of Chaco Canyon: An Eleventh-Century Pueblo Regional Center*, edited by Stephen H. Lekson, pp. 3–44. Santa Fe, NM: SAR Press.

2009   *A History of the Ancient Southwest*. Santa Fe, NM: SAR Press.

2010   The Good Gray Intermediate: Why Native Societies in North American Can't Be States. In *Ancient Complexities*, edited by Susan M. Alt, pp. 177–182. Salt Lake City: University of Utah Press.

2014   Southwest New Mexico and the Land Between. In *Between Mimbres and Hohokam*, edited by Henry D. Wallace, pp. 501–516. Anthropological Papers 52. Tucson: Archaeology Southwest.

Forthcoming   *The Southwest in the World*. Salt Lake City: University of Utah Press.

Lekson, Stephen H., ed.

2006   *The Archaeology of Chaco Canyon: An Eleventh-Century Pueblo Regional Center*. Santa Fe, NM: SAR Press.

2007   *The Architecture of Chaco Canyon, New Mexico*. Salt Lake City: University of Utah Press.

Lekson, Stephen H., Michael Bletzer, and A. C. MacWilliams
  2004   Pueblo IV in the Chihuahuan Desert. In *The Protohistoric Pueblo World,
          A.D. 1275–1600*, edited by E. Charles Adams and Andrew I. Duff, pp. 53–61.
          Tucson: University of Arizona Press.

Lekson, Stephen H., and Catherine M. Cameron
  1995   The Abandonment of Chaco Canyon, the Mesa Verde Migrations, and the
          Reorganization of the Pueblo World. *Journal of Anthropological Archaeology*
          14:184–202.

Lekson, Stephen H., John R. Stein, Thomas Windes, and W. James Judge
  1988   The Chaco Canyon Community. *Scientific American* 259(1):100–109.

Lekson, Stephen H., Thomas C. Windes, and Patricia Fournier
  2007   The Changing Face of Chetro Ketl. In *Architecture of Chaco Canyon*, edited by
          Stephen H. Lekson, pp. 155–178. Salt Lake City: University of Utah Press.

Lekson, Stephen H., Thomas C. Windes, and Peter J. McKenna
  2006   Architecture. In *The Archaeology of Chaco Canyon*, edited by Stephen H.
          Lekson, pp. 67–116. Santa Fe, NM: SAR Press.

Levin Rojo, Danna A.
  2014   *Return to Aztlan: Indians, Spaniards, and the Invention of Nuevo Mexico.*
          Norman: University of Oklahoma Press.

Lewis, David
  1994   *We, the Navigators: The Ancient Art of Landfinding in the Pacific.* 2nd edition.
          Honolulu: University of Hawaii Press.

Lightfoot, Kent G.
  1979   Food Redistribution among Prehistoric Pueblo Groups. *Kiva* 44(4):319–339.

Lipe, William D.
  2006   Notes from the North. In *The Archaeology of Chaco Canyon*, edited by
          Stephen H. Lekson, pp. 261–313. Santa Fe, NM: SAR Press.
  2010   Lost in Transit: The Central Mesa Verde Archaeological Complex. In *Leaving
          Mesa Verde*, edited by Timothy A. Kohler, Mark D. Varien, and Aaron M.
          Wright, pp. 262–284. Tucson: University of Arizona Press.

Lister, Florence C.
  1997   *In the Shadow of the Rocks: Archaeology of the Chimney Rock District in
          Southern Colorado.* Durango, CO: Durango Herald Small Press.

Lister, Robert C.
  1958   *Archaeological Excavations in the Northern Sierra Madre Occidental,
          Chihuahua and Sonora, Mexico.* University of Colorado Studies, Series in
          Anthropology 7. Boulder: University of Colorado Press.
  1978   Mesoamerican Influence at Chaco Canyon, New Mexico. In *Across the
          Chichimec Sea: Papers in Honor of J. Charles Kelley*, edited by Carroll L. Riley
          and Basil C. Hedrick, pp. 233–241. Carbondale: Southern Illinois University
          Press.

Lister, Robert C., and Florence C. Lister
  1987   *Aztec Ruins on the Animas*. Albuquerque: University of New Mexico Press.

Lockhart, James
  1992   *The Nahuas after the Conquest: A Social and Cultural History of the Indians of Central Mexico, Sixteenth through Eighteenth Centuries*. Stanford, CA: Stanford University Press.

Love, Marian F.
  1975   A Survey of the Distribution of T-Shaped Doorways in the Greater Southwest. In *Collected Papers in Honor of Florence Hawley Ellis*, edited by Theodore R. Frisbie, pp. 296–311. Papers of the Archaeological Society of New Mexico 2. Santa Fe, NM: Archaeological Society of New Mexico.

Lumholtz, Carl
  1973 [1902]   *Unknown Mexico*. Glorieta, NM: Rio Grande Press.

Malville, J. McKim, ed.
  2004   *Chimney Rock: The Ultimate Outlier*. Lanham, MD: Lexington Books.

Malville, J. McKim, and W. James Judge
  1993   The Uses of Esoteric Astronomical Knowledge in the Chaco Regional System. Paper presented at the Fourth Oxford International Conference on Archaeoastronomy, Stara Zagora.

Malville, J. McKim, and Nancy J. Malville
  2001   Pilgrimage and Periodic Festivals as Processes of Social Integration in Chaco Canyon. *Kiva* 66:327–344.

Malville, Nancy J.
  2001   Long-Distance Transport of Bulk Goods in the Pre-Hispanic American Southwest. *Journal of Anthropological Archaeology* 20:230–243.

Marcus, Joyce, and Jeremy A. Sabloff, eds.
  2008   *The Ancient City*. Santa Fe, NM: SAR Press.

Marshall, Michael P.
  1997   The Chacoan Roads: A Cosmological Interpretation. In *Anasazi Architecture and American Design*, edited by Baker H. Morrow and V. B. Price, pp. 62–74. Albuquerque: University of New Mexico Press.

Marshall, Michael P., and Christina L. Marshall
  2008   *Double H Ranch, Lion Mountain Unit Survey*. Cibola Research Consultants Report 442. Corrales, NM: Cibola Research Consultants.

Marshall, Michael P., John R. Stein, Richard W. Loose, and Judith E. Novotny
  1979   *Anasazi Communities of the San Juan Basin*. Santa Fe, NM: Historic Preservation Bureau.

Martin, Paul S., and Fred Plog
  1973   *The Archaeology of Arizona*. Garden City, NY: Doubleday/Natural History Press.

Mathien, Frances Joan
  1986   External Contact and the Chaco Anasazi. In *Ripples in the Chichimec Sea: New Considerations of Southwestern-Mesoamerican Interactions*, edited by Frances Joan Mathien and Randall H. McGuire, pp. 220–242. Carbondale: Southern Illinois University Press.
  1993   Exchange Systems and Social Stratification among the Chaco Anasazi. In *The American Southwest and Mesoamerica: Systems of Prehistoric Exchange*, edited by Jonathan E. Ericson and Timothy G. Baugh, pp. 27–63. New York: Plenum Press.
  2005   *Culture and Ecology of Chaco Canyon and the San Juan Basin.* Studies in Archaeology 18H. Santa Fe, NM: National Park Service.

Mathiowetz, Michael Dean
  2011   The Diurnal Path of the Sun: Ideology and Interregional Interaction in Ancient Northwest Mesoamerica and the American Southwest. PhD dissertation, University of California, Riverside.

Maxwell Museum
  2011   *Testimony of the Hands.* https://hands.unm.edu/63–50–123.html.

McCluney, Eugene B.
  1968   A Mimbres Shrine at the West Baker Site. *Archaeology* 21(3):196–205.

McGrayne, Sharon Bertsch
  2011   *The Theory That Would Not Die.* New Haven, CT: Yale University Press.

McGuire, Randall H.
  1980   The Mesoamerican Connection in the Southwest. *Kiva* 46(1–2):3–38.
  1989   The Greater Southwest as a Periphery of Mesoamerica. In *Center and Periphery: Comparative Studies in Archaeology*, edited by Timothy C. Champion, pp. 40–66. London: Unwin Hyman.
  1993a   Charles Di Peso and the Mesoamerican Connection. In *Culture and Contact, Charles C. Di Peso's Gran Chichimeca*, edited by Anne I. Woosley and John C. Ravesloot, pp. 23–38. Albuquerque: University of New Mexico Press.
  1993b   The Structure and Organization of Hohokam Exchange. In *The American Southwest and Mesoamerica: Systems of Prehistoric Exchange*, edited by Jonathan E. Ericson and Timothy G. Baugh, pp. 95–119. New York: Plenum Press.

McKenna, Peter J.
  1998   The Cultural Landscape of Aztec Ruins, New Mexico. Paper presented at the 63rd Annual Meeting of the Society for American Archaeology, Seattle.

McKenna, Peter J., and James E. Bradford
  1989   *The TJ Ruin, Gila Cliff Dwellings National Monument.* Southwest Cultural Resources Center Professional Paper 21. Santa Fe, NM: National Park Service.

McKenna, Peter J., and H. Wolcott Toll
  1992   Regional Patterns of Great House Development among the Totah Anasazi, New Mexico. In *Anasazi Regional Organization and the Chaco System*, edited by David E. Doyel, pp. 133–143. Papers of the Maxwell Museum of

Anthropology 5. Albuquerque: Maxwell Museum of Anthropology, University of New Mexico.

McKusick, Charmion R.
2001   *Southwest Birds of Sacrifice*. Phoenix: Arizona Archaeological Society.

McPherson, Robert S.
1992   *Sacred Land, Sacred View: Navajo Perceptions of the Four Corners Region.* Charles Redd Center for Western Studies. Provo, UT: Brigham Young University Press.
2014   *Viewing the Ancestors: Perceptions of the Anaasází, Mokwič, and Hisatsinom.* Norman: University of Oklahoma Press.

Metcalf, Mary P.
2003   Construction Labor at Pueblo Bonito. In *Pueblo Bonito*, edited by Jill E. Neitzel, pp. 72–79. Washington, DC: Smithsonian Books.

Michell, J.
1974   *The Old Stones of Land's End*. London: Garnstone Press.
1977   Statistical Leyhunting. *The Ley Hunter* 74:11–12.

Mills, Barbara J.
2002   Recent Research on Chaco: Changing Views on Economy, Ritual, and Society. *Journal of Archaeological Research* 10(1):65–117.

Mills, Barbara J., Jeffrey J. Clark, Matthew A. Peeples, W. R. Haas Jr., John M. Roberts Jr., J. Brett Hill, Deborah L. Huntley, Lewis Borck, Ronald L. Breiger, Aaron Clauset, and M. Steven Shackley
2013   Transformation of Social Networks in the Late Pre-Hispanic US Southwest. *Proceedings of the National Academy of Science* 110(15):5785–5790.

Mindeleff, Victor
1891   A Study of Pueblo Architecture: Tusayan and Cibola. In *Eighth Annual Report of the Bureau of American Ethnology, 1886–87*. Washington, DC: Government Printing Office.

Minnis, Paul E.
1984   Regional Interaction and Integration on the Northeastern Periphery of Casas Grandes. *American Archaeology* 4(3):181–193.
1985   *Social Adaptations to Food Stress: A Prehistoric Southwestern Example.* Chicago: University of Chicago Press.
1988   Four Examples of Specialized Production at Casas Grandes, Northwestern Chihuahua. *Kiva* 53:181–193.
1989   The Casas Grandes Polity in the International Four Corners. In *The Sociopolitical Structure of Prehistoric Southwest Societies*, edited by Steadman Upham, Kent G. Lightfoot, and Roberta A. Jewett, pp. 269–305. Boulder, CO: Westview Press.

Minnis, Paul E., and Michael E. Whalen
2010   The First Prehispanic Chile (Capsicum) from the U.S. Southwest/Northwest Mexico and Its Changing Use. *American Antiquity* 75(2):245–257.

Morgan, Lewis Henry
1965 [1881]   Houses and House-Life of the American Aborigines. Reprint;
                   Chicago: University of Chicago Press.

Morgan, William N.
1994   Ancient Architecture of the Southwest. Austin: University of Texas Press.

Morris, Earl H.
1919   The Aztec Ruin. Anthropological Papers of the American Museum of Natural
            History 26(1). New York: American Museum of Natural History.
1921   The House of the Great Kiva at the Aztec Ruin. Anthropological Papers of the
            American Museum of Natural History 26(2). New York: American Museum
            of Natural History.
1924a   Burials in the Aztec Ruin. Anthropological Papers of the American Museum of
            Natural History 26(3). New York: American Museum of Natural History.
1924b   The Aztec Ruin Annex. Anthropological Papers of the American Museum of
            Natural History 26(4). New York: American Museum of Natural History.
1928   Notes on Excavations in the Aztec Ruin. Anthropological Papers of the
            American Museum of Natural History 26(5). New York: American Museum
            of Natural History.

Motsinger, Thomas N.
1998   Hohokam Roads at Snaketown, Arizona. Journal of Field Archaeology 25:89–
            96.

Moulard, Barbara L.
2005   Archaism and Emulation in Casas Grandes Painted Pottery. In Casas Grandes
            and the Ceramic Art of the Ancient Southwest, edited by R. F. Townsend, pp.
            66–97. Chicago: Art Institute of Chicago.

Mountjoy, Joseph B.
2001   The Aztatlan Complex. In Archaeology of Ancient Mexico and Central
            America, edited by Susan Toby Evand and David L. Webster, pp. 57–59. New
            York: Garland.

Multhauf, Robert P.
1985   Early Instruments in the History of Surveying: Their Use and Their Invention.
            In Plotter and Patterns of American Land Surveying: A Collection of Articles
            from the Archives of the American Congress on Surveying and Mapping, edited
            by Roy Minnick, pp. 57–70. Rancho Cordova, CA: Landmark Enterprises.

Nabokov, Peter
1996   Native Views of History. In The Cambridge History of the Native Peoples of the
            Americas, edited by Bruce G. Trigger and Wilcomb E. Washburn, pp. 1–59.
            Cambridge: Cambridge University Press.

Naranjo, Tessie
1995   Thoughts on Migration by Santa Clara Pueblo. Journal of Anthropological
            Archaeology 14(2):247–250.

Naylor, Thomas H.
1995   Casas Grandes Outlier Ballcourts in Northwest New Mexico. In *The Gran Chichimeca: Essays on the Archaeology and Ethnohistory of Northern Mesoamerica*, edited by Jonathan E. Reyman, pp. 224–239. Aldershot: Avebury.

Needham, Joseph
1959   *Science and Civilization in China*, vol. 3: *Mathematics and the Sciences of the Heavens and Earth*. Cambridge: Cambridge University Press.

Neitzel, Jill E.
1989a   Regional Exchange Networks in the American Southwest: A Comparative Analysis of Long-Distance Trade. In *The Sociopolitical Structure of Prehistoric Southwestern Societies*, edited by Steadman Upham, Kent G. Lightfoot, and Roberta A. Jewett, pp. 149–195. Boulder, CO: Westview Press.
1989b   The Chacoan Regional System: Interpreting the Evidence for Sociopolitical Complexity. In *The Sociopolitical Structure of Prehistoric Southwestern Societies*, edited by Steadman Upham, Kent G. Lightfoot, and Roberta A. Jewett, pp. 509–556. Boulder, CO: Westview Press.
2010   Landscapes of Complexity in Middle Range Societies: Peer Polities and the Hohokam and Chacoans in the U.S. Southwest. In *Ancient Complexities: New Perspectives in Pre-Columbian North America*, edited by Susan Alt, pp. 153–176. Salt Lake City: University of Utah Press.

Neitzel, Jill E., ed.
2003   *Pueblo Bonito: Center of the Chacoan World*. Washington, DC: Smithsonian Books.

Nelson, Ben A.
1995   Complexity, Hierarchy, and Scale: A Controlled Comparison between Chaco Canyon, New Mexico and La Quemada, Zacatecas. *American Antiquity* 60(4):597–618.
1997   Chronology and Stratigraphy at La Quemada, Zacatecas, Mexico. *Journal of Field Archaeology* 24(1):85–109.
2000   Aggregation, Warfare, and the Spread of the Mesoamerican Tradition. In *The Archaeology of Regional Interaction*, edited by Michelle Hegmon, pp. 317–337. Boulder: University Press of Colorado.
2006   Mesoamerican Objects in Chaco Contexts. In *Archaeology of Chaco Canyon*, edited by Stephen H. Lekson. Santa Fe, NM: SAR Press.

Nelson, Ben A., and Roger Anyon
1996   Fallow Valleys: Asynchronous Occupations in Southwestern New Mexico. *Kiva* 61(3):275–294.

Nelson, Margaret C.
1999   *Mimbres during the Twelfth Century*. Tucson: University of Arizona Press.

Nelson, Richard S.
1981   The Role of a Pochteca System in Hohokam Exchange. PhD dissertation, Department of Anthropology, University of Arizona, Tucson.

1986   Poctecas and Prestige: Mesoamerican Artifacts in Hohokam Sites. In *Ripples in the Chichimec Sea: New Considerations of Southwestern-Mesoamerican Interactions*, edited by Frances Joan Mathien and Randall H. McGuire, pp. 155–182. Carbondale: Southern Illinois University Press.

Nials, Fred, John Stein, and John Roney
1987   *Chacoan Roads in the Southern Periphery: Results of Phase II of the BLM Chaco Roads Project*. Cultural Resource Series 1. Albuquerque, NM: Bureau of Land Management.

Ortiz, Alfonso
1972   Ritual Drama and the Pueblo World View. In *New Perspectives on the Pueblos*, edited by Alfonso Ortiz, pp. 135–161. Albuquerque: University of New Mexico Press.

Osterholtz, Anna
2013   Hobbling and Torture as Performative Violence: An Example from the Prehistoric Southwest. *Kiva* 78(2):123–144.

Parmentier, Richard J.
1979   The Pueblo Mythological Triangle: Poseyemu, Montezuma, and Jesus in the Pueblos. In *Handbook of North American Indians*, vol. 9: *Southwest*, edited by Alfonso Ortiz, pp. 609–622. Washington, DC: Smithsonian Institution.

Parsons, Elsie Clews
1996   *Pueblo Indian Religion*. Boulder, CO: Bison Books. Originally published by University of Chicago Press, 1939.

Pauketat, Timothy R.
2007   *Chiefdoms and Other Archaeological Delusions*. Lanham, MD: AltaMira Press.

Pennick, Nigel, and Paul Devereux
1989   *Lines on the Landscape: Leys and Other Linear Enigmas*. London: Robert Hale.

Pepper, George H.
1920   *Pueblo Bonito*. Anthropological Papers of the American Museum of Natural History 27. New York: American Museum of Natural History.

Phillips, David A., Jr.
1989   Prehistory of Chihuahua and Sonora, Mexico. *Journal of World Prehistory* 3(4):373–401.

Pippin, Lonnie C.
1987   *Prehistory and Paleoecology of Guadelupe Ruin, New Mexico*. University of Utah Anthropological Papers 107. Salt Lake City: University of Utah Press.

Pitezel, Todd A., and Michael T. Searcy
2013   Understanding the Viejo Period. In *Collected Papers from the 17th Biennial Mogollon Conference*, edited by L. C. Ludeman. Silver City: Western New Mexico University.

Plog, Stephen
1997   *Ancient Peoples of the American Southwest*. London: Thames and Hudson.
2008   *Ancient Peoples of the American Southwest*. 2nd edition. London: Thames and Hudson.

Plog, Stephen, and Carrie Heitman
    2010   Hierarchy and Social Inequality in the American Southwest, A.D. 800–1200. *Proceedings of the National Academy of Science* 107(46):19619–19626.

Potter, James M.
    2010   *Final Synthetic Report.* Animas-La Plata Project 16. SWCA, Inc.

Potter, James M., and Jason Chuipka
    2007a   *Blue Mesa Excavations.* Animas-La Plata Project 3. SWCA, Inc.
    2007b   Early Pueblo Communities and Cultural Diversity in the Durango Area: Preliminary Results from the Animas–La Plata Project. *Kiva* 72:407–430.

Powers, Robert P., William B. Gillespie, and Stephen H. Lekson
    1983   *The Outlier Survey: A Regional View of Settlement in the San Juan Basin.* Reports of the Chaco Center 3. Albuquerque, NM: National Park Service.

Publ, Helmut
    1985   Prehispanic Exchange Networks and the Development of Social Complexity in Western Mexico: The Aztatlan Interaction Sphere. PhD dissertation, Anthropology, Southern Illinois University, Carbondale.
    1990   Interaction Spheres, Merchants, and Trade in Prehispanic West Mexico. *Research in Economic Anthropology* 12:201–242.

Putsavage, Kathryn Jane
    2008   Mesa Verde Style Mugs: An Analysis of Domestic and Ritual Functions. MA thesis, Museum and Field Studies, University of Colorado, Boulder.

Rakita, Gordon F. M., and Gerry R. Raymond
    2003   The Temporal Sensitivity of Casas Grandes Polychrome Ceramics. *Kiva* 68(3):153–184.

Ravesloot, John C.
    1988   *Mortuary Practices and Social Differentiation at Casas Grandes, Chihuahua, Mexico.* Anthropological Papers of the University of Arizona 49. Tucson: University of Arizona Press.

Reed, Paul F.
    2004   *The Puebloan Societies of Chaco Canyon.* Westport, CT: Greenwood Press.
    2006   Chronology of Salmon Pueblo. In *Thirty-Five Years of Archaeological Research at Salmon Ruins, New Mexico,* vol. 1: *Introduction, Architecture, Chronology and Conclusions,* edited by Paul F. Reed, pp. 287–296. Tucson, AZ: Center for Desert Archaeology/Bloomfield, NM: Salmon Ruins Museum.

Reed, Paul F., ed.
    2000   *Foundations of Anasazi Culture: The Basketmaker-Pueblo Transition.* Salt Lake City: University of Utah Press.
    2006   *Thirty-Five Years of Archaeological Research at Salmon Ruins, New Mexico,* vol. 1: *Introduction, Architecture, Chronology and Conclusions.* Tucson: Center for Desert Archaeology.
    2008   *Chaco's Northern Prodigies: Salmon, Aztec, and the Ascendancy of the Middle San Juan Region after AD 1100.* Salt Lake City: University of Utah Press.

Reyman, Jonathan E.
  1985   A Reevaluation of Bi-wall and Tri-wall Structures in the Anasazi Area. In
          Contributions to the Archaeology and Ethnohistory of Greater Mesoamerica,
          edited by William J. Folan, pp. 293–333. Carbondale: Center for
          Archaeological Investigations, Southern Illinois University.
  1987   Priests, Power, and Politics: Some Implications of Socioceremonial Control.
          In *Astronomy and Ceremony in the Prehistoric Southwest*, edited by John B.
          Carlson and W. James Judge, pp. 121–147. Papers of the Maxwell Museum of
          Anthropology 2. Albuquerque: Maxwell Museum of Anthropology, University
          of New Mexico.

Richter, Daniel K.
  2011   *Before the Revolution: America's Ancient Pasts*. Cambridge, MA: Harvard
          University Press.

Richert, Roland
  1964   *Excavations of a Portion of the East Ruin, Aztec Ruin National Monument,
          New Mexico*. Southwestern Monuments Association Technical Series 4.
          Arizona: Globe.

Riley, Carroll L.
  1976   *Sixteenth Century Trade in the Greater Southwest*. Mesoamerican Studies 10,
          Research Records of the University Museum. Carbondale: Southern Illinois
          University.
  1995   *Rio del Norte: People of the Upper Rio Grande from Earliest Times to the
          Pueblo Revolt*. Salt Lake City: University of Utah Press.

Riley, Carroll L., and Joni L. Manson
  1991   The Sonoran Connection: Road and Trail Networks in the Protohistoric
          Period. In *Ancient Road Networks and Settlement Hierarchies in the New
          World*, edited by Charles D. Trombold, pp. 132–144. Cambridge: Cambridge
          University Press.

Roberts, David
  1996   The Old Ones of the Southwest. *National Geographic* 189(4):86–109.
  2015   *The Lost World of the Old Ones*. New York: Norton.

Roberts, Frank H. H.
  1929   *Shabik'eschee Village: A Late Basketmaker Site in the Chaco Canyon*. Bulletin
          92. Washington, DC: Bureau of American Ethnology.

Robinson, William J., and Bruce G. Harrill
  1974   *Tree-Ring Dates from Colorado V, Mesa Verde Area*. Tucson: Laboratory of
          Tree-Ring Research.

Roney, John R.
  1992   Prehistoric Roads and Regional Integration in the Chacoan System. In
          Anasazi Regional Organization and the Chaco System, edited by David E.
          Doyel, pp. 123–131. Papers of the Maxwell Museum of Anthropology 5.
          Albuquerque: Maxwell Museum of Anthropology, University of New Mexico.

1995   Mesa Verdean Manifestations South of the San Juan River. *Journal of Anthropological Archaeology* 14(2):170–183.

1996   The Pueblo III Period in the Eastern San Juan Basin and the Acoma-Laguna Areas. In *The Prehistoric Pueblo World, A.D. 1150–1350*, edited by Michael A. Adler, pp. 145–169. Tucson: University of Arizona Press.

Rupke, Nicolaas A.

2008   *Alexander von Humboldt: A Metabiography*. Chicago: University of Chicago Press.

Ruppe, Reynold J., Jr.

1953   The Acoma Culture Province. PhD dissertation, Harvard University, Cambridge, MA.

Saitta, Dean J.

1997   Power, Labor, and the Dynamics of Change in Chacoan Political Economy. *American Antiquity* 62(1):7–26.

Sando, Joe S.

1992   *Pueblo Nations: Eight Centuries of Pueblo Indian History*. Santa Fe, NM: Clear Light Publishers.

Santley, Robert S., and Rani T. Alexander

1992   The Political Economy of Core-Periphery Systems. In *Resources, Power and Interregional Interaction*, edited by Edward M. Schortman and Patricia A. Urban, pp. 23–49. New York: Plenum Press.

Sauer, Carl

1932   *The Road to Cibola*. Ibero-Americana 3. Berkeley: University of California Press.

Sauer, Carl, and Donald Brand

1932   *Aztatlan: Prehistoric Mexican Frontier on the Pacific Coast*. Ibero-Americana 1. Berkeley: University of California Press.

Schaafsma, Curtis F.

1979   The "El Paso Phase" and Its Relationship to the "Casas Grandes Phenomenon." In *Jornada Mogollon Archaeology*, edited by Patrick H. Beckett and Regge N. Wiseman, pp. 383–388. Las Cruces: New Mexico State University.

Schaafsma, Polly, ed.

1994   *Kachinas in the Pueblo World*. Albuquerque: University of New Mexico Press.

Schelberg, John D.

1984   Analogy, Complexity, and Regionally-Based Perspectives. In *Recent Research on Chaco Prehistory*, edited by W. James Judge and John D. Schelberg, pp. 5–21. Reports of the Chaco Center 8. Albuquerque, NM: National Park Service.

1992   Hierarchical Organization as a Short-Term Buffering Strategy in Chaco Canyon. In *Anasazi Regional Organization and Chaco System*, edited by David E. Doyel, pp. 59–74. Papers of the Maxwell Museum of Anthropology 5. Albuquerque: Maxwell Museum of Anthropology, University of New Mexico.

Schmidt, Robert H., Jr., and Rex E. Gerald
 1988   The Distribution of Conservation-Type Water-Control Systems in the Semi-Arid Northern Sierra Madre Occidental. *Kiva* 53:165–179.

Sebastian, Lynne
 1991   Sociopolitical Complexity and the Chaco System. In *Chaco and Hohokam: Prehistoric Regional Systems in the American Southwest*, edited by Patricia L. Crown and W. James Judge, pp. 109–134. Santa Fe, NM: School of American Research Press.
 1992   *The Chaco Anasazi: Sociopolitical Evolution in the Prehistoric Southwest.* Cambridge: Cambridge University Press.
 2004   Understanding Chacoan Society. In *In Search of Chaco*, edited by David G. Noble, pp. 93–99. Santa Fe, NM: SAR Press.
 2006   The Chaco Synthesis. In *The Archaeology of Chaco Canyon*, edited by Stephen H. Lekson, pp. 393–422. Santa Fe, NM: SAR Press.

Sedig, Jakob W.
 2015   Surface Survey of Woodrow Ruin, Grant County, New Mexico. *Kiva.*

Seymour, Deni J., ed.
 2012   *From the Land of Ever Winter to the American Southwest: Athapaskan Migrations, Mobility, and Ethnogenesis.* Salt Lake City: University of Utah Press.

Shafer, Harry J.
 1995   Architecture and Symbolism in Transitional Pueblo Development in the Mimbres Valley, SW New Mexico. *Journal of Field Archaeology* 22(1):23–47.
 1999   The Mimbres Classic and Postclassic: A Case for Discontinuity. In *The Casas Grandes World*, edited by Curtis Schaafsma and Carroll Riley, pp. 121–133. Salt Lake City: University of Utah Press.
 2003   Mimbres Archaeology at the NAN Ranch Ruin. Albuquerque: University of New Mexico Press.

Silko, Leslie Marmon
 1995   Interior and Exterior Landscapes: The Pueblo Migration Stories. In *Landscape in America*, edited by George F. Thompson, pp. 155–169. Austin: University of Texas Press.

Smith, Michael E.
 2000   "Aztec City States." In *A Comparative Study of Thirty City-State Cultures*, edited by Mogens Herman Hansen, pp. 581–595. Copenhagen: Royal Danish Academy of Sciences and Letters.
 2008   *Aztec City-State Capitals.* Gainesville: University Press of Florida.
 2011   Tula and Chichen Itza: Are We Asking the Right Questions? In *Twin Tollans*, edited by Jeff Karl Kowalski and Cynthia Kristan-Graham, pp. 469–499. Washington, DC: Dumbarton Oaks.

Smith, Michael E., and Francis F. Berdan, eds.
 2003   *The Postclassic Mesoamerican World.* Salt Lake City: University of Utah Press.

Snow, Meradeth, Harry Shafer, and David Glenn Smith
2011   The Relationship of the Mimbres to Other Southwestern and Mexican Populations. *Journal of Archaeological Science* 38:3122–3133.

Snygg, John, and Tom Windes
1998   Long, Wide Roads and Great Kiva Roofs. *Kiva* 64(1):7–25.

Sobel, Dava
1995   *Longitude.* New York: Walker and Company.

Sofaer, Anna
1997   The Primary Architecture of the Chacoan Culture: A Cosmological Expression. In *Anasazi Architecture and American Design*, edited by Baker H. Morrow and V. B. Price, pp. 88–132. Albuquerque: University of New Mexico Press.

Sofaer, Anna, Michael P. Marshall, and Rolf M. Sinclair
2008   The Great North Road: A Cosmographic Expression of the Chaco Culture of New Mexico. In *Chaco Astronomy: An Ancient American Cosmology*, edited by Anna Sofaer, pp. 129–142. Santa Fe, NM: Ocean Tree Books.

Somerville, Andrew D., Ben A. Nelson, and Kelly J. Knudson
2010   Isotopic Investigation of pre-Hispanic Macaw Breeding in Northwest Mexico. *Journal of Anthropological Archaeology* 29:125–135.

Spence, Michael W.
2000   From Tzintzuntzan to Paquimé: Peers or Peripheries in Greater Mesoamerica? In *Greater Mesoamerica*, edited by Michael S. Foster and Shirley Gorenstein, pp. 255–261. Salt Lake City: University of Utah Press.

Stanislawski, Michael
1963   Wupatki Pueblo: A Study in Cultural Fusion and Change in Sinagua and Hopi Prehistory. PhD dissertation, University of Arizona, Tucson.

Stein, John R.
1987   An Archaeological Reconnaissance in the Vicinity of Aztec Ruins National Monument, New Mexico. Santa Fe, NM: National Park Service.
1989   The Chaco Roads. *El Palacio* 94(3):5–17.

Stein, John R., and Andrew Fowler
1996   Looking beyond Chaco in the San Juan Basin and Its Peripheries. In *The Prehistoric Pueblo World A.D. 1150–1350*, edited by Michael A. Adler, pp. 114–130. Tucson: University of Arizona Press.

Stein, John R., Richard Friedman, Taft Blackhorse, and Richard Loose
2007   Revisiting Downtown Chaco. In *Architecture of Chaco Canyon*, edited by Stephen H. Lekson, pp. 199–223. Salt Lake City: University of Utah Press.

Stein, John R., and Stephen H. Lekson
1992   Anasazi Ritual Landscapes. In *Anasazi Regional Organization and the Chaco System*, edited by David E. Doyel, pp. 87–100. Papers of the Maxwell Museum of Anthropology 5. Albuquerque: Maxwell Museum of Anthropology, University of New Mexico.

Stein, John R., and Peter J. McKenna
1988   *An Archaeological Reconnaissance of a Late Bonito Phase Occupation Near Aztec Ruins National Monument, New Mexico.* Santa Fe, NM: National Park Service.

Stein, John R., Judith E. Suiter, and Dabney Ford
1997   High Noon at Old Bonito: Sun, Shadow, and Geometry in the Chaco Complex. In *Anasazi Architecture and American Design*, edited by Baker H. Morrow and V. B. Price, pp. 133–148. Albuquerque: University of New Mexico Press.

Stewart, Joe D., Jane H. Kelley, A. C. MacWilliams, and Paula J. Reimer
2005   The Viejo Period of Chihuahua Culture in Northwestern Mexico. *Latin American Antiquity* 16:169–192.

Stirling, Matthew W.
1942   Origin Myths of the Acoma and Other Records. *Bureau of American Ethnology Bulletin* 135. Washington, DC: Bureau of American Ethnology.

Storey, Glenn, ed.
2006   *Urbanism in the Preindustrial World.* Tuscaloosa: University of Alabama Press.

Sullivan, Mary, and J. McKim Malville
1993   Clay Sourcing at Chimney Rock: The Chemistry and Mineralogy of Feather Holders and Other Ceramics. In *The Chimney Rock Symposium*, edited by J. McKim Malville and Gary Matlock, pp. 29–34. USDA Forest Service Rocky Mountain Forest and Range Experiment Station General Technical Report RM-227. Fort Collins, CO.

Swanson, Steven J.
2003   Documenting Prehistoric Communication Networks: A Case Study in the Paquimé Polity. *American Antiquity* 68:753–767.

Tainter, Joseph A.
1988   *The Collapse of Complex Societies.* Cambridge: Cambridge University Press.

Tainter, Joseph A., and Fred Plog
1994   Strong and Weak Patterning in Southwestern Prehistory: The Formation of Pueblo Archaeology. In *Themes in Southwestern Prehistory*, edited by George Gumerman, pp. 109–134. Santa Fe, NM: School of American Research Press.

Tainter, Joseph A., and Bonnie Bagley Tainter
1996   *Evolving Complexity and Environmental Risk in the Prehistoric Southwest.* Santa Fe Institute Studies in the Sciences of Complexity Proceedings 24. Reading, MA: Addison-Wesley.

Tassin, Wirt
1902   The Casas Grandes Meteorite. *Proceedings of the U.S. National Museum* 25:69–74.

Taylor, John R.
1982   *An Introduction to Error Analysis: The Study of Uncertainties in Physical Measurements.* Oxford: Oxford University Press.

Teague, Lynn S.
1993   Prehistory and the Traditions of the O'Odham and Hopi. *Kiva* 58(4):435–454.

Tedlock, Dennis, trans.
1972   *Finding the Center: Narrative Poetry of the Zuni Indians.* New York: Dial Press.

Todd, Brenda K., and Stephen H. Lekson
2011   Chimney Rock Stabilization Project, Chimney Rock Great House (5AA83), Archuleta County, CO. Report submitted to USDA Forest Service San Juan National Forest. Boulder: University of Colorado.

Toll, H. Wolcott
1990   A Reassessment of Chaco Cylinder Jars. In *Clues to the Past*, edited by Meliha S. Duran and David T. Kirkpatrick, pp. 273–305. Albuquerque: Archaeological Society of New Mexico.
1991   Material Distributions and Exchange in the Chaco System. In *Chaco and Hohokam: Prehistoric Regional Systems in the American Southwest*, edited by Patricia L. Crown and W. James Judge, pp. 77–107. Santa Fe, NM: School of American Research Press.

Trigger, Bruce G.
1972   Determinants of Urban Growth in Pre-Industrial Societies. In *Man, Settlement, and Urbanism*, edited by Peter J. Ucko, Ruth Trigham, and G. W. Dimbleby, pp. 579–599. Cambridge: Schenkman.
2003   *Understanding Early Civilizations: A Comparative Study.* Cambridge: Cambridge University Press.

Trombold, Charles D.
1990   A Reconsideration of Chronology for the La Quemada Portion of the Northern Mesoamerican Frontier. *American Antiquity* 55(2):308–324.

Turner, Christy G., II
1993   Southwest Indian Teeth. *National Geographic Research and Exploration* 9(1):32–53.
1999   The Dentition of Casas Grandes with Suggestions on Epigenetic Relationships among Mexican and Southwestern U.S. Populations. In *The Casas Grandes World*, edited by Curtis F. Schaafsma and Carroll L. Riley, pp. 229–233. Salt Lake City: University of Utah Press.

Turner, Christy G., II, and Jacqueline A. Turner
1999   *Man Corn: Cannibalism and Violence in the Prehistoric American Southwest.* Salt Lake City: University of Utah Press.

Tyler, Hamilton A.
1991   *Pueblo Birds and Myths.* Flagstaff, AZ: Northland Publishing. Originally published by University of Oklahoma Press, 1979.

Utah State Parks
2014   Edge of the Cedars State Park. http://stateparks.utah.gov/park/edge-of-the-cedars-state-park-museum.

Van Dyke, Ruth M.
  2003   Memory and the Construction of Chacoan Society. In *Archaeologies of Memory*, edited by Ruth M. Van Dyke and Susan E. Alcock, pp. 180–200. Oxford: Blackwell.
  2004   Memory, Meaning, and Masonry: The Late Bonito Chacoan Landscape. *American Antiquity* 69:413–431.

Van West, Carla
  1994   *Modeling Prehistoric Agricultural Productivity in Southwestern Colorado: A GIS Approach*. Reports of Investigations 67. Pullman: Department of Anthropology, Washington State University.
  1996   Agricultural Potential and Carrying Capacity in Southwestern Colorado, A.D. 901 to 1300. In *The Prehistoric Pueblo World A.D. 1150–1350*, edited by Michael A. Adler, pp. 214–227. Tucson: University of Arizona Press.

Vansina, Jan
  1985   *Oral Tradition as History*. Madison: University of Wisconsin Press.

Vargas, Victoria D.
  1995   *Copper Bell Trade Patterns in the Prehispanic US Southwest and Northwest Mexico*. Archaeological Series 187. Tucson: Arizona State Museum.

Varien, Mark D., William D. Lipe, Michael A. Adler, Ian M. Thompson, and Bruce A. Bradley
  1996   Southwestern Colorado and Southeastern Utah Settlement Patterns: A.D. 1100 to 1300. In *The Prehistoric Pueblo World A.D. 1150–1350*, edited by Michael A. Adler, pp. 86–113. Tucson: University of Arizona Press.

Varien, Mark D., and Richard H. Wilshusen, eds.
  2002   *Seeking the Center Place: Archaeology and Ancient Communities in the Mesa Verde Region*. Salt Lake City: University of Utah Press.

Villagrá, Gaspar Pérez de
  1992   *Historia de la Nueva Mexico, 1610: A Critical and Annotated Spanish/English Edition*. Translated and edited by Miguel Encinias, Alfred Rodríguez, and Joseph P. Sánchez. Albuquerque: University of New Mexico Press.

Vivian, Gordon
  1959   *The Hubbard Site and Other Tri-Wall Structures in New Mexico and Colorado*. Archaeological Research Series 5. Washington, DC: National Park Service.
  1960   *The Great Kivas of Chaco Canyon*. School of American Research Monographs 22. Santa Fe, NM: School of American Research.

Vivian, Gordon, and Tom W. Mathews
  1964   *Kin Kletso: A Pueblo III Community in Chaco Canyon, New Mexico*. Technical Series 6(1). Southwest Parks and Monuments Association. Arizona: Globe.

Vivian, Gordon, and Paul Reiter
  1960   *The Great Kivas of Chaco Canyon*. School of American Research Monographs 22. Santa Fe, NM: School of American Research.

Vivian, R. Gwinn
  1990   *The Chacoan Prehistory of the San Juan Basin.* San Diego: Academic Press.
  1991   Chacoan Subsistence. In *Chaco and Hohokam: Prehistoric Regional Systems in the American Southwest,* edited by Patricia L. Crown and W. James Judge, pp. 57–75. Santa Fe, NM: School of American Research Press.
  1997a   Chacoan Roads: Morphology. *Kiva* 63(1):7–34.
  1997b   Chacoan Roads: Function. *Kiva* 63(1):35–67.
  2001   Chaco Reconstructed: A Review of *The Chaco Meridian. Cambridge Archaeological Journal* 11(1):142–144.

Ware, John A.
  2014   *A Pueblo Social History: Kinship, Solidarity, and Community in the Northern Southwest.* Santa Fe, NM: SAR Press.

Washburn, Dorothy K.
  2008   The Position of Salmon Ruins in the Middle San Juan, AD 1000–1300: A Perspective from Ceramic Design Structure. In *Chaco's Northern Prodigies,* edited by Paul F. Reed, pp. 284–308. Salt Lake City: University of Utah Press.

Washburn, Dorothy K., William N. Washburn, Petia A. Shipkova, and Mary Ann Pelleymounter
  2014   Chemical Analysis of Cacao Residues in Archaeological Ceramics from North America: Considerations of Contamination, Sample Size and Systematic Controls. *Journal of Archaeological Science* 50:191–207.

Weigand, Phil C., and Garman Harbottle
  1993   The Role of Turquoises in the Ancient Mesoamerican Trade Structure. In *The American Southwest and Mesoamerica: Systems of Prehistoric Exchange,* edited by Jonathan E. Ericson and Timothy G. Baugh, pp. 159–177. New York: Plenum Press.

Whalen, Michael E., A. C. MacWilliams, and Todd Pitezel
  2010   Reconsidering the Size and Structure of Casas Grandes, Chihuahua, Mexico. *American Antiquity* 75(3):527–550.

Whalen, Michael E., and Paul E. Minnis
  1996a   Ball Courts and Political Centralization in the Casas Grandes Region. *American Antiquity* 61(4):732–746.
  1996b   Studying Complexity in Northern Mexico: The Paquimé Regional System. In *Debating Complexity,* edited by Daniel A. Meyer, Peter C. Dawson, and Donald T. Hanna, pp. 282–289. Calgary: Archaeological Association of the University of Calgary.
  1996c   The Context of Production in and Around Paquimé, Chihuahua, Mexico. In *Interpreting Southwestern Diversity,* edited by Paul R. Fish and J. Jefferson Reid, pp. 173–182. Anthropological Research Papers 84. Tempe: Arizona State University.
  2001   *Casas Grandes and Its Hinterland: Prehistoric Regional Organization in Northwest Mexico.* Tucson: University of Arizona Press.
  2003   The Local and the Distant in the Origin of Casas Grandes, Chihuahua, Mexico. *American Antiquity* 68:314–332.

2009   *The Neighbors of Casas Grandes: Excavating Medio Period Communities of Northwest Chihuahua, Mexico.* Tucson: University of Arizona Press.

Whalen, Michael E., and Paul E. Minnis, eds.
2015   *Ancient Paquimé and the Casas Grandes World.* Tucson: University of Arizona Press.

White, Leslie A.
1932   The Acoma Indians. In *47th Annual Report of the Bureau of American Ethnology for the Years 1929–1930*, pp. 17–192. Washington, DC: Bureau of American Ethnology.

Whitecotton, Joseph W., and Richard A. Pailes
1986   New World Precolumbian World Systems. In *Ripples in the Chichimec Sea: New Considerations of Southwestern-Mesoamerican Interactions*, edited by Frances Joan Mathien and Randall H. McGuire, pp. 183–204. Carbondale: Southern Illinois University Press.

Wilcox, David R.
1993   The Evolution of the Chacoan Polity. In *The Chimney Rock Archaeological Symposium*, edited by J. McKim Malville and Gary Matlock, pp. 76–90. USDA Forest Service Rocky Mountain Forest and Range Experiment Station General Technical Report RM-227. Fort Collins, CO.
1996a   The Diversity of Regional and Macroregional Systems in the American Southwest. In *Debating Complexity*, edited by Daniel A. Meyer, Peter C. Dawson, and Donald T. Hanna, pp. 375–390. Calgary: Archaeological Association of the University of Calgary.
1996b   Pueblo III People and Polity in Relational Context. In *The Prehistoric Pueblo World A.D. 1150–1350*, edited by Michael A. Adler, pp. 241–254. Tucson: University of Arizona Press.
1999a   A Preliminary Graph: Theoretical Analysis of Access Relationships at Casas Grandes. In *The Casas Grandes World*, edited by Curtis F. Schaafsma and Carroll L. Riley, pp. 93–104. Salt Lake City: University of Utah Press.
1999b   A Peregrine View of Macroregional Systems in the North American Southwest, A.D. 750–1250. In *Great Towns and Regional Polities in the American Southwest*, edited by Jill Neitzel, pp. 115–141. Albuquerque: University of New Mexico Press.

Wilcox, David R., T. Randall McGuire, and Charles Sternberg
1981   *Snaketown Revisited.* Archaeological Series 155. Tucson: Arizona State Museum.

Wilcox, David R., and Lynette O. Shenk
1977   *The Architecture of the Casa Grande and Its Interpretation.* Archaeological Series 115. Tucson: Arizona State Museum.

Williamson, Tom, and Liz Bellamy
1983   *Ley Lines in Question.* Kingswood: World's Work.

Wills, W. H.
  2000   Political Leadership and the Construction of Chaco Great Houses. In
          Alternative Leadership Strategies in the Prehispanic Southwest, edited by
          Barbara J. Mills, pp. 19–44. Tucson: University of Arizona Press.

Wills, W. H., and Wetherbee Bryan Dorshow
  2012   Agriculture and Community in Chaco Canyon: Revisiting Pueblo Alto.
          Journal of Anthropological Archaeology 31(2):138–155.

Wills, W. H., and Thomas C. Windes
  1989   Evidence for Population Aggregation and Dispersal during the Basketmaker
          III Period in Chaco Canyon, New Mexico. *American Antiquity* 54:347–369.

Wills, W. H., F. Scott Worman, Wetherbee Dorshow, and Heather Richards-Rissetto
  2012   Shabik'eschee Village in Chaco Canyon: Beyond the Archetype. *American
          Antiquity* 77(2):326–350.

Wilshusen, Richard H.
  1991   Early Villages in the American Southwest: Cross-Cultural Perspectives. PhD
          dissertation, University of Colorado, Boulder.

Wilshusen, Richard H., and Scott G. Ortman
  1999   Rethinking the Pueblo I Period in the San Juan Drainage: Aggregation,
          Migration, and Cultural Diversity. *Kiva* 64:369–399.

Wilshusen, Richard H., and Ruth Van Dyke
  2006   Chaco's Beginnings. In *The Archaeology of Chaco Canyon*, edited by Stephen
          H. Lekson, pp. 211–259. Santa Fe, NM: SAR Press.

Windes, Thomas C.
  1984   A New Look at Population in Chaco Canyon. In *Recent Research on Chaco
          Prehistory*, edited by W. James Judge and John D. Schelberg, pp. 75–87.
          Reports of the Chaco Center 8. Albuquerque, NM: National Park Service.
  1987a   *Investigations at the Pueblo Alto Complex, Chaco Canyon, New Mexico*, vol. 1:
          Summary of Tests and Excavations at the Pueblo Alto Complex. Publications in
          Archaeology 18F. Santa Fe, NM: National Park Service.
  1987b   *Investigations at the Pueblo Alto Complex, Chaco Canyon, New Mexico*, vol. 2,
          pt. 1: *Architecture and Stratigraphy*. Publications in Archaeology 18F. Santa
          Fe, NM: National Park Service.
  2007   Gearing Up and Piling On: Early Great Houses of the Interior San Juan Basin.
          In *The Architecture of Chaco Canyon*, edited by Stephen H. Lekson, pp. 45–92.
          University of Utah Press, Salt Lake City.
  In press *Basketmaker Sites of Chaco Canyon*. Archaeological Papers. Tucson: Arizona
          State Museum.

Windes, Thomas C., and Dabney Ford
  1996   The Chaco Wood Project: The Chronometric Reappraisal of Pueblo Bonito.
          American Antiquity 61(2):295–310.

Wiseman, Regge N., and J. Andrew Darling
  1986   The Bronze Trail Site Group: More Evidence for a Cerrillos-Chaco Turquoise
          Connection. In *By Hands Unknown: Papers on Rock Art and Archaeology*,

edited by Anne Poore, pp. 115–143. Papers of the Archaeological Society of New Mexico 12. Santa Fe, NM: Ancient City Press.

Woosley, Anne I., and John C. Ravesloot, eds.
1993   *Culture and Contact: Charles C. Di Peso's Gran Chichmeca.* Amerind Foundation New World Studies Series 2. Albuquerque: University of New Mexico Press.

Yoffee, Norman
2001   The Chaco "Rituality" Revisited. In *Chaco Society and Polity*, edited by Linda S. Cordell and W. James Judge, pp. 63–78. NMAC Special Publication 4. Albuquerque: New Mexico Archaeological Council.

Young, M. Jane
1987   Issues in the Archaeoastronomical Endeavor in the American Southwest. In *Astronomy and Ceremony in the Prehistoric Southwest*, edited by John B. Carlson and W. James Judge, pp. 219–232. Papers of the Maxwell Museum of Anthropology 2. Albuquerque: Maxwell Museum of Anthropology, University of New Mexico.

Zeilik, Michael
1987   Anticipation in Ceremony: The Readiness Is All. In *Astronomy and Ceremony in the Prehistoric Southwest*, edited by John B. Carlson and W. James Judge, pp. 25–41. Papers of the Maxwell Museum of Anthropology 2. Albuquerque: Maxwell Museum of Anthropology, University of New Mexico.

Zuidema, R. Tom
1982   Bureaucracy and Systematic Knowledge in Andean Civilization. In *The Inca and Aztec States 1400–1800: Anthropology and History*, edited by George A. Collier, Renata I. Rosaldo, and John D. Wirth, pp. 419–458. New York: Academic Press.

Index

Note: Page numbers followed by *f* indicate figures.

About the Author

Stephen H. Lekson received his BA from Case Western Reserve University and his PhD in anthropology from the University of New Mexico in 1988. His principal mentors were David Brose at the former and Lewis Binford at the latter, although both were happily unaware of their roles. James Fitting, Linda Cordell, George Gumerman, Alden Hayes, and Jim Judge were highly influential in his training. Lekson's obstinate independence renders them all blameless.

His archaeological fieldwork focuses on the ninth- to fifteenth-century Southwest: Mimbres, Chaco, Mesa Verde, Tucson Basin Hohokam, Salado, Casas Grandes, and Rio Grande Abajo. This research has been reported in a dozen books and monographs, sixty book chapters and articles, several popular books, and museum exhibits.

Lekson was born at West Point, New York, to a military family. Movement was constant; his formative years were spent, one or two years at a time, in Austria, Italy, Korea, and various southeastern United States. His father, John S. Lekson, retired as a major general; his mother, Gladys M. (Pecsok) Lekson, had an equally successful career in military society; his brother, J. Michael Lekson, retired from Foreign Service.

Lekson is married to Catherine M. Cameron, a Southwestern archaeologist of impeccable reputation—not responsible for the intellectual foibles and follies of her husband. They live in Boulder and work at the University of Colorado, where Lekson is a semiretired curator of archaeology and Cameron is a fully employed professor of anthropology. Cameron drinks herbal tea; Lekson drinks cognac.